SIMPLIFIED MANAGEMENT SKILLS

Lessons from the Ramayana

Dr. Atul Kumar Bansal

BLUEROSE PUBLISHERS
India | U.K.

Copyright © Dr. Atul Kumar Bansal 2024

All rights reserved by author. No part of this publication may be reproduced, stored in a retrieval system or transmitted in any form or by any means, electronic, mechanical, photocopying, recording or otherwise, without the prior permission of the author. Although every precaution has been taken to verify the accuracy of the information contained herein, the publisher assumes no responsibility for any errors or omissions. No liability is assumed for damages that may result from the use of information contained within.

BlueRose Publishers takes no responsibility for any damages, losses, or liabilities that may arise from the use or misuse of the information, products, or services provided in this publication.

For permissions requests or inquiries regarding this publication,
please contact:

BLUEROSE PUBLISHERS
www.BlueRoseONE.com
info@bluerosepublishers.com
+91 8882 898 898
+4407342408967

ISBN: 978-93-6261-951-8

Cover design: Shivam
Typesetting: Namrata Saini

First Edition: June 2024

Acknowledgments

This journey of writing a book turned out to be far better than I could ever define. I've come to realize that the entire world glows with new vigor when people go into growth and leadership, and it glows much brighter when they pay the price of time to mentor other people. So, my humble thanks to all those who are ready to move ahead with dedication towards growth and sharing with others.

First of all, thanks are owed to my lovely wife, Preeti Bansal, for her selfless support, reading early drafts, and being instrumental in offering invaluable advice on cover designs—as graciously as a little one kept from me getting work done by diverting my attention to editing.

I owe my deepest debt to our Hon'ble CMD, of Gateway Distriparks Limited Shri Prem Kishan Gupta, and my colleagues for their unconditional support and inspiration through their real-time life experiences and encouragement. Without their guidance, this manuscript would be a dream unfulfilled.

A myriad of people generously contributed their time, and thoughts and played a pivotal role in this book to come alive. I offer my sincere thanks to all. This book wouldn't be the best version of itself without their invaluable input.

My sincere thanks go to my dedicated beta readers. Your meticulous feedback and thoughtful comments have undoubtedly enriched the pages of this book.

I would like to extend my deepest gratitude to Ms. Tanya Singh and my daughter Aditi Bansal for her remarkable suggestions and long hours of dedicated proofreading work, which surely enhanced the quality of this book.

I would like to dedicate this book to the memory of my late beloved Mother and Father. Their love & blessings remain the cornerstone of everything I strive to achieve.

Last but not least, I would like to thank all the readers of this book. It is because of you, that I have had the opportunity to bring **Simplified Management Skills—Lessons from the Ramayana**.

Thank you all, from the bottom of my heart.

Introduction

In modern-day settings, where strategies change in waves and tasks emerge to serve obstacles, effective leadership often involves navigating through uncharted waters. Yet, amidst the whirlwind of contemporary management theories and business lexicon, there exists a reservoir of timeless wisdom offering profound insights into the art of leadership and organizational excellence. Welcome to "***Simplifying Management Skills: Lessons from Ramayana***". In this transformational journey, we will venture into a timeless narrative that transcends epochs and the boundaries of our understanding of leadership and management, drawing inspiration from one of the world's most esteemed epics: **The Ramayana**. As a flagship of Indian tradition, the Ramayana is no mere tale of heroism and righteousness; it, indeed, stands as a classical text, bringing into harmony managerial doctrines that remain timeless, proving a treasure trove of lessons for managers engaged in the intricate journey of leadership in the corporate world.

We will be able to dissect the intricacies of leadership as we wade deeper into the essence of this epic saga and see a panoply of characters in the narrative of the Ramayana, each representing one or another form of leadership - from unconditional loyalty to brilliant strategy, from such ethical decision-making as to make any leader proud to steadfast perseverance. Through the prism of the Ramayana, we unwind the complexities of leadership, which reveals timeless truths that resonate across generations and cultures.

Our journey starts with a study of history, in which management principles were not limited to boardrooms and presentations but woven into the very fabric of societal governance. We reflect on how this ancient wisdom has a pertinent application in today's business scenario and how such enduring principles only bring out the best of management practices leading to the growth and success of organizations.

Central to our exploration is the power of storytelling, a tool that transcends time and space, weaving together the threads of wisdom passed down to generations. We immerse ourselves in the narrative of the Ramayana and uncover in it a unique route to learning, in which timeless truths are veiled in myth and legend, waiting to be discovered by discerning leaders.

As we traverse the path, we encounter an array of archetypal characters who each showcase invaluable lessons about the multifaceted realm of leadership. From the steadfast commitment of Lord Rama to the visionary leadership of Hanuman, from the strategic alliances forged by Sugriva to the ethical dilemmas faced by Ravana, we glean lessons that transcend time and culture boundaries, illuminating the path toward effective leadership and organizational success.

In **"Simplifying Management Skills: Lessons from Ramayana**," we embark on a journey of transformation where ancient wisdom combines with modern management principles, where timeless truths get distilled into actionable insights, and where the epic narrative of the Ramayana serves as our guiding light to exemplary leadership.

Table of Contents

Chapter 1: Introduction to Management Lessons from Ramayana.................1

Understanding the Relevance of Ancient Wisdom in Modern Management..................2

Overview of Key Leadership Principles from the Ramayana......4

The Importance of Storytelling in Conveying Management Lessons..................7

Chapter 2: Commitment and Fulfilling Promises..........11

Ram's Commitment to Exile and Its Corporate Parallels..........13

Navigating Unexpected Challenges While Honoring Commitments......................15

Fostering a Culture of Commitment in the Workplace.............18

Chapter 3: Team Motivation and Leadership................25

1. Jamvant's Motivational Leadership Style...............27
2. Developing a Visionary Leadership Approach.....................29
3. Building Trust and Loyalty Within a Team........................32

Chapter 4: Strategic Alliances and Managerial Skills....37

Sugriva's Managerial Characteristics and Their Application in the Business World 39

Creating and Nurturing Strategic Alliances............................40

Building Effective Relationships with Stakeholders...................43

Chapter 5: Value Your Subordinates and Listening Skills..................49

Recognizing the Signs of Poor Leadership through Ravana's Example..................51

Signs of Poor Leadership:........................51

The Importance of Active Listening in Leadership 52
Key Principles of Active Listening: 53
Holding Teams Together Through Effective Communication . 54

Chapter 6: Trusting Your Team and Confidence 58
Balancing Trust and Accountability in Leadership: 60
Developing Confidence in Challenging Situations: 64
The Impact of Trust on Team Performance: 66

Chapter 7: Moving Out of the Comfort Zone and Leadership Perception 72
Embracing Discomfort for Professional Growth 73
Leaders as Active Participants in Their Organizations 75
Understanding and Adapting to Changing Environments 77

Chapter 8: Excellence in Execution and Wisdom 80
Hanuman's Wisdom in Executing Plans: 81
Lessons in Strategic Execution from the Ramayana: 83
Achieving Goals through Focused and Disciplined Execution: . 85

Chapter 9: Putting a Premium on Values and Ethical Leadership 89
Applying Rama's Principles to Business: 91
Balancing Ethical Considerations in Business Decisions 91
Upholding Core Values During Challenging Times 94

Chapter 10: Leadership Skills 98
Analyzing Ram's Leadership Qualities in Depth 99
Translating Leadership Skills from the Ramayana to the Corporate World 102
Leadership Lessons from Various Characters in the Epic 105

Chapter 11: Delegation of Responsibility and Effective Task Assignment 109

The Art of Effective Delegation: 111
Selecting the Right People for Specific Tasks: 113
Balancing Responsibility and Authority in Delegation: 115

Chapter 12: Teamwork and Collaboration 120

Lessons in Collaboration from Building the Ram Setu Bridge: 121
Fostering a Culture of Teamwork Within an Organization: 124
Achieving Collective Success through Effective Collaboration: 127

Chapter 13: Ethics and Righteous Decision-Making ... 131

Rama's Ethical Considerations in Decision-Making 132
Applying Righteous Principles to Contemporary Business Dilemmas 134
Fair Labor Practices and Corporate Social Responsibility 134

Chapter 14: Time Management and Planning 139

Strategic Planning Lessons from Ram's 14-Year Exile: 140
Timely Production and Delivery in a Corporate Context: 142
The Importance of Time Management in Achieving Organizational Goals: 144

Chapter 15: Decision-Making and Quick Thinking 148

Developing Quick Decision-Making Skills in Leadership 150
Adapting Hanuman's Quick Thinking to Modern Business Scenarios 153
Overcoming Decision-Making Challenges Through Effective Strategies 156

Chapter 16: Coordination and Collaborative Efforts ... 161
Nal and Neel's Coordination in Bridge Construction............. 163
Coordinating Complex Projects Within an Organization 166
Lessons in Effective Communication for Better Coordination. 168

Chapter 17: Values and Upholding Principles 173
The Role of Values in Shaping Corporate Culture................ 174
Encouraging Employees to Align with Organizational Values 176
Upholding Principles During Organizational Challenges 179

Chapter 18: Effective Communication and Leadership 184
Rama's Communication Style and Its Impact on Leadership.. 185
Enhancing Communication Skills for Effective Leadership..... 188
Communicating a Vision to Inspire and Motivate Teams....... 191

Chapter 19: Conflict Resolution and Team Collaboration 196
Resolving Conflicts through Open Dialogue and Equitable Solutions.. 197
Strategies for Promoting Healthy Collaboration within Teams 199
Building Conflict Resolution Skills for Effective Leadership.... 201

Chapter 20: Trust and Empowerment in Leadership .. 205
Building Trust Through Consistent and Transparent Leadership... 206
Empowering Employees with Autonomy for Increased Engagement 208
Creating a Culture of Trust Within an Organization............. 210

Chapter 21: Managing Change and Adaptability 214
Adapting to Change Through Rama's Experiences 215
Guiding Teams Through Organizational Change 216
Proactive Approaches to Managing Change Effectively 218

Chapter 22: Resilience and Perseverance in Leadership 222
Cultivating Resilience in Leaders During Challenging Times. 223
Motivating and Supporting Teams Through Adversity 225
The Role of Perseverance in Achieving Long-Term Goals 227

Chapter 23: Setting an Example Through Leadership Behavior 231
Leading by Example Through Fair, Respectful, and Humble Behavior 232
Developing Leadership Behavior that Fosters Loyalty 234
Emulating Positive Leadership Traits for Organizational Success 235

Chapter 24: Networking, Relationship Building, and Strategic Alliances 239
Building Relationships with Different Stakeholders 240
Creating Strategic Alliances for Business Growth 243
Networking Skills for Effective Leadership 244

Chapter 25: Pushing Beyond Limits and Employee Dedication 248
Encouraging Employees to go Above and Beyond Job Descriptions 249
Motivating Teams to Contribute to Organizational Growth .. 251
Cultivating a Culture of Dedication and Excellence Within a Team 252

Chapter 26: Continuous Improvement, Learning, and Resource Management 256
    Lifelong Learning for Leaders 257
    Creating a Culture of Continuous Improvement 259
    Empowering Employees 260
    Rama's Resource Management Skills during the War With Ravana 261

Chapter 1

Introduction to Management Lessons from Ramayana

In the modern world, which is developing at breakneck speed due to technological progress and constant variations in business, having good management skills is vital. However, what if we could learn some practical lessons from an epic story that has been there since time immemorial ? A world of management lessons from the Ramayana, a well-known ancient Indian epic.

Therefore, the world is changing very rapidly due to technological innovations, and organizations are required to respond to such changes at a similar speed. wherein efficient management is required. It turns out that we can learn quite useful things about our lives from an ancient Indian tale called the Ramayana.

The journey is a trip back in time to an era when there were no smartphones or computers, yet interestingly, the lessons from that period can assist us in the current day and age. The Ramayana is not just a fun adventure story about a man named Rama but also offers great ideas on how to be a good leader and manager.

We are introduced to Lord Rama in Ramayana who is portrayed as a savior in the story. He helps us understand the right way to do things, even when it is hard. This notion of what is righteous, or "dharma", is something leaders today can hopefully still learn from when they come face to face with decisions that are difficult.

The story also reveals that cooperation is very significant. Rama has a partner who is a monkey - God named Hanuman who helps him accomplish great feats. This team-building concept is yet highly relevant in modern offices, where people have to work together and be faithful to each other to deliver results.

Further, smart decision-making is a concept that keeps us cool while reading the Ramayana. There is this part where Rama's father has to make the toughest decision which makes us understand how leaders should be careful of making decisions that they think will affect them in the future.

Apart from being a neat story, the Ramayana also has intelligent thoughts on planning and execution. When Rama's army builds a bridge, it is a step-by-step plan and cooperation of people to achieve big goals. This can perfectly be relevant in the way teams conduct projects in organizations today.

In brief, the Ramayana is a repository of valuable concepts that guide one to perform tasks productively. It is the connection between the past and present day, with everlasting knowledge that can help leaders resolve challenges and success in this fast-evolving world. Therefore, despite being an old story, the Ramayana has much impart about being good leaders and managers in the current age.

Understanding the Relevance of Ancient Wisdom in Modern Management

Imagine a Timeless Wisdom:

Setting off on this journey to delve into timeless wisdom, it is necessary to define how ancient learning relates to our modern era. The Ramayana, which dates back millennia, reveals timeless universal laws of human behavior, leadership, and ethics. This is because its timeless teachings to cross the temporal chasm, echoing the immutability of humanity. As the world today is complicated, the challenges that were faced by the epic's characters also reflect those we find in our modern offices.

Despite the enormous temporal and cultural distances, the Ramayana serves as a corridor between antiquity and modernity, presenting timeless lessons that remain relevant. Whether it is ancient epics or contemporary organizational environments, human nature with the pursuits, dilemmas, and ethic conundrums, is a constant factor that binds them together. The teachings of the Ramayana act as a source of wisdom to guide us in various perspectives of leadership, ethical decision making, and human relations that prove essential in guiding men and women through the complexities of our dynamic world.

Universal Themes in the Ramayana:

The Ramayana is timeless in its heroic themes, and it has transcended its ancient origins to become a source of universal truths that strike a chord with eternal relevance. It is more than just a story as it unfolds a veritable repository of the eternal wisdom, exploring basic aspects of the human condition. Themes of relationships, peace-making, decision-making, and a higher purpose are interlaced in the story making it a wise book on contemporary life.

Relationships in the Ramayana include family ties, friendship, and alliances; these aspects show how humans are affected by other human beings despite time and space. The theme of conflict resolution is an important part of the epic, as it encompasses complex approaches that reverberate to this day, offering insightful tips for resolving conflicts in both personal and professional contexts.

Furthermore, the Ramayana explores decision-making using it as an avenue to discuss how choices bear consequences and the moral dilemmas that come with leadership. These motifs, as if a reflection of the dilemmas we encounter in contemporary decision-making landscapes, still represent moral considerations and the desire to pursue a greater purpose.

Adapting to Change:

In the Ramayana, characters travel through a narrative world that is full of doubt and changeability, which resembles the difficulties that are embedded in our modern business settings. The epic is a source of knowledge that provides invaluable lessons required for adaptation is critical in the fast-moving waters of change in today's business environment.

This is why analyzing the reactions of the characters to adversity gives us a practical viewpoint through which we can acquire usable knowledge. The unshakeable steadfastness of Lord Rama in holding fast to dharma amidst the most profound disruptions stands as a testament to the need for constant values during times of chaos. The resilience of Sita to stay calm and respond with calculated defiance while captive illustrates the importance of keeping cool under pressure and tactful disposition during unexpected changes.

In addition to that, Hanuman's ability to be resourceful and agile in dealing with challenges is an excellent foundation for a proactive mindset when adapting to changing business environments. The epic makes the reader think about the strength of working together, as is evident from the Rama-Sugriva alliance, and the importance of the right alliances for achieving common ends.

Overview of Key Leadership Principles from the Ramayana

Rama: The Ideal Leader

At the core of the Ramayana is the archetypal leader, Lord Rama, who as a character surpasses all time as an unsurpassed ideal leader. Lord Rama's leadership is distinguished by the firm devotion to dharma, which represents the ideals of righteousness that help leaders even in different eras. This dedication to maintaining high moral values, regardless of the circumstances, makes him a timeless symbol of inspiration to the leaders entrusted with that responsibility.

The leadership style of Rama is characterized by a strong sense of integrity which forms the foundation on which he bases his decision-making. His knowledge to lead by precept, which was based on the highest moral values, is a standard for leaders who face their own challenges. In addition, Rama's empathetic personality as he interacts with people from all walks of life also reflects the need for one to understand and resonate with the concerns of those being led.

An element of duty is an integral part of Rama's leadership, which shows a dedication that transcends individual needs and focuses on the broader interests. His ardent work is a lesson to leaders aiming at creating a culture of responsibility and accountability within their organizations. Essentially, Lord Rama's leadership in the Ramayana gives a timeless model to leaders, who must not only display integrity and empathy but also a strong determination to accomplish what is right.

Sita's Strength:

The character of Sita as demonstrated within this text is a representation of resilience in the face of adversity and adaptation, which serve as valuable lessons for leaders who operate in volatile environments. Her unwavering support for Rama in times of adversity reveals the importance of a strong support system to all leaders. Sita's unwavering loyalty proves that such strength comes from a united partnership, stressing the need for each other for the fulfillment of common objectives.

In times of difficulty, Sita remains poised and composed despite the challenges that she faces. This is a quality that leaders can learn from when they are navigating their professional path. Her ability to manage any situation with grace and elegance despite the uncertainties portrays the need to keep calm. Leaders can be inspired by the power of Sita's courage, acknowledging the importance of flexibility and unwavering support in establishing a culture of strong leadership that leads to long-term success in the field of organizational challenges.

Hanuman's Devotion:

Hanuman is a monkey God who represents devotion in the Ramayana, and his story teaches us about the power of loyalty and unselfish service. His long-term loyalty to Lord Rama portrays the power that loyalty can bring with leadership. Leaders can learn from the example of Hanuman, as they know that bringing loyalty to the team makes them perform better.

The modesty of Hanuman in the light of his superhuman potential emphasizes the necessity of remembering modesty as a leader's core value. The leaders who adopt this humility foster a culture of cooperation and interdependence. They encourage selfless service instead of personal favors: they inspire their team members to a shared purpose of collective success. Thus, the loyalty of Hanuman provides leaders with a path to design organizational cultures that are resilient and collaborative based on faithfulness, modesty, and a desire for shared goals.

Lakshmana's Loyalty:

In the Ramayana, Lakshmana, who is also the brother of Lord Rama and an unwavering loyalist personifies the core concept of trust and loyalty as a significant aspect of leadership. His unwavering dedication to Rama's cause highlights the magnitude of trust and loyalty in affecting the way the team interacts which, in return, can lead to the success of an organization.

Lakshmana's unflinching loyalty is a powerful message for leaders on the transformative potential of developing interpersonal networks among team members. By creating an atmosphere of trust, leaders can encourage loyalty that is more than just sticking to one's role but it is a commitment towards common goals. So this loyalty, which is not just in words but in actions, becomes a driving force for improved cooperation between team members, better communication, and increased overall team unity. The example of Lakshmana, therefore, brings light to the fact that trust and loyalty are essential ingredients in leadership that raises a whole lot to the achievement of organizational objectives.

The Importance of Storytelling in Conveying Management Lessons

The Power of Narrative:

The strength of storytelling as a vehicle for communicating management lessons is illustrated in the Ramayana, an unending epic that has lived for generations with its rich narrative. Stories hold/possess a power that no other medium can match—the ability to hold someone's attention, to move people emotionally, and to make lessons more memorable. The Ramayana, with the dramatic plot of its sound, is a great tool for transferring sophisticated management concepts in a simple yet entertaining way.

Through interlacing management theories into the fiber of the mythical epic, the Ramayana brings abstract principles to life in an easy-to-understand scenario. The difficulties that characters like Rama, Sita, Lakshmana, and Hanuman had to go through are transformed into allegorical responses to real-life puzzles of leadership. This narrative approach not only improves understanding but also leaves a powerful mark on the audience's consciousness, making the theoretical lessons embedded in stories long-lasting and universally applicable across various organizational environments. The ability of the Ramayana to tell a story in a way that cements its place as one of the best management tools proves that whatever is said by telling stories has a deeper meaning and stays for a long time in the minds of the audience.

Making Lessons Memorable:

Cognition is specifically designed to remember stories, and using this cognitive bias improves the memorability and relatability of management lessons. Weaving management principles into the Ramayana's narrative cloth is a successful tactic in this respect. Regardless of the concepts mentioned, whether elucidating ethical decision-making or effective communication, embedding these lessons within a narrative framework sets up an irresistible linkage between the audience and the core message.

The narrative structure of the Ramayana not only entertains the audience but also provokes emotional reactions, allowing for deeper engagement and learning of the managerial concepts. This strategy allows one to translate abstract principles into concrete situations making it possible for individuals to correlate the challenges that epic characters had to cope with, into the business realities. Briefly, the process of merging management lessons within the storytelling model of the Ramayana is consistent with the tendency in neurological to recall a narrative. This integration guarantees that the lessons become memorable and relatable stories that become rooted in a manager's mind, a deeper and more permanent understanding of critical managerial concepts.

Cultural Significance:

The Ramayana is not just a story; it is a grand cultural heritage that goes beyond generations. By using this well-known and respected story, we are not merely trying to communicate management lessons – we are engaging with a universal cultural phenomenon that is deeply embedded in the lives of people from different backgrounds. The collectivization of the Ramayana's significance in culture also enhances the effectiveness of management lessons transmitted.

Through this shared cultural reservoir, the lessons enshrined within the epic become more than managerial insights; they become values and wisdom that are common to both. The ramifications of the Ramayana in several cultural settings bring about a universal understanding, thus making sure that the management principles discussed are not only understandable but also very meaningful to many people of different cultures. Through this, the value of the cultural significance of the Ramayana turns out to be a medium through which lessons on management are transferred and by doing so, one enriches the learning process with a shared heritage above all backgrounds and views.

Engaging and Inspiring:

Using stories, especially through the lens of Ramayana, becomes a dynamic approach not only to educate but also to be moved to action. This narrative mode helps to impart management insights interestingly, ensuring the relevance of such lessons and their connection between the experience and each individual's life and career.

With the rich narrative background that is provided by the Ramayana, it is easy to see how this setting could be captivating and appealing to audiences. We then weave management principles into this esteemed epic creating a storyline that elevates above theoretical constructs, rendering the lessons more palpable and applicable. The built-in inspiring nature of stories ensures that not only does an individual understand the managerial lessons but also adopts them in their life and career path.

Basically, the narrative allure of the Ramayana becomes an engine of engagement that ignites an inspiring force that moves people to apply management principles in practice and thereby contribute to positive transformation.

Conclusion

The voyage into the relics of leadership, decision-making, cooperation, and flexibility that can be drawn from the timeless tale of the Ramayana provides an insightful exploration of management lessons. In general, as the world races through the advancements in technology and quick business changes, we realize the need for old knowledge more than ever. All things considered, the Ramayana – a cultural legacy that has been inherited from one generation to another – appears as a fountain of timeless wisdom whose truths effortlessly span the gap between time and contemporary times.

The interwoven tales of Lord Rama, Sita, Lakshmana, and Hanuman represent allegorical lights and as such offer universal lessons that continue to reverberate throughout cultural institutions and organizational terrains. Lord Rama's unvarying dedication to dharma serves as an eternal benchmark for leaders that exemplifies the transcendent nature of integrity, empathy, and duty. In the context of Sita and Hanuman's power of perseverance in the face of adversity and extreme loyalty, the importance of a substantive support system and selfless service in leadership is highlighted.

The power of narration that the Ramayana holds results in its ability to carry these management lessons becomes an irresistible channel to deliver these messages. Stories, which are woven into the fabric of human thought, transform abstract concepts into situations that can be related to, and doing so results in a deeper and more lasting comprehension. Through such cultural implications of the Ramayana, these lessons become more than mere managerial insights—they transform into shared values and wisdom that go beyond the divides of diverse cultures.

As we journey through the universal motifs in the Ramayana relationships, conflict resolution, decision-making, and change management we find a source of wisdom that navigates leaders through the turbulence of the modern business environment. The epic stands as a bridge between past and present, providing a timeless guidepost to lead through the constant changes in leadership. As a testament to the fact that human experiences are eternal and the lessons drawn from their stories are universal, this travel from ancient wisdom to modern-day management principles, the Ramayana signifies its glorious past. It is the leaders in any cultural and professional setting that can find inspiration and practical advice within the pages of this epic, transcending temporal gaps and enhancing their leadership with personal insights that have survived the test of time. However, the Ramayana is anything but a simple and meaningless story. It becomes a living handbook that connects the ancient via the contemporaries to offer leaders a light in the complicated seas of change and complexity of today's business world.

End of Chapter 1

Chapter 2

Commitment and Fulfilling Promises

In this chapter, we shall aim to uncover the basic concepts of commitment and reasons why, a promise must be kept, once made. The significance of these concepts cuts across diverse areas including relationships and businesses among others. Through relevant examples and comprehensive language, we attempt to clarify these ideas for a wider audience.

Commitment is a dedication or obligation to a purpose, goal, or relationship. It involves being truthful to one's word and honoring the promises that one makes. In personal commitments, trust, security, and emotional intimacy get promoted. By way of instance, partners in a romantic relationship rely on each other's commitment to construct a solid foundation of trust and loyalty. In friendship, commitment shows up through mutual support and dependability as well.

In the professional realm, dedication is paramount in the attainment of organizational goals and the creation of a thriving work environment. Dedicated employees are diligent, reliable, and accountable. This level of commitment manifests itself as improved productivity, higher work satisfaction, and team unity. Employers appreciate committed individuals because of their commitment and reliability, which add to the success of the organization.

Keeping undertakings is another part of the list of commitments. When we take an oath, we imply assumptions and duties, not only for the parties involved but also for each and everyone involved. If these commitments are not met, one can feel disappointed, become skeptical, and curate strained relationships. Hence, we should be alert of the promises we give and put the required efforts into achieving them.

In personal relationships, the promises tie individuals together and ensure trust either through a pledge to be there for a friend in moments of need or through the endeavors to take out time for family, the confirmation taking relevance in the action. On the other hand, repeatedly breaking promises will destroy trust and damage relationships beyond repair.

Consequently, in the professional setting, the delivery of promises forms the basis of the preservation of credibility and integrity. Employees that live up to their commitments with clients, colleagues, and supervisors, strengthen their reputation and dependability. This then facilitates the creation of solid professional connections and ensures that the industry views one favorably. Commitments and fulfilling promises come into play in this example. Think of a team that is in charge of a project that is critical and has to be completed under a tight deadline. Each team member agrees to meet their deadlines and work collectively to achieve the end result. Having said that, if one team member persistently fails to meet their commitments through missing deadlines or delivering average quality work, the project is bound to fail and the team's trust as well as cohesion will be seriously undermined.

Contrarily, when all team members adhere to their responsibilities and honor their engagements, they display reliability and responsibility. It creates an environment of collaboration where people trust each other and therefore, the completion of the project is achieved.

Ram's Commitment to Exile and Its Corporate Parallels

The Story of Ram

Ancient mythology's Ram, a prince, showed unshakable loyalty and concern for his family when he solemnly promised his father, the king, that he would go into exile for fourteen years and give up his legal claim to the throne.

Being committed and keeping vows is very important, as shown by Ram's choice to follow his father's order even though it cost him personally. His absence brought him many hardships and problems, but he stayed determined. His steadfast dedication was a compass that helped him face the difficulties with strength and honesty.

What happened to Ram is a timeless example of how dedication can change things. Honesty and duty came before his own goals, which showed the noble virtues of devotion and sacrifice. In addition to showing how honest he was, his unwavering dedication to his father's orders set the stage for a legacy that will last forever.

The main idea of Ram's story is that commitment has a lasting effect on fate and character. For generations, his unwavering determination showed how important it is to keep vows, encouraging others to live by similar standards of honesty and loyalty.

Lessons from Ram's Commitment

Having vowed to his father, the king of ancient mythology, Ram, exhibited remarkable dedication as he decided to live in a fourteen-year exile sacrificing his rightful throne. This vow represented his unchangeable commitment and filial piety.

Ram's resolution to respect his father's order irrespective of personal loss emphasizes the great importance of commitment and keeping promises. During his tenure of exile, he was tested many times but never wavered. That dedication was in itself a guiding principle, allowing him to wade through the challenges with bravery and dignity.

The tale of Ram is an instance of the cross-time ability of the commitment. Thus, duty and honor as his priority over his own desires were the model of the noble virtues of loyalty and sacrifice. His unfailing loyalty to his father's wish not only re-stressed his own integrity but also started a line of such traits that lasted forever.

Thus, the tale of Ram depicts the lasting influence of dedication on destiny and a person. He was living proof of the power of keeping promises, motivating people to observe the same in their own lives in years to come.

Corporate Implications

In the business world, commitments span across different areas such as project deadlines, deliverables, and client engagements. In the same manner as the Rams's serious vow, observance of such pledges is very important in building trust, dependability, and reputation in teams and organizations.

Reliability and accountability are displayed when individuals and teams keep their promises meet project deadlines and achieve the outcome they had promised. This dependability is crucial in instilling confidence between the members of the team as well as the stakeholders hence guaranteeing seamless working together and successful implementation of tasks.

Also, keeping promises to the customers is indispensable for creating and maintaining long-term relationships. Consistent delivery of promises improves the reputation of the organization and strengthens its market position. Clients prefer to and are willing to do business with companies that show reliability and commitment to meet their obligations.

Similarly, while Ram's commitment represented integrity and loyalty within the personal domain, keeping commitments within the corporate setting is fundamental in creating a culture of trust and accountability, which results in the success and sustenance of organizations.

Navigating Unexpected Challenges While Honoring Commitments

Challenges Encountered by Ram

While in exile Ram had to surmount a number of obstacles such as encounters with powerful demons and finding his way through treacherous terrains. Though these hurdles were quite overwhelming, he was determined to honor his pledge to his father.

The challenges Ram faces during his exile represent the tests that people encounter in their personal and professional lives. Resilience is required to pass through unexpected setbacks, determination to take on daunting adversaries, and resolve to survive adversity.

Ram's determination to face and be victorious over these impediments is proof of his strong character and high level of commitment. He faced numerous obstacles but did not falter in his resolve to keep his word, thereby confirming that perseverance and determination are instrumental in reaching one's objectives.

Prominently, the journey of Ram represents the transforming nature of resilience and determination in beating the obstacles. His steadfast determination is an eternal inspiration, and it calls for remembering the power of sticking to our obligations even when the circumstances are harsh.

Lessons Learned

The meaning of Ram's journey is a syllabus on resilience and flexibility. Given the emergence of an unexpected problem, preservation of commitment will need not only a resolute but also an innovative approach to address the problem.

The flexibility of Ram to accept unforeseeable situations emphasizes the role of this vital quality and creative thinking in overcoming problems. He did not see setbacks as obstacles but as stepping stones to development and knowledge gain. He was always ready to look for alternative solutions and to change his tactics, this is how he managed to win over adversity and to be loyal to his promises.

Additionally, Ram's pilgrimage symbolizes the importance of determination in striving for accomplishments. Having faced many hurdles on his way he was steadfast in his determination not to turn aside. His persistence is an example of what is required for overcoming adversity and attaining success.

In the end, Ram's journey teaches us that commitment is the art of not only staying on the path but also to change and rebound with strength and purpose. By bringing such qualities into our lives we can successfully overcome challenges and achieve our goals as well as honoring our obligations.

Strategies for Overcoming Challenges

In the corporate world unanticipated issues like resource constraints, technical problems, and market volatility can easily lead to the failure to meet an obligation. To meet these challenges, the teams can use strategic approaches that revolve around communication, cooperation, and contingency planning.

In the first place, the creation of open and transparent communication avenues among the team is necessary for the early detection of challenges and formulation of suitable solutions. By enabling members of a team to speak out about their concerns and give insights, leaders will be able to acquire valuable insights and collectively brainstorm solutions to overcome the hurdles.

In the corporate sector, collaboration is also a major factor in the process of overcoming challenges. The use of different expertise and strengths of team members enables organizations to generate holistic solutions that cover different eventualities. When a team solves problems in cooperation, it creates a feeling of ownership and works as a driving force for all common efforts.

Further, a proactive approach in the development of contingencies assists in minimizing the impact of unanticipated challenges on compliance. Through the identification of probable threats and designing of alternate plans, organizations can minimize interruptions and continue progression towards their objectives even in adverse situations.

In this case, through ensuring effective communication, collaboration, and contingency planning the teams will be able to steer unanticipated challenges in the business environment and eventually conclude with timely delivery. All these strategic approaches enable organizations to learn and to act in response to changing circumstances, and to stay focused on their objectives come what may.

Corporate Parallels

Like Ram, organizations have to demonstrate persistence and flexibility to keep promises in fast-changing business contexts. Accepting challenges as growth opportunities reinforces the commitment culture within teams.

Just like Ram's journey, organizations undergo several challenges, from market volatility to technological disruptions. To overcome these challenges, they should be flexible and strong, reacting properly to unpredictable conditions but not losing sight of their objectives.

Accepting challenges as chances for development nurtures a culture of ongoing improvement among the institutions. Obstacles, instead of discouraging teams, can be used as learning opportunities, which provide important information to be used in future decision-making and strategy creation.

In addition, resilience in adversity enhances confidence and trust in stakeholders. Graceful response to challenges by organizations strengthens their promise of delivery and success.

In fact, it was that very and perseverance of Ram that defined the path to victory, and in the same breath, organizations can only taste success when they accept challenges, show perseverance, and stand by their commitments in the ever-changing business landscape. By adopting this resilience and determination ethos, organizations will flourish in uncertainty and live their objectives assured.

Fostering a Culture of Commitment in the Workplace

Leadership Influence

Leaders have immense power to mold the organizational culture through their acts and behavior. Through qualities such as dedication and ethical standards, leaders show a magnetic example for others.

Consistent demonstration of leadership responsibility and duty will breed confidence and reliability in the organization. Leaders are the role models for employees and therefore when they see their leaders making and keeping commitments, they tend to realize that those are values being emphasized in the organization.

Additionally, leaders who demonstrate integrity in their decisions and interactions promote openness and responsibility. Leaders that practice ethical standards as well as uphold their words are respected and admired because of their behaviors, thereby deepening the trust core in the organization.

In addition, leaders who value transparency and open communication enable an atmosphere where the employees are free to voice out their concerns and give their input. It cultivates an atmosphere of teamwork and tolerance, where dedication to common objectives is the main priority.

Basically, leaders are role models of some values of the organization like dedication and honesty. Emulating these traits in their actions and behaviors, leaders create a culture that promotes these values, and in the end, the organization is propelled to success and sustainability.

Establishing Clear Expectations

Clear expectations and objectives are the key fundamentals to building commitment in an organization. When employees are clearly aware of what they are supposed to be doing, they are more capable of performing effectively by their commitments.

Clarity in expectation communication gives employees clear information about what they are supposed to do, thus bringing down ambiguity and misunderstandings. Through clear goal setting, deadlines, and performance measures, leaders enable their staff to direct efforts toward the organization goals.

In addition, when individual employees have a clear picture of how their unique inputs contribute the organization's overall targets, they tend to be more committed and accountable to their work. Expected activities help in defining the purpose of what the team is supposed to do and thus provide direction to the team members making them feel like part of the team.

In addition, clear communication promotes transparency and confidence within the organization. When leaders openly articulate their expectations and give routine feedback, employees feel appreciated and nurtured resulting in improved engagement and morale.

Basically, the ability of effective communication to provide clear expectations cannot be overemphasized in creating a culture of commitment where employees are empowered to perform their duties with clarity and confidence. Leaders create a framework for success and continuity by ensuring that individual efforts are aligned with the organizational goals.

Accountability Mechanisms

Enforcing accountability mechanisms is key to actually getting commitments met and performance standards kept in an organization. Through setting clear expectations and consequences, leaders can create an environment of accountability which leads to loyalty and high performance.

Feedback loops are opportunities for an employee to receive critical input on performance and adjust as required. The feedback ensures that accountability increases since workers know where they stand, concerning expectations and areas of improvement.

Performance appraisals are the official evaluations of individual and team successes to set targets. Through conducting continuous performance reviews, leaders may objectively assess progress, identify strengths and weaknesses, and offer actionable feedback that supports ongoing improvement.

In addition, the identification and rewarding of achievements maintain the accountability aspect through the promotion of an outstanding performance. Recognition of an employee's contribution in public or through rewards and incentives makes an individual want to live up to such recognition and also reiterates the organizational culture of appreciating excellence.

Fundamentally, the tools of accountability such as feedback, performance appraisals, and mechanisms of recognizing achievements are vital in encouraging a culture of responsibility and accountability within teams. Through the accountability of individuals and teams for their actions and outcomes, organizations will boost performance, create a culture of excellence, and meet their strategic goals efficiently.

Recognizing and Rewarding Commitment

The recognition and awarding of individuals and teams that are committed to the organization is fundamentally necessary for growing a culture of gratitude and motivation within an organization. Be it in the form of verbal commendations, concrete rewards, or professional advancement chances, appreciation is a tool that helps in fortifying values and desired behaviors.

Oral praise and public recognition are simple yet effective ways to appreciate dedication. When a leader appraises employees' commitment and accountability in public, such as during meetings or near the end of the month, it rewards them and motivates other employees to act the same way. This promotes an environment where commitment is honored and cherished.

Moreover, the prospect of clear rewards and benefits reinforces the significance of commitment. Be it financial rewards, additional vacation time, or other benefits, tangible rewards are a way of presenting appreciation for employees' dedication and hard work. Such stimulants encourage the staff to perform well and hence become dedicated and excellent employees.

In addition, offering professional development opportunities as a way of recognition serves as proof of the investment of the organization in the growth and success of the employees. Be it in the form of providing sponsorship for training programs, availing mentorship opportunities, or promoting career advancement, such opportunities enable the employees to upgrade their skills and knowledge, enhancing their sense of worth and loyalty to the organization.

Basically, identifying and compensating for loyalty not only appreciates the efforts of an individual or a team but also promotes a culture where faithfulness and dependability are honored. Giving both intrinsic and extrinsic rewards, an organization can stimulate and encourage employees to fulfill their commitments and thus, become an important part of the success of the organization as a whole.

Encouraging Open Communication

Open communication is important for the development of an environment in which employees are in power to voice their problems and ask for help, breeding trust and cooperation within the organization. Openness leads to the expressing of concerns and ideas by the employees which helps in creating a culture of transparency and mutual respect.

The interactive format allows for a preventative approach to problem-solving as the issues are addressed at an early stage and possible barriers to commitment fulfillment are avoided. Through open discussion of challenges, the root causes are identified, solutions are brainstormed, and effective strategies are developed that allow teams to overcome obstacles together.

In addition, open communication leads to the establishment of trust between colleagues, employees, and management. This indicates a leader's dedication to ensuring a conducive and inclusive working atmosphere when they truly listen to employee feedback and take their concerns seriously. This further strengthens the employees' connection with their organization, consequently improving morale and engagement.

Open communication styles also foster innovation and creativity in teams. The freer the employees feel to pass along their thoughts and perspectives, the better the chances of new insight and solution being discovered, and this leads to organizational growth and success.

Open communication positively influences the achievement of commitment fulfillment and organizational effectiveness through the effective use of collective intelligence and creativity, proactive response, trust construction, as well as collaboration culture.

Conclusion

To sum up, the investigation of commitment and keeping promises in private and business life demonstrates the pivotal role of these notions in creating trust, responsibility, and achievements. In this chapter, we have looked into the importance of commitment in different spheres of life, from personal relationships to the corporate world, and analyzed the links between individual loyalty and organizational strength.

In essence, commitment is a devotion or responsibility to a cause, objective, or relationship that involves the qualities of sincerity and keeping of promises. In personal commitments, for instance, in romantic relationships or friendships, trust and emotional intimacy are developed when both partners support each other and are dependable. Likewise, in the professional domain, commitment is the key to success in accomplishing organizational objectives and the development of a healthy working environment. Dedicated employees promote better productivity, work satisfaction, and team unity which in turn, make the organization attractive to the market and successful.

But commitment goes further than mere dedication; it also involves the action of delivering on one's promises. Fulfilling promises is necessary for the preservation of trust, respect, and positive relations in both personal and working environments. In all areas, be it personal relationships or business transactions, failing to deliver on promises creates problems by fostering skepticism and a lack of trust. Consequently, people and even organizations get to exercise discipline in the promises they make and work towards keeping them.

Ram is an eternally relevant portrayal of unsparing loyalty and sacrifice, demonstrating how dedication turns destiny and makes our characters. The prevailing loyalty of Ram to his father's command in all the adversities that he undergoes during his exile highlights the noble qualities of devotion and sacrifice. His unyielding fortitude prepares us to abide by the same plans of truth and loyalty in our own lives, reiterating the eternal effect of commitment on destiny and character.

Additionally, in the corporate arena, commitment serves as the basis of trust and credibility, the pushers of success and longevity. Reputation and reliability are strengthened through honoring commitments to clients, colleagues, and supervisors, which facilitates solid professional connections and industry favorability.

Effective communication, collaboration, and contingency planning become strategic tools for negotiating unexpected hurdles while honoring responsibilities. Fostering open communication within teams helps create transparency, trust, and innovation, facilitating proactiveness in problem-solving which, in turn, acts against the potential obstacles to the completion of the commitment.

In general, the development of a performance culture at the workplace entails leadership influence, defined performance expectations, mechanisms of accountability, and recognition of commitment. Through these philosophies and promoting an environment where commitment is appreciated and rewarded, organization can produce excellence, promote teamwork, and comfortably meet their strategic objectives with confidence and integrity.

By providing real-life illustrations and practical approaches, this book exposes the significance of integrity, agility, and effective communication in honoring obligations.

End of Chapter 2

Chapter 3

Team Motivation and Leadership

On the current dynamic management scene, the significance of leadership beats strongly, the catalyst for team motivation, and the compass that guides them towards success. In this chapter, we explore the invaluable importance of leadership in identifying motivation, trust, and loyalty within a team. Through a complex exploratory journey through various leadership paradigms and strategies, our aim is to supply you with the arsenal to ignite the flare of inspiration among your team members and culminate in an environment saturated with unity and productivity. At the core of every successful team is a leader who guides not only tasks but guides people to realize their fullest potential. However, leadership is more than just being the holder of some influential position. It is all about influencing, motivating, and empowering other people with a common objective. So, the variegated leadership styles lie at the root of every team's dynamics and become paramount in the effort to achieve meaningful outcomes. The characteristics and implications of different leadership styles are as follows: Autocratic leadership, characterized by centralized decision-making and strict control, might work in certain contexts where there is a necessity for quick action, but at the cost of dousing creativity and not encouraging any sense of ownership within team members. On the other hand, democratic leadership encourages participation and collaboration to explore ideas and solutions for innovation and challenges. Further, transformational leadership has been lauded for its ability to influence far-reaching organizational change and enhance team morale on the merit of vision, inspiration, and individualized concern.

While effectiveness in leadership extends beyond its adoption of a single style but needs a flexible and adaptive approach that would be suited to the needs of the team as well as the context of their work, The situational leadership theory has provided that a leader adjusts his or her style according to the readiness and maturity of the followers. To this end, by adjusting leadership behaviors to the developmental stage of the team members, leaders get the most effective and most facilitating growth. Besides leadership style, what makes effective leadership is the seeding of trust. Trust is the currency of relationships that frees up open communication, collaboration, and possible risk-taking with the team. A leader looking at trust building could guarantee that team members will have space in which they can offer their thoughts, air their concerns, and calculate risks without fear of judgment or prosecution. More effectively, effective leadership involves nurturing a sense of commitment and loyalty among members of the team. This fosters a sense of belonging and shared vision and a partnership wherein team members respect and care for one another. Showing concern and appreciation towards team members will give them a sense of loyalty, regardless of their affiliation with the organization. This breeds loyalty, resilience, and readiness to go the extra mile in making collective goals a reality.

Finally, good management relies on strong leadership to drive team motivation, trust, and loyalty. Leaders who embrace varied leadership styles and methods can motivate their teams to outperform expectations and prosper in today's competitive environment. As you explore the complexities of leadership, keep in mind that true leadership is about empowering others to reach their full potential and create greatness together, rather than about authority or control.

1. Jamvant's Motivational Leadership Style

Let us introduce Jamvant, a fictional leader known for his amazing inspiring leadership style. Jamvant embodies the ethos of motivated leadership with three essential principles:

Leading by Example:

Jamvant, in essence, is an exemplar that epitomizes the values and work ethic he hopes his team members to apply. Jamvant is not just a delegate; he actively participates in the tasks, showcasing the commitment and dedication he has toward them. Be it working late into the night to hit deadlines or holding difficult projects with his team, Jamvant's actions speak volumes, the inspiration for his team to emulate his zeal and passion. His hands-on approach fosters a sense of camaraderie and mutual respect among the team as they see his willingness to roll up his sleeves and tackle challenges head-on. In leading from the front, Jamvant shows a very high benchmark for performance and professionalism. His team members get motivated by his level of dedication, knowing that he is not asking them to do anything that he would not do himself. This style of leadership provides a platform where the team operates in accountability and ownership, their a sense of pride around whatever they are doing, and they strive to reach excellence. Jamvant's leadership style is not by commanding authority but by earning respect through action. His willingness to work alongside his team, sharing both successes and failures and celebrate achievements creates a sense of unity and purpose. In the end, Jamvant's leadership is a clear example of how effective leading by example can be in reaching new heights of performance and success.

Recognition and Appreciation:

Jamvant being well aware of the relevance of acknowledgment in team motivation, places due recognition of the contribution to his team's activities, irrespective of magnitude. Every accomplishment is celebrated; whether through heartfelt "thank yous" or public appreciation during team meetings, Jamvant assures that every individual is valued. Through this practice, he enhances team morale and cultivates a profound sense of achievement and positive behavior among his team members. Jamvant's commitment to recognition extends beyond mere formality; it is a reflection of his genuine appreciation for his team's hard work and dedication. By taking the time to express gratitude, he fosters a culture of appreciation and respect within the team. That culture itself motivates team members to go above and beyond in their efforts knowing that their contributions will be recognized and valued. Moreover, Jamvant recognizes that appreciating collective successes equally enhances a sense of unity and belonging that is integral to team unity and success. Essentially, Jamvant's emphatic impact of recognition and appreciation for nurturing a culture of team members positively and motivated in various initiatives serves as an influential set of approaches. Indeed, Jamvant's genuine expressions of gratitude increase morale and forge among team members feelings of belonging and pride. Through his deeds, Jamvant demonstrates that a simple "thank you" can do much in stimulating and empowering a high-performing team.

Creating a Positive Work Environment:

Jamvant is great at constructing a positive environment at work, one in which positivity, support, and camaraderie not only reside but also flourish. Being open to communication and cherishing diverse points of view, he fosters collaboration. Team building and regular check-ins with his team, along with a friendly leadership style, provide an environment where the team members feel valued, respected, and even more motivated to bring their A-game. Jamvant realized that motivation is one of the important factors that can impact team dynamics and performance. Through empathy, authenticity, and a clear sense of purpose, Jamvant sets up the team that will be motivated and engaged, on its way to success. His emphasis on open communication assures that every team member is heard and understood, thereby promoting trust and transparency within the team. Through collaboration, Jamvant taps the collaborative force and adds their collective intelligence to solve problems or innovate. Moreover, his respect for diversity of perspectives breeds a culture of inclusivity and creativity, where people feel empowered to express their unique strengths and ideas. Through thoughtful team-building activities and regular check-ins, Jamvant strengthens the bonds among team members, nurturing a sense of belonging and mutual support. His approachable leadership style further reinforces this culture of positivity, making it easy for team members to approach him with questions, concerns, or ideas. In essence, Jamvant's wholehearted commitment to creating a positive working environment will underscore his conviction inthe transformative nature of motivation. By creating a positive environment for motivation, he helps foster a culture of support and collaboration that will result in higher performance and enhance the working lives of his employees.

2. Developing a Visionary Leadership Approach

Visionary leadership promotes organisational growth and innovation. It entails presenting a compelling vision, inspiring others to support it, and empowering them to make important contributions towards its realisation. Here's how to create a visionary leadership approach:

Clarify Your Vision:

A leader who envisions is the one who first frames up a particular and powerful vision for the future. This vision can be the same beacon of light to bind the team to a common sense of mission and purpose. This vision needs to be a powerful one in terms of resonating with the aspirations and values of the team. The power to articulate this vision for inspiration and motivation of others is central to the role of a visionary leader. He motivates and encourages the team by painting a beautiful picture of what success would look like. Furthermore, the vision acts as a constant reminder of the big picture; it aids in determining the decisions being made and the priorities being set, even against all odds or uncertainty.

In addition to clarity, the vision should be inspiring. It should make it quite tangible in ways that have some kind of credibility and uniqueness. Just the same, that vision makes every team member feel personally invested in its attainment. The element of the vision that requires constant communication and reinforcement by the visionary leader is to take forward the vision periodically. This can involve regular meetings, feedback, celebration of progress, etc. to ensure that the vision does not fade into oblivion but keeps lingering at the front of the collective consciousness of the team, thus reaffirming its significance and relevance.

Effective Communication:

Proper communication of the vision is required for its success. A visionary leader excels in conveying the vision in a captivating and relatable way, which ignites passion and enthusiasm among his/her team members. Leveraging storytelling, visual aids, and interactive discussions, the leader represents the future in a vivid manner and clarifies what the roles of each team member should be in realizing it.

Storytelling, a strong weapon in the arsenal of a visionary leader, ensures that people feel an emotional connection to the narrative and the probable impact of the vision. By weaving these stories in stories that illustrate the potential future vision, the leader gets his/her team inspired and motivated, by making them feel a sense of purpose and urgency towards the shared goal.

Visual aids often come in handy during the communication process of the vision, as this comes in handy for comprehension and retention purposes. Whether it is through slides, diagrams, or multimedia materials, the leader has had a visual element of use that supports key messages and simplifies complex concepts into one coherent theme. The visual representations of the desired future are made to make the team members visualize the contribution and how the efforts made out of it take part in the bigger scheme.

Interactive discussions further deepen understanding and engagement with the vision. In this way, the leader encourages active participation and seeks feedback from the team members. This promotes a sense of ownership and commitment towards the vision, where the people feel valued and empowered to give input and opinions that can propel forward the vision.

Empower Your Team:

The power of a visionary leader rests in empowering its members. He has emissaries of deep faith in team members and enables them to take up, in effect, the charge of their work, effect self-rule, and contribute unique talents and perspectives toward the realization of shared vision. Offering the resources, support, and opportunities of growth, he fosters a culture of accountability, creativity, and collective perspectives and empowers individuals to be at the forefront in showcasing their full potential.

Visionary leadership is initiated and shaped through the belief in the latent abilities of every member. A visionary leader realizes that individuals who are encouraged with authority and responsibility are motivated to surpass their wildest imaginations, resulting in leveraging their creativity and problem-solving skills. This autonomy not only pushes job satisfaction but also cranks up the sense of ownership and commitment towards meeting the goals that the organization collectively sets out to achieve.

Moreover, the leader's support is instrumental in bringing out success at the individual and team levels. Be it through mentorship, feedback, or advocacy for professional development, the leader proves a genuine concern for the well-being and growth of his subordinates. Such support encourages risk-taking and experimentation, thereby creating an environment that fuels innovation and continues to evolve.

More so, visionary leaders fully understand the importance of collaboration. They allow free communication among members of the team, ideas to be exchanged, and cross-functional teamwork to bring about an even flow of ideas toward innovation and enhanced creativity.

Ultimately, the fabric of visionary leadership is strengthened by the power of empowerment; one is thus able to thrive and excel in an environment of trust, support, and teamwork. An empowered team member will be able to take initiative and show their strength in their unique sense. This sets a platform whereby innovation can flourish and collective success is not only envisioned but also realized.

3. Building Trust and Loyalty Within a Team

Trust and loyalty are essential components of robustness, resilience, and high-performing teams. They facilitate effective communication, collaboration, and mutual support, promoting psychological safety and cohesion. Here's how to create trust and loyalty among your team members:

Lead with Integrity:

Leading with integrity is key to establishing trust in leadership. A person who is committed to ethical standards, honesty, and transparency among interactions is facilitating a culture of trust and respect towards his team members. They are role models, ensuring alignment between their words and actions and taking responsibility for their decisions and conduct even when met with difficulties. The following stands as a great part of leading with integrity: the commitment to ethical principles. While such principles are witnessed in all leaders' behavior, this kind of behavior incites a lot of respect and followers' confidence. Leaders, through such passion, create a culture where individuals feel safe and valued. This is because integrity must be demonstrated by example to the extent that many individuals present themselves with the same. Leadership with integrity, which has been effective, sets an example, encouraging others to lead by the same standards and behavior.

Furthermore, leaders who can lead with integrity always lead by example. Honesty, fairness, and accountability are reflective of such actionable leaders who inspire their team into the same level of uncertainty. Their consistency in what they say and what they do builds credibility that increases trust, leading to strong and long-lasting relationships within the team.

Much more, leaders who lead with integrity are never afraid to face difficult situations and communicate openly with their team members. They do not shy away from delivering bad news or negative feedback; they address conflicts with transparency. By having transparency and tackling issues face-on, these leaders foster a culture of trust and collaboration, where team members feel comfortable in expressing their concerns and contribute to collective problem-solving.

Leading with integrity is important for establishing trust and respect in leadership. Ethics, such as consistency between words and action, and candidness create an environment where people feel safe, respected, and motivated to work to achieve common goals together.

Foster Open Communication:

Open communication nurtures trust and fosters a culture of transparency and cooperation in a team. In that vein, leaders who prioritize open communication and positive dialogue that is constructive in nature set the standard for honest dialogue, active listening, and constructive feedback to enable team members to feel valued, heard, and respected. Such leaders tend to nurture transparency, ensuring that conflicts are resolved quickly and that concerns are addressed appropriately.

Encouraging open communication, therefore, is a concern for the kind of safe space for honest dialogue that comes with it. Leaders who encourage their team members to express their thoughts, ideas, and concerns without fear of judgment or reprisal demonstrate their commitment to building trust and mutual respect. Active listening by leaders towards their team members shows that what they think and feel of an organization is relevant and will be for the betterment of the team.

In addition, more leaders ensure that transparency is promoted through the consistent sharing of pertinent information and updates within their teams. Keeping everyone updated on organizational goals, challenges, and decisions makes the team members aware and aligned in an orderly and rational way for the achievement of common goals. This will help prevent the generation of inaccurate information and the spread of false rumors, thus stimulating a sense of ownership and accountability amongst the members of the team.

Moreover, leaders ought to be proactive in resolving conflicts and treating issues that pertain to them. Doing so is an indication of devotion in building a supportive and inclusive work environment. Through empathetic conflict resolution, leaders are able to build trust and nurture bonds within the team for smooth cooperation and addressing of issues.

To sum up, open communication is critical to the development of trust and collaboration in a team. Leaders, by giving time and energy towards the right kind of open communication and encouraging transparency, often foster an environment in which team members feel valued, respected, and empowered to help the team to achieve its objectives.

Lead by Example:

Leadership is an example to follow, and trust is not gifted but earned through continuous actions. When a leader trusts his team through delegation of responsibilities and empowering them to make decisions, it reflects his confidence in their capabilities. By granting autonomy, recognition of achievements, and commemoration of successes, leaders foster loyalty and commitment within the team members, nurturing a culture that is based on mutual trust, respect, and reciprocity. Trust, leading by example, is established through examples rather than mere words. Through their actions, the leader communicates that the task is within the abilities and capabilities of the team member. A leader who empowers others with leadership positions ensures that a sense of ownership and accountability prevails by providing them with authority to carry out work. This, in turn, leads to motivation and commitment by the team members.

Furthermore, recognition and appreciation of achievements maintain and strengthen the culture of trust within the team. In a way, a leader's appreciation of what is done at work by team members creates a sense of respect and appreciation for these team members. It improves morale, further enhancing the sense of belonging and pride, thus increasing loyalty and commitment to the team's goals.

In addition, leaders who give autonomy and recognition create an environment of reciprocity. A sense of being valued and respected emerges when team members are entrusted with responsibilities and appreciated for their contributions. This mutual trust and respect creates a cohesive and high-performing team, one where members collaborate, innovate, and push themselves toward excellence. In effect, leading by example means demonstrating trust through actions, empowering team members, and honoring their successes. It creates a culture where mutual trust, respect, and reciprocity motivate team members to contribute towards the goals of the team to eventually achieve success.

Conclusion

In the end, the exploration, discovery, and empowerment journey through team motivation and leadership have brought forth a rich tapestry of knowledge and experience in both theory and practice. In this chapter, we have endeavored to illuminate the fundamental role leadership plays in driving motivation, trust, and loyalty within a team. We have cut across the varied landscape of leadership styles and identities for the foundations of effective leadership. Leadership should never be seen as a process of being but as a state of inspiration and motivation to other people in order to achieve their maximum performance. Leadership is about leading by example, exhibiting integrity, and fostering a culture of trust, respect, and cooperation. Effective leaders recognize that vision, communication, and recognition for milestones create the foundation for the bestowment of excellence in team performance and success.

As we reflect on the observations made in this chapter, it becomes clear that leadership is not straightforward and can be narrowed down to several parameters that are dynamic. Effective leadership, for instance, varies and is dependent on a lot of special factors related to team members' needs and ambitions. Through some of the varied leadership styles and approaches, leaders can navigate the complexities of the modern world of work and inspire their teams to achieve greatness.

The success of any organization, its strength comes from the power of its leaders. Leaders who make their members' well-being and development their priority to form an environment where individuals can thrive, work together, and innovate. They understand that effective leadership is not about power or authority but about empowering others to attain their potential and contribute towards a group's common good.

You will carry on through your leadership journey having the motivation and inspiration you need to impact people in a positive way. Placing principles of trust, integrity, and empowerment in your leadership, you'll create the kind of teams that are not only motivated but also resilient and adaptable in the face of challenges.

To sum up, we hope to lead with purpose, passion, and authenticity in knowing that the actions we undertake today can shape not just the leaders of tomorrow but also a brighter future for all.

End of Chapter 3

Chapter 4

Strategic Alliances and Managerial Skills

As a businessperson, your success often depends on how well you can build and handle strong strategic partnerships. By working together with other businesses or groups, strategic alliances can create new chances, reach more customers, and encourage new ideas. A wide range of skills and strategies are needed for managers to effectively handle these partnerships.

Imagine that each piece of the puzzle is a different part of your business or field. Connecting with other businesses through strategic partnerships is like finding the last piece missing from a puzzle. Understanding the most important parts of making and managing these partnerships is necessary to reach this goal.

Firstly, it's important to find possible partners. Locate businesses that can help you fill in the gaps in your business and play to your skills. Partnering with a hardware manufacturer, for example, can help your product line and market exposure if you are a software developer.

It's important to set common goals once you've found suitable partners. Therefore, everyone is on the same page and moving towards the same goal. Communication is important because it keeps everyone on the same page and avoids mistakes.

Constructing trust is another important part of managing strategic partnerships. To have a good partnership, you need to be open, honest, and dependable with your partners. Meeting your obligations, being honest about your plans, and keeping things private when needed are all examples of this.

Forging partnerships also requires effective communication. Communication stays open with regular meetings, reports, and feedback sessions. Any problems or issues are dealt with quickly. Additionally, being flexible is very important because it lets you deal with changing situations and meet your partner's wants. The success of the alliance must be constantly evaluated. This means regularly checking the partnership against set criteria to make sure it's yielding the desired outcomes. Being ready to make changes if they are needed and working together with your partners to reach your goals will help everyone succeed.

In addition to managing alliances, it's also important to have good ties with stakeholders. Customers, workers, investors, suppliers, and people in the community are all examples of stakeholders.

Locating important people and learning what they want and need is the first step. Communication with stakeholders on a regular basis and including them in decision-making processes helps build trust and make sure their opinions are heard. Openness is important in dealing with stakeholders because it helps build trust and confidence. Honesty and openness about your choices and actions and how they affect others build trust and a good friendship.

Managing relationships between stakeholders also includes figuring out how to solve conflicts. While disagreements are normal, it's important to deal with them quickly and in a productive way. Dealing with disagreements and improving relationships can be done by listening to everyone, looking for shared ground, and working toward a solution that works for everyone.

Sugriva's Managerial Characteristics and Their Application in the Business World

A character from old Indian mythology named Sugriva can teach us important lessons about how to be a good manager that can be used in the modern business world. Sugriva was known for being a good boss because he did things like:

Clear Communication:

It's like the glue that holds a team together, and Sugriva was a great example of this skill in the past. Just like Sugriva made sure his team knew what he wanted them to do, today's businesses do best when leaders talk to their teams clearly. Clear communication of goals and plans helps everyone work together toward a shared goal, avoiding confusion and building unity. When it comes to business, clear communication makes sure that everyone knows what is expected of them, how their work fits into the bigger picture, and what needs to be done to succeed. It encourages team members to be open and honest, builds trust, and works well together, which makes the business more productive and achieves better results overall.

Strategic Thinking:

As Sugriva showed, strategic thinking means seeing beyond the present and imagining what the future will be like. Just like Sugriva carefully planned what he was going to do, managers today need to think strategically to deal with the complicated market. Knowing what problems and chances might come up ahead of time helps managers make plans and use resources wisely. Businesses can stay ahead of the curve, adjust to new situations, and make money off of new trends by thinking strategically. It includes looking at data, finding patterns, and making decisions based on that information that are in line with long-term goals. Strategic thinking helps managers stay flexible and quick to respond to changes in the market, moves by competitors, and customer tastes in a business world that is always changing. In the end, encouraging a mindset of strategic thinking within a business leads to new ideas, resilience, and long-term growth.

Empowerment:

Trust in your team, as Sugriva does, is a key part of being a good leader in today's companies. Just like Sugriva gave his team members responsibility, giving workers today that same level of freedom creates a culture of creativity and ownership. Employees are more likely to take the lead, try new things, and contribute creatively to the success of the company if they feel trusted and given the freedom to do so. Employees who are empowered feel like they own their work and are responsible for it, which makes them proud of it and drives them to do their best. It also promotes teamwork and collaboration because everyone feels valuable and appreciated for what they bring to the table. Businesses can use the many skills and points of view of their employees to drive creativity and long-term growth by decentralizing decision-making and letting workers make their own decisions.

Adaptability:

As Sugriva's quick response to changing situations shows, adaptability is a key skill for success in today's lightning-fast business world. Similar to how Sugriva quickly dealt with new problems, businesses need to be able to adapt to the constantly changing market conditions and customer wants. Staying rigid and unwilling to change can cause you to miss chances and become less relevant in today's competitive world. Businesses must make adaptability a core value and create an environment that supports new ideas and trials. Staying open to new ideas and ways of doing things helps businesses take advantage of new chances, deal with new threats, and stay ahead of the curve. Additionally, being flexible helps companies listen to what their customers say and change their goods and services to match changing needs and preferences. Organizations that put an emphasis on being flexible, ultimately do better in a business world that is always changing and unpredictable.

Creating and Nurturing Strategic Alliances

When companies form strategic partnerships, they work together to get benefits for both of them. Here's how to make and keep these kinds of alliances:

Identify Complementary Partners:

Finding similar partners is like finding the last piece of a puzzle that makes the whole picture complete. Within the business world, this means seeking out companies whose strengths match your own. For instance, if your business is making software applications, working with a hardware maker could be very helpful. By using your knowledge of software, you can make their hardware goods more useful, making them a more appealing option for customers. Both you and the hardware manufacturer can benefit from using each other's goods. You can use each other's skills to reach more customers, come up with new ideas, and gain a competitive edge by working with partners that complement yours. In addition to helping your business, this method also makes the ecosystem stronger, which encourages growth and development across all fields.

Establish Common Goals:

Choosing shared objectives is like making a map for your trip. All sides must be on the same page and working toward the same goals by setting clear alliance objectives and outcomes. Establishing shared objectives gives partners a sense of togetherness and purpose, which encourages them to work together and take action as a group. It is important to communicate clearly throughout this process so that there are no mistakes and everyone starts off on the same page. All sides working together toward common goals make it easier to make decisions, reduce disagreements, and make the alliance more effective. Furthermore, having common goals gives a structure for judging success and the alliance's performance over time. You can build a strong foundation for a successful and mutually beneficial relationship by setting common goals right from the start.

Build Trust:

Trusting someone is like putting down a strong base for a house. Trust is the essential building block of any strong partnership. Prioritize openness, honesty, and integrity in your relationships if you want to build trust with your partners. Transparency means being honest about your plans, actions, and choices, so there are no surprises or hidden goals. Being honest means telling the truth and being true to what you say, even if it's hard or causes discomfort. Being reliable and responsible means keeping your promises. Collaboration and problem-solving work better when partners trust each other. When you don't care for and develop your trust, it can easily be lost. Adopting honesty and trust as top priorities in your union builds a strong base for long-term success and mutual benefit.

Effective Communication:

Effective communication is like the lifeline that keeps the alliance going. Maintaining open lines of communication with your alliance partners is critical to ensuring that information flows freely and that everyone is informed. Regular updates, meetings, and feedback sessions provide an opportunity to check in, share progress, and address any issues or concerns that may arise. By maintaining continual communication, you promote transparency and trust within the alliance, resulting in a collaborative environment in which ideas can be discussed openly and problems solved swiftly. Furthermore, efficient communication aids in aligning efforts toward common goals, reducing misunderstandings, and increasing the effectiveness of collaborative action. It is not enough to simply communicate; you must also actively listen to your partners, comprehend their points of view, and collaborate to discover mutually beneficial solutions. Prioritizing excellent communication strengthens your relationships with alliance partners and increases the possibility of joint success.

Flexibility:

Flexibility, or the capacity to bend without breaking, is critical for negotiating the twists and turns that come with any arrangement. It is critical to be willing to adjust and compromise when unanticipated obstacles arise, which they frequently do in the dynamic world of business. This entails being open to new ideas, techniques, and solutions, even if they diverge from your initial objectives. By displaying flexibility, you demonstrate your willingness to collaborate with your partners to overcome hurdles and reach shared goals. This could entail altering timeframes, reallocating resources, or revising tactics to better reflect changing circumstances. Cooperation from all parties is essential in these situations because it allows for creative problem-solving and keeps the alliance robust in the face of adversity. By embracing flexibility, you not only increase the agility of the alliance, but also improve relationships between partners, cultivating a spirit of trust, cooperation, and mutual support.

Continuous Evaluation:

Continuous evaluation is similar to regularly checking the compass to ensure you're still on the right track. Regularly assessing the alliance's performance against set measures is critical for determining its success and identifying opportunities for improvement. Setting explicit goals and benchmarks from the start provides a framework for measuring performance and evaluating progress over time. Regular evaluation enables you to monitor important performance metrics, detect trends, and pinpoint areas where the alliance may be falling short of expectations. This allows you to make educated judgments and take corrective action as needed, ensuring that the alliance remains focused on its goals and objectives. Furthermore, regular review promotes a culture of accountability and learning inside the partnership, pushing all parties to strive for excellence and continually improve their performance. By focusing on constant evaluation, you position the alliance for long-term success and sustainability in a continuously changing business environment.

Building Effective Relationships with Stakeholders

Stakeholders are persons or groups who are interested in your company's success. Here's how you can develop and keep positive relationships with them.

Identify Key Stakeholders:

Identifying key stakeholders is similar to creating a guest list for a party—you want to ensure that every one crucial is invited. In business, stakeholders are persons or groups who have a vested interest in your organization's success. This encompasses not only consumers and staff, but also investors, suppliers, and the larger society. Each stakeholder group has unique demands, expectations, and concerns that may differ depending on their relationship with your company. Identifying and understanding these stakeholders allows you to adjust your tactics and actions to their individual needs and preferences. Customers, for example, may place more value on product quality and customer service, whilst investors may be more concerned with financial success and ROI. By proactively engaging with stakeholders and addressing their problems, you may generate trust, loyalty, and a positive community reputation for your company. Finally, understanding and prioritizing the requirements of important stakeholders is critical to long-term success and viability.

Engagement and Communication:

Stakeholder engagement and communication require care and attention, like relationships. It's important to notify stakeholders about new product releases, strategic initiatives, and corporate policy changes. They feel included and respected, which builds trust in your company. When appropriate, including stakeholders in decision-making can improve results and increase buy-in. You demonstrate that you value their thoughts and are devoted to meeting their requirements by asking for and listening to criticism. It increases your business's interaction with stakeholders and helps you make well-informed decisions that benefit them. Effective engagement and communication develop trust and collaboration, enabling long-term success and mutual gain.

Transparency:

To build trust and understanding in relationships between stakeholders, Transparency is like sunlight—it shines on things and gets rid of shadows. Honesty and openness about the reasons behind your business choices and how they might affect stakeholders are part of being transparent in your actions and decisions. Maintaining communication with stakeholders and giving clear reasons for choices makes people trust your organization's honesty and dependability. Additionally, openness promotes a culture of responsibility by pushing leaders to own up to their actions and giving stakeholders the details they need to hold them responsible. Stakeholders will admire and be loyal to you if you put transparency first because it shows that you are committed to ethical behavior and good governance. In the end, disclosure is the most important thing for building trust among stakeholders, which is necessary for working together and achieving success for everyone.

Manage Expectations:

Planning a show is a lot like managing expectations—you want to make sure that everyone knows what to expect and that you keep your promises. Communicating clearly what you can and cannot offer based on your resources and abilities is part of setting realistic expectations with your stakeholders. Fairness, honesty, and a deep knowledge of the wants and needs of stakeholders are needed to do this. Sharing clear information about what your group will do to meet their needs will help avoid disappointment and confusion in the future. Furthermore, aiming to meet or beat these standards shows that you are dedicated to providing value and gaining the trust of your clients. Managing expectations is an ongoing process that needs constant conversation and feedback, though. Open lines of communication and active listening to stakeholder concerns will allow you to make changes to your plans and actions as needed to keep expectations in line with reality. Effectively managing expectations helps build good relationships with stakeholders and, in the long run, improves your organization's credibility and image.

Conflict Resolution:

Conflict resolution is like untangling a knot; it needs time, comprehension, and a will to compromise. When conflicts emerge among stakeholders, it is critical to handle them quickly and constructively to keep them from growing and inflicting greater harm. This entails listening to all people involved and comprehending their viewpoints, concerns, and goals. Active listening demonstrates respect and empathy, which can assist in reducing tension and create a more conducive climate for dispute resolution. Finding common ground is essential for reaching a mutually acceptable solution that serves the requirements and interests of all parties concerned. To bridge differences and establish a settlement that is acceptable to all parties, compromise, flexibility, and creative problem-solving strategies may be required. Furthermore, it is critical to approach conflict resolution with a long-term relationship preservation mindset rather than a concentration on quick successes. Addressing issues in an open and collaborative manner helps enhance stakeholder's trust, communication, and cooperation, providing the framework for future success and collaboration.

Value Creation:

Value creation is similar to planting seeds that bloom into flourishing gardens; it is about sustaining relationships and providing meaningful outcomes for stakeholders. To demonstrate how your efforts, provide value, highlight the beneficial influence your company has on stakeholders' lives and livelihoods. This could be accomplished by delivering high-quality products and services that meet and exceed client expectations, resulting in increased satisfaction and loyalty. Furthermore, providing returns for investors through consistent financial success and development displays your dedication to long-term value and prosperity. Furthermore, giving back to the community through corporate social responsibility activities, philanthropy, and environmental stewardship demonstrates your company's dedication to making a positive influence beyond profit margins. Focusing on achieving positive outcomes for all parties involved

fosters trust, goodwill, and reputation, all of which are necessary for long-term success and sustainability. Finally, value creation involves developing mutually beneficial relationships and cultivating a culture of shared wealth and success.

Understanding Sugriva's managerial traits and combining them with successful techniques for forming alliances and managing stakeholder interactions will help you simplify management skills and achieve business success.

Conclusion

In the corporate world, success frequently depends on the capacity to form solid partnerships and maintain positive connections with stakeholders. Strategic partnerships provide chances for growth, innovation, and wider market reach, and efficient stakeholder management ensures that all parties' requirements and expectations are met. Throughout this chapter, we have examined numerous tactics and managerial abilities required for navigating these crucial components of business management.

From identifying ideal partners to cultivating trust and effective communication, the process of forming and managing strategic alliances needs meticulous planning, collaboration, and flexibility. Businesses can form partnerships by exploiting complementary skills, defining common goals, and stressing transparency and flexibility. Continuous evaluation ensures that alliances are still aligned with their goals and adaptive to changing conditions, ensuring resilience and sustainability in a dynamic business environment.

Similarly, developing good relationships with stakeholders entails understanding their needs and expectations, communicating openly and transparently, and addressing disagreements constructively. Businesses may improve their reputation in the community by identifying important stakeholders, managing expectations, and prioritizing value creation.

Furthermore, learning from Sugriva's managerial characteristics might provide useful lessons for modern corporate executives. Clear communication, strategic thinking, empowerment, and adaptability are critical skills for success in today's competitive environment. By combining these characteristics with successful alliance-building and stakeholder management strategies, managers can simplify management skills and achieve long-term growth in their firms. Finally, mastering the art of building strategic alliances and managing stakeholder relationships necessitates a combination of abilities, strategies, and personal characteristics. Businesses that prioritize cooperation, openness, and value creation can negotiate obstacles, seize opportunities, and lay the groundwork for long-term success. As we progress in a quickly changing business environment, the ideas stated in this chapter provide a road map for simplifying management abilities and reaching excellence in business management.

End of Chapter 4

Chapter 5

Value Your Subordinates and Listening Skills

Managing well means showing your employees you value them and getting better at listening. This chapter goes into great detail on these important topics. Making the workplace a good place to be, improving teamwork, and achieving company success all depend on these basic traits. In more depth, let's look at these ideas. In order to be a good boss, you need to value your subordinates. This isn't just a nice thing to do. Managers create an environment of respect and acceptance when they value and acknowledge the unique skills, accomplishments, and points of view of each team member. Because of this, employees feel like they fit in and are loyal, which makes them happier at work and more engaged.

Because they are driven by a sense of purpose and being noticed, employees who feel appreciated are more likely to go above and beyond in their jobs. Additionally, they are more open to working together, discussing ideas, and taking responsibility for their own tasks. When workers feel unappreciated or underpaid, on the other hand, they might lose interest in their work and be less dedicated to it.

Another important part of being a good manager is being a good listener. Actively trying to understand other people's points of view, worries, and feelings is part of listening to what they have to say. People who manage teams show they care and value their employees by listening carefully. This builds trust and makes relationships stronger.

Employers learn a lot about their workers' wants, needs, and problems when they listen to their workers. This lets them deal with problems before they happen, give members of the team the help they need, and adapt their leadership style to each person. Employees who feel heard and respected are more likely to share their thoughts, give feedback, and help make decisions when they are actively listening. Managers can make the workplace a good place to work where people feel respected, given the freedom to do their best, and motivated to achieve by showing they value their employees and learning how to listen well. This boosts happiness and job satisfaction, as well as the interaction between team members and the work that gets done. People are more likely to work well together, come up with new ideas, and reach common goals if they feel like their contributions are valued and their opinions are being heard.

Managers need to change how they act and what they do in order to show that they value their employees and listen well. Regular one-on-one meetings with management can be used to check in, give feedback, and talk about ways for team members to advance in their careers. On top of that, they can promote open communication by asking for ideas, and comments, and participating in team discussions.

When managers talk to their team members, they can set a good example by showing understanding, respect, and active listening. Making the whole company feel good about these values sets a good example for the culture at work. And finally, managers can make the company more successful by putting the health and growth of their employees first. This will lead to a more welcoming, cooperative, and productive team.

Overall, two important parts of being a good manager are showing respect for your employees and getting better at listening. Bosses can make the workplace a better place to be, improve teamwork, and get better results for their company by realizing how important these traits are and actively using them in their leadership style.

Recognizing the Signs of Poor Leadership Through Ravana's Example

Leadership is more than just having power; it's also about being responsible and caring about the people you lead. To make our point, we use the figure Ravana from old stories to show how this works. Ravana was very powerful, but he didn't care about or understand his workers. Similarly, leaders who aren't good at their job often don't think about how their choices will affect their team.

Signs of Poor Leadership:

Lack of Empathy:

Leaders who don't have empathy don't care about their team members' feelings and worries, which makes people distrustful and less motivated. When leaders don't understand or handle the feelings and needs of their team, it can make it harder for people to work together and lower morale and productivity as a whole. Empathy is important for creating a good work atmosphere where everyone feels valued, understood, and supported, which ultimately helps the company succeed.

Micromanagement:

Micromanagement is when a boss keeps too much of an eye on every part of their team's work, which limits their freedom and creativity. This way of doing things hurts trust and faith in the team because it makes it harder to come up with new ideas and grow. Leaders who don't give tasks to their team members and let them own their work can make them frustrated and lose interest in their job. Giving advice and support while letting team members make choices and share their own skills and ideas is an important part of being a good leader. This encourages a mindset of independence and responsibility, which is important for driving success and making sure employees are happy.

Poor Communication:

Misunderstandings and lack of trust happen when leaders don't deliver information clearly. As a result of communication routes that aren't clear or don't work consistently, team members may become confused and irritated. Poor guidance and clear instructions can cause people to do their jobs wrong or not at all, which lowers morale and output. Concerns that aren't heard or handled by team members can also hurt trust in leadership and make it harder for people to work together. Clear, honest, and trusting communication within the team is important for creating a positive and productive work environment.

Ignoring Feedback:

When leaders don't listen to or act on feedback from their team members, it can stop growth and progress. Leaders who don't show appreciation for feedback send the word that people's thoughts and ideas are not important. This can make team members lose interest and get angry, which can stop them from working together and being creative. Leaders miss chances to make things better and don't use different ideas and skills on their team when they don't listen to comments. Accepting feedback as a way to improve creates a culture of constant innovation and improvement, which leads to success and higher employee happiness.

It's important for leaders to be aware of these signs in themselves and take action to fix them. How well a leader can relate to, talk to, and involve their team members has a direct effect on the team's total output and happiness.

The Importance of Active Listening in Leadership

Active listening is one of the most important skills for leaders to have. Listening alone isn't enough; you have to really be interested in and understand what other people are saying. Leaders show that they value their team members' ideas by constantly listening and encouraging open communication.

Key Principles of Active Listening:

Pay Attention:

To give someone your full attention, you have to block out all other sounds and interruptions. This lets you actively listen and understand what they are saying. Focusing only on the speaker's message shows respect and interest, which leads to trust and open communication. By avoiding distractions like phone calls or other conversations, you can make sure the person speaking feels important and heard. This amount of attention helps you understand what the other person is saying more deeply, which makes communication and teamwork easier. In turn, this leads to better relationships and a happier workplace, which improves teamwork and the success of the company.

Show Interest:

Using nonverbal cues, like nodding and keeping eye contact, to show attention is an important part of being attentive. These actions let the person speaking know that their words are being paid attention to and appreciated. Maintaining eye contact builds trust and a sense of closeness, while nodding shows that you agree and understand. By using these kinds of nonverbal cues, viewers make the space supportive and interesting, which makes speakers more likely to speak freely. This helps people on the team talk to each other better and builds stronger relationships between them. Ultimately, using nonverbal cues to show interest make it easier for people to work together and create a good work environment that encourages productivity and new ideas.

Clarify and Summarize:

Clarifying and summarizing are important parts of good communication that make sure both the speaker and the viewer understand. To clear up any questions or doubts about the message, asking for clarification is helpful. Rephrasing key points shows that you have heard and understood them. By summarizing and clarifying, viewers make sure they understand what the speaker is saying, which lowers the chance of misinterpretation. This helps to make things clear and consistent, which makes communication easier and teamwork better. In the end, these habits help build a culture of respect and understanding between people, which leads to better teamwork and greater success for the company.

Respond Thoughtfully:

Responding carefully means taking a moment to think about what was said, pausing before answering, and then giving a thoughtful answer. This pause gives the viewer time to think about what was said, different point of views, and how to respond in a well-thought-out way. By pausing to think, viewers show that they value the speaker's thoughts and feelings, which leads to a better understanding and more meaningful conversation. Thoughtful answers show that you understand and care, which builds trust and friendship within the team. This method supports honest talking and helpful feedback, which makes interactions more useful and results that are good. In the end, responding with care leads to a culture of mutual respect and teamwork, which is what makes a company successful.

Leaders and their teams get along better and trust each other more when they listen actively. It gets people involved, helps them work together, and makes them feel like they fit on the team.

Holding Teams Together Through Effective Communication

Teamwork depends on being able to talk to each other clearly. It involves more than just getting knowledge across. It also involves helping team members understand each other, work together, and respect each other.

Strategies for Effective Communication:

Clarity and Conciseness:

It is very important to be clear and to the point when communicating, so use simple, clear wording to get your point across without adding extra complexity. Speakers make sure that their words are clear for everyone by using simple, direct language. This lowers the chance of confusion or misinterpretation. Using less jargon and academic language makes the message even clearer and easier for a wide range of people to understand. This method encourages clear conversation and makes it easy for team members to share information. Ultimately, being clear and to the point helps everyone understand the goals and standards, which leads to alignment and teamwork toward common goals.

Openness and Transparency:

Trustworthy and open communication are key to creating a supportive work atmosphere where everyone feels comfortable sharing their thoughts, worries, and feedback. Promoting an open culture helps leaders make a secure area where everyone feels valued and accepted, allowing them to share their unique ideas without worrying about being judged or punished. Clear communication throughout the team builds trust and strengthens relationships, which encourages working together and coming up with new ideas. As a result of feeling heard and respected, team members are more involved and motivated, which boosts morale and productivity. Encouraging truth and honesty are the building blocks of a strong and effective team.

Feedback and Recognition:

Feedback and praise are important parts of a healthy team culture because they encourage everyone to keep getting better and show appreciation for what each person does. Giving constructive comments is a great way to help people grow and develop, and it can also help your team achieve excellence. Recognizing and appreciating the work of each team member also gives them a feeling of accomplishment and motivation, which increases their engagement and commitment. Leaders create a supportive atmosphere that values learning and growth by making feedback and praise a regular part of work. This creates a culture of excellence and encourages everyone on the team to do their best, which leads to the team's total success.

Lead by Example:

As an example for others to follow, leading by example means communicating openly and honestly with your team. Effective leaders build trust and confidence by communicating openly and honestly with their teams, encouraging a culture of honesty and integrity. This method promotes open communication, helpful comments, and respect between team members. Leadership that values honesty and openness builds trust and loyalty, which encourages others to follow suit. Overall, setting a good example creates a positive work environment where communication soars, which boosts teamwork, efficiency, and overall success.

Leaders can encourage teamwork, settle disagreements, and motivate people to work together to reach shared goals by putting an emphasis on good communication.

Conclusion

In this chapter, we looked at the essential concepts of efficient management, such as appreciating your subordinates and improving your listening skills. These simple yet strong characteristics are critical for cultivating a healthy work atmosphere, encouraging teamwork, and achieving organizational success.

Managers can foster an environment of respect and acceptance in the workplace by understanding the significance of employee value. When employees feel valued and acknowledged for their accomplishments, they are more engaged, motivated, and loyal. This sense of belonging motivates them to go above and beyond their responsibilities, resulting in higher productivity and job satisfaction. Similarly, active listening is essential for establishing trust and improving relationships within teams. Managers that actively listen to their people display care and respect, which promotes open communication and collaboration. Managers who understand their team members' viewpoints, problems, and feedback can handle issues proactively, provide required support, and tailor their leadership style to match individual needs.

Recognizing the signs of weak leadership, such as a lack of empathy, micromanagement, poor communication, and disregarding feedback, is also critical for good managing. Managers may foster a culture of continuous improvement and innovation by avoiding these mistakes and adopting a leadership style marked by empathy, trust, and transparency.

Managers may ultimately build a workplace where employees feel valued, supported, and inspired to succeed by respecting them and practicing active listening. This leads to improved teamwork, increased production, and better overall organizational outcomes.

To summarize, being a good manager entails more than simply having authority; it entails cultivating a culture of respect, collaboration, and continuous learning. Managers that embrace and incorporate these values into their leadership approach can create a workplace wherein everyone feels respected, heard, and empowered to offer their best.

End of Chapter 5

Chapter 6

Trusting Your Team and Confidence

Effective leadership does not only entail giving orders; it includes building trust and having confidence in both yourself and your team members. These are foundational pillars for creating a positive work environment and driving organizational success. In this chapter, we delve into the crucial functions played by trust and confidence in the leadership and team environment.

Trust is truly the lifeblood for any successful team. It means confidence in their abilities, understanding, or perceptions of judgment, and integrity. When leaders put confidence in their team, they create a climate of cooperation, releasing energy for empowerment and mutual respect. It means team members are respected and valued, which greatly increases their morale and motivation. Trust also encourages people to work independently by taking the initiative to express their opinions, work alone, and express what they believe in, promoting innovation and productivity within the team.

However, trust needs to be tempered with accountability. Equally important as trusting your team is holding them accountable for their actions. This balance allows things to be done efficiently and for responsibilities to be discharged. Clear expectations have to be established, active and frequent communication has to be established, and members of the teams receive support from leaders. When accountability is evident, it further fortifies trust within the team and shapes a culture of responsibility and ownership.

Another element of effective leadership is confidence. Firstly, it starts with the confidence within yourself and extends to the confidence in your team members' abilities. Leaders who exhibit confidence in their team inspire trust and motivate them to reach their maximum. With confidence, the leader will enable himself or herself to be resilient and handle the challenges faced by the team and with motivation, they would improve the team's self-belief and optimism. It encourages individuals to go beyond their comfort zones, take risks, and embrace opportunities for growth and learning.

Building confidence in the team is also equally important. Leaders can boost confidence within their team by providing support, encouragement, and recognition. Empower the team members to be a part of new challenges and decision-making that fosters a sense of ownership and investment in the success of the team. Leaders who believe in their team's capabilities instill a sense of value, motivation, and empowerment within the team that ultimately leads to organizational success.

Trust and confidence go a long way in performance by the team. Trusts in collaboration, teamwork, and free communication among team members. Trust and respect of their fellow team members and leader encourage the sharing of ideas, feedback, and problem-solving, hence improved team collaboration. Such an open and collaborative approach tends to bring about increased creativity, productivity, and overall team performance.

The boosting of trust and confidence also has consequences on morale and engagement in the team. When people feel secure, they will more often feel respected and treated, and therefore will be engaged in the work. This feeling of belonging and purpose is a catalyst for individual and collective achievements that ultimately leads to organizational success.

Balancing Trust and Accountability in Leadership:

Understanding Trust:

The backbone of effective teamwork and leadership is trust. It is more than sheer dependency; it is having belief in abilities, integrity, and judgment. Trust among the team under the respective leader sets the premises for working together in a collaborative and empowered working environment. First, trust causes a feeling of empowerment on the part of the team members. When the leader believes in them, their ability, and the judgment of things, they feel empowered to take initiative and take decisions without any approval. This empowerment becomes a fuel for a culture in which team members feel valued and respected, thus creating higher morale and satisfaction in work. Secondly, trust leads to cooperation and teamwork. When people trust one another and their leader, they share ideas, offer feedback, and work together toward common goals. This process of working together with diverse talents and perspectives within the team leads to fruitful solutions and better results.

Thirdly, trust breeds ownership and accountability. When a person is trusted, then he takes ownership of his job with full responsibility, including its outcomes. Such ownership accounts for more involvement and commitment towards common objectives.

In essence, trust is the pillar that truly establishes successful teams. It sets up an environment of empowerment, ownership, and accountability where members at all levels feel inclined and ready to bring their best efforts, driven by a shared purpose for working towards common goals. The fostering of trust among team members by the leaders is the way to unlock the full potential of the team members and drive organizational success.

Establishing Accountability:

It is necessary to have accountability within a team so as to be assured of one completing the assigned task effectively and for one to achieve goals. While trust is the basic ingredient for a strong team, accountability becomes the framework that ensures reliability and consistency in performance. From this assertion, leaders need to strike a balance between trust and accountability. In so doing, trusting team members to go ahead and do their jobs without directing them unnecessarily lays a great platform for enabling them to act independently and independently, growing in confidence. On the other hand, accountability assures that there is no misplaced trust because it holds an individual responsible for their actions and outcomes.

To establish accountability within a team, one should define roles and responsibilities and performance objectives clearly. Clarity on such issues promotes team members' autonomy and accountability with the stakeholders. In addition, individuals need to know how their work contributes toward realizing the goal of the organization. When members understand how their work supports overall organizational performance, it enhances motivation. The goals should be set to a level that is achievable for the team to help grow competence and skill throughout the team.

Furnishing needed assistance and resources is another equally crucial factor in encouraging accountability. If team members have tools and necessary information and training to fulfill their responsibilities successfully, then it is assured that they will deliver outcomes effectively. Leaders are to lead, mentor, and guide whenever necessary, give assistance to team members in achieving their goals.

Accountability involves offering constructive feedback at the same time. Such feedback is important as it helps to recognize achievements and offer possible ways to overcome difficulties. Such evaluation ensures that the individual is aware of the impact that the actions have on team performance and therefore leads to continuous improvement.

Generally, accountability makes the individual, indeed the whole team, take ownership of their actions and the consequences. This kind of ownership inculcates in the members to be responsible for their activities as well as their results. This sense of ownership of one's work inspires one to perform better, individually and collectively, hence increasing the sense of productivity and innovation toward success. Between the associated trust and accountability that can be a working culture fostering high performance and accountability for a better organizational success rate, balancing trust with accountability proves imperative.

Clear Communication:

A team needs to have accountability that would see them perform effectively and meet their goals. Even though trust comes first, it is a structure and framework for teams to deliver results on a consistent basis. First, accountability provides a clear understanding of what tasks and responsibilities mean to every team member. This helps the team to focus and brings clarity of what should be done, reducing misunderstandings and conflicts among the team members. Secondly, accountability is one-way team members are motivated to perform their responsibilities to the best of their abilities and sometimes even go the extra mile to achieve specific objectives. This sense of accountability fosters a high-performance culture and a culture for continuous improvement in a team.

Moreover, accountability requires leaders to offer adequate support and resources for the team members to fulfill their roles or sometimes expectations. In providing guidance and training in addition to feedback, leaders will offer the team members with an opportunity to have all the necessary tools and knowledge at their disposal for performing effectively. The support shows the commitment of leaders to the team's success and adds trust and confidence among the team members.

Clear Communication:

Effective communication is the basic foundation of any team's success. This, in turn, creates the foundation for maintaining trust, fostering accountability, and promoting collaborative approaches among team members. Effective communication involves not just passing on information but also ensuring that it is understood, accepted, and given action.

In the first place, clear communication is how leaders articulate their expectations, goals, and objectives to their team. Through this, they give members clear roles and responsibilities, as well as guidelines about their general performance, leading to motivation and providing clarity to them so that they understand what is expected of them, and thus they can direct their energies towards a common goal. Alignment of purpose and unity within the team is promoted through this alignment.

Moreover, while feedback can be used to give constructive feedback, to give corrective measures, to give the feedback to be constructive, among others, the openness of feedback sessions. Hence, by providing constructive feedback, leaders can recognize achievement, identify things needed to be improved, and offer support to growth and development. Feedback also encourages open discussion and bi-directional communication to facilitate expression of ideas and considering the experiences or challenges of each other.

Open and transparent communication builds trust among team members and their leader. When the information is communicated openly and honestly, it builds the culture of transparency and honesty within the team. Team members feel valued and respected when they are given the proper information about any great decisions, changes, or developments affecting their work. This builds credibility and builds relationships, hence increasing trust and cooperation.

Clear communication helps in avoiding misunderstandings and conflicts within the team. By making the expectations and goals clear, it can bring down the chance of confusion or ambiguity. By clarity in communication, members will know what is expected of them, and therefore the issues raised will be addressed. Furthermore, open communication develops mutual respect and understanding between the team members, leading to a positive and supportive work environment.

Developing Confidence in Challenging Situations:

Self-Confidence:

Self-confidence is the bedrock upon which effective leadership is built. It arises from a profound conviction in oneself—in one's talents, strengths, and potential to overcome obstacles and achieve desired outcomes. Effective leaders possess a confident attitude with their decisions, problem-solving, and handling of uncertain situations with great finesse and determination. Self-confidence is the backbone of any successful leader.

Self-awareness plays a pivotal role in cultivating self-confidence. Leaders with an understanding of their strengths and weaknesses can use the same to the maximum. By recognizing areas of expertise and areas to be improved, leaders are in a position to make informed decisions, delegate tasks optimally, and seek support or development when required. This self-awareness instills a sense of authenticity and credibility, enhancing their confidence in being able.

However, confidence is not about arrogance or false humility; instead, it's the courage to take on calculated risk and embrace challenges with optimism and resilience. A leader who exudes confidence inspires trust and respect among his team. When leaders demonstrate confidence in their own capabilities, it instills belief and assurance in their team members.

Further, self-confidence enables leaders to lead by example, influence, and set a good tone for their team. The confidence level of a leader, exhibited with regard to his vision and capabilities, inspires confidence in his or her team. Positive attitudes in behavior, communication, and innovation are created within the team that can empower people and account for team members.

Team Confidence:

Team confidence plays a vital part in developing and maintaining good team dynamics, and leaders play a pivotal role in promoting and building it within their teams. It can be summarized in a collective sense of confidence that their achievements can be completed and that they will be successful in confronting challenges alongside each other. Leaders facilitate the building of team confidence by offering support, encouragement, and recognition. When a leader is supportive of the team member, he/she tends to remain motivated and appreciated. Celebrating group and individual accomplishments shows appreciation and validation, which propel morale and confidence.

Another thing that strengthens team confidence is empowerment. Leaders empower people by assigning authority, asking them to take on roles, and giving them a lot of time to work independently. When people feel ownership and invested in the success of their team, they tend to be more confident and motivated to contribute at a higher level.

Allowance to take on new challenges and make decisions fosters a culture of growth and learning within the team. Leaders who offer opportunities for skill development, professional growth, and innovation inspire confidence and instill a sense of purpose and excitement among team members. By empowering team members to contribute ideas and solutions, leaders use the collective expertise and creativity of the team for innovation and problem-solving.

Leaders with the belief in their team, empower people to take action and be heard because leaders believe they can do anything. A leader who shows faith in his team's abilities confirms their skills and talents and makes them feel proud of what they do. This belief in the team's capabilities fosters a positive and collaborative atmosphere, where people are supported and encouraged to achieve maximum potential.

Embracing Challenges:

This gullible confidence forms the bedrock of well-functioning teamwork, where the gears of a leader's influence run prime in coordinating and shaping his team's dynamics for ultimate success. This team confidence manifests as a collective group's faith, belief, and trust in each other's mutual and sustainable success, according to their shared goals and struggles.

Leaders can foster and sustain team confidence by offering support, motivation, and recognition. When team members feel supported by their leader, they feel more valued and driven to perform to the best of their abilities. Timely rewards for both individual and team successes create an atmosphere of esteem and appreciation that provides the team members with a sense of confidence and motivation.

However, empowerment is another important factor contributing to building team confidence. Leaders enable team members through delegation of authority, entrusting them with responsibilities, and fostering a work environment where ownership and a sense of commitment to the success of the team is felt. Empowered team members carry a sense of ownership and investment in the success of the team, driving higher levels of engagement and commitment.

Also, providing opportunities for growth, development, and innovation within the team motivates an atmosphere of growth and learning. Leaders who give opportunities for skill development, professional growth, and innovation inspire confidence and instill a sense of purpose and excitement among the team members. Also, leaders tap into the collective expertise and creativity of the team by empowering them to contribute ideas and solutions.

Leaders who believe in their team's capability find themselves in an environment where individuals feel valued and empowered to achieve their full potential. When leaders bring confidence in the capabilities of their team members, this validates their skills and talents, creating pride and confidence in their work. This kind of belief in the team's capability makes the atmosphere cheerful and collaborative, where one is encouraged to go beyond and achieve excellence.

The Impact of Trust on Team Performance:

Collaboration and Innovation:

Collaboration and innovation are both very imperative in today's fast-paced and dynamic business environment. Trust helps in creating an environment where collaboration flourishes and innovation takes place. A culture of collaboration occurs because team members trust each other and the leader under whom they work. The trusting environment gives team members the confidence to share ideas, take risks, and collaborate in a very effective manner.

This openness and truth leads to open communication, whereby one can share information openly, hence developing a relationship of trust. At this level, the team members collect ideas, skills, and perspectives from each one of them to help and tackle these problems and develop ideas that can lead to newer innovations.

In a culture of feedback, an environment of constant learning and improvement, through sharing past experiences and opinions with one another, is where teams develop creative and intelligent solutions to pressing problems.

Creative collaboration enforces a team spirit and reinforces the collective effort to meet the goals and objectives. Working together, each member draws from the areas of strengths and competence among team members and blends them together into overall excellence. With pooled resources and talents, collectively, the team may put in more output to achieve significantly much better success.

Moreover, trust enables individuals to take calculated risks and experiment with new ideas and approaches. When people trust one another and their leader, confidence builds up in them towards daring to undertake bold initiatives or try innovative solutions to problems. This courage to take risks inculcates a spirit of innovation, where creative invention and experimentation are rewarded.

Finally, collaboration and innovation fueled by trust are the key drivers of organizational growth and success. When leaders create an environment where everyone feels safe to share ideas, take risks, and collaborate efficiently, they can bring out the best in their teams, achieving significant progress and driving meaningful change. In this regard, in today's rapidly changing business environment, organizations that emphasize trust, collaboration, and innovation are better positioned to adapt and thrive.

Open Communication:

Open communication is essential for any successful teamwork and collaboration in every organization. Trust is the most critical factor that will prove to be vital in ensuring open communication because it assumes an environment wherein people are free to express their views, thoughts, concerns, and ideas openly without any fear of judgment or any retribution. When a person is confident that they are trusted and respected by other team members and by the leader/s , they are more likely to communicate freely, thus making the communication open and transparent. In this way, they set a culture where people feel authorized to give their viewpoints, give feedback, and engage in constructive discussions.

Open communication promotes accountability and mutual respect within the team. When one feels valued and respected, they are likely to take ownership of their actions and responsibilities. Transparent leadership promotes an environment in which team members feel like they can perform at their best. Team members will hence be held responsible for their actions.

Moreover, open communication strengthens the team's cohesion and performance. When team members feel listened to and valued, they find effective collaboration toward shared goals. Fostering an environment of open communication and leadership develops a sense of unity and shared purpose among team members, which therefore encourages members to collaborate and innovate.

Leaders prioritizing open communication create a platform where individuals can have open communication as part of the team. In turn, leaders create an open and active forum to listen to and take on feedback from their team members. In this regard, leaders demonstrate their commitment to transparency and inclusivity. This gives a sense of psychological safety within the team; which encourages individuals to offer their ideas and opinions without fear of retaliation.

Morale and Engagement:

Trust, therefore, is the bedrock on which morale and engagement lay, all that is fundamental to a high-performing team. When members of the team trust each other and the leader, they build up a good working environment with people who are valued, respected, and are free to contribute according to their potential. Trust creates a sense of belonging and camaraderie within the team. When one trusts others, that person is ready and able to collaborate effectively and support one another towards achieving common goals. This unity comes out of creating a supportive and inclusive work cultures where team members feel like they belong and are appreciated for their contribution.

Trust also enhances individual and collective engagement in a team. When a leader is trusted, it will motivate and commit team members to their work. This sense of trust and security makes them focus on their tasks and worry less about micromanagement and unwanted scrutiny. They are, therefore, more engaged, proactive, and committed to shared objectives.

Moreover, trust fosters creativity and innovation within the team. When team members feel trusted and respected, they tend to take up risk-taking behaviors, idea sharing, and creative thinking. This willingness to experiment and explore new possibilities results in innovative solutions and continuous improvement in the team.

Leaders who invest in building strong relationships and fostering a culture of trust and respect make such contributions possible within the work environment. These leaders lay down a platform that empowers the employees to speak up, take initiative, and contribute towards the team's success.

Conclusion

Trust and confidence are indispensable elements for the effective leadership and dynamics of a team. It would be difficult to think of any successful team built upon any foundation other than this. This chapter has explored how these two pillars form the bedrock of a positive working environment and drive organizational success.

Trust is the foundation for building successful teams; this enables empowerment, collaboration, and accountability within the team and increases morale, motivation, and productivity. Leadership developed with trust that allows the workers to trust the team members creates an environment where individuals value, respect, and feel empowered to contribute their best efforts toward achieving common goals.

However, this trust must be balanced with accountability to ensure that tasks are executed effectively and responsibilities are met. Clear expectations should be discussed; support and resources needed should be provided; constructive feedback should be given if the work cannot be done; it would help foster accountability within the team. Accountability strengthens trust and promotes a culture of responsibility and ownership.

Confidence—self-confidence and team confidence—are equally important to effective leadership and team performance. A leader who has a sense of confidence within themselves will instill confidence and trust within his team members. Likewise, by instilling confidence in his team, a leader will create an environment where people feel valued, motivated, and empowered to be themselves.

Trust and confidence within a team pave the way for taking up challenges and fostering an environment that encourages collaboration and innovation. When individuals feel trusted and confident, they turn towards doing risky things and sharing ideas that would lead to a culture where they are motivated to do better and increase productivity. This culture of collective actions will help them in achieving competitive productivity.

Furthermore, to maintain trust, accountability, and engagement within the team, open communication is an essential element. When team members feel respected and trusted, they are more likely to communicate openly, share ideas, and participate in constructive discussions. Such free exchange of information builds trust, strengthens relationships, and helps boost team cohesion and performance.

In essence, trust and confidence are the two pillars of effective leadership and team dynamics. By incorporating confidence, accountability, and trust within the team, leaders can cultivate a supportive environment where team members feel enabled and valued to succeed in their roles. This, in turn, leads to enhanced morale, engagement, and successful organizational outcomes.

End of Chapter 6

Chapter 7

Moving Out of the Comfort Zone and Leadership Perception

Leadership isn't an endpoint but a journey—a continuous process of learning, development, and adaptation to new challenges and opportunities. At the core, effective leadership requires willingly stepping into discomfort, and being willing to endure temporary discomfort as a pathway toward personal and professional growth.

In essence, the venture into discomfort is more than just willingness to sustain brief moments of unease; it's a mindset shift that opens the door to new opportunities and potentials. It requires leaders to confront their fears, insecurities, and limitations head-on, realizing that true growth often resides on the other side of discomfort.

To stop within their comfort zones, leaders expose themselves to new experiences, perspectives, and thought processes. They become more resilient, adaptable, and innovative because of the tools and insights they gather from their explorations in the complex terrain of the modern business environment.

Additionally, it encourages a continuous improvement culture in the organization. When leaders lead by example and embrace the uncomfort, they inspire others to do the same. This, in turn, creates a culture of experimentation, creativity, and innovation—a culture where failure does not stand in the way but is embraced as a natural part of the learning process.

Eg; Of course, there is also a part where effective leadership support cultivates an active participantion within the organization. This understanding is paramount, for leadership is not a passive role but an active participation in people, processes, and challenges that define organizational life.

By being present, engaged, and accessible to their teams, leaders engender trust, encourage collaboration, and drive organizational success. They lead not from a position of power but from a place of authenticity and humility, earning the respect and loyalty of their colleagues through their actions.

Effective leaders understand that there is the need to comprehend and adapt to a changing world. The way things are in the fast-moving, unstable business world today, agility and adaptability are paramount leadership attributes.

By staying ahead of the curve concerning the industry trends, market dynamics, and emerging technologies, leaders can predict and foresee changes to proactively position their organization for success. Besides, they remain flexible and willing to shift strategies when needed to either accommodate or seize opportunities that their changing landscape presents.

Embracing Discomfort for Professional Growth

Embracing discomfort is as good as getting ready to embark on a new course into the unknown. It involves courage, resilience, and willingness to challenge oneself. In the domain of leadership, this voyage often begins with taking calculated risks. Risk-taking is not about reckless behavior; rather, it's stepping outside the confines of familiarity and getting ready to venture into the realm of possibility.

Taking Calculated Risks:

There are continual decisions in leadership: every decision carries with it some risks and threats. Good leaders discern this calculus of proper decision from imprudent adventures. Calculated risks are not impulsive leaps into uncertainty but rather careful analysis on the basis of strategic vision and acceptance of failure. The acceptance of possible outcomes, and outcomes being a feature of, calculated risk-taking by leaders. By the course of calculated risks, leaders try out new prospects, break through ordinary boundaries, making developments and advances possible. They understand that progress often lies beyond the comfort zone, and therefore, there is an acceptance to cross into new territories in order to uncover new opportunities. Calculated risk-taking spawns a creative, enduring culture within organizations. It inspires employees to challenge conventional methods, produce new ideas, and aim for greater achievements. Calculated risk-taking does not point to reckless abandon; it points to strategic decisions guided by a clear vision for the future. It is through calculated risks that leaders push their organizations ahead, making innovations and sustainable growth possible on a day-to-day business basis.

Learning from Failure:

Failure, though most dreaded, plays a pivotal role as a catalyst towards positive change and progress. Successful leaders have always understood that failure is not an end in itself, but an opportunity on the journey towards greater heights. For successful leaders, failure never turns into a dead end; rather, failure becomes a stepping stone towards greater achievements. In fact, while most have cringed with misgivings when faced with failure, effective leaders do not dwell on setbacks but rather view them as opportunities for learning and development. Failure provides a leader with the opportunity to discover what does and does not work for him and subsequently fine-tune his strategies. In fact, each failure becomes a lesson to help leaders sharpen their skills, refine approaches, and finally help themselves land up stronger and wiser. More importantly, effective leaders know that the failure is not a reflection of their abilities but rather a testament to the courage to try, which manifests as a natural by-product of innovation and experimentation—a normally important aspect of a journey towards growth and success. When this new understanding holds power, even failure can lead to valuable learning opportunities for leaders, as well as inspire resilience and continuous improvement within their organizations. These leaders therefore encourage their teams to take calculated risks, knowing that even in failure, there are valuable lessons to be learned. This culture of resilience will help the organization not only to withstand pressure but also drive innovation and sustain growth over a long time.

Leaders as Active Participants in Their Organizations

Being a leader is not passive engagement, but active attention to the several facets of organizational life. Effective leaders know that being present, engaged, and accessible is essential to their teams. They lead with their physical presence on the frontlines, showcasing their commitment and dedication through their actions.

Active Listening:

Active listening is one of the most crucial aspects of good leadership, serving as a pillar that ensures collaboration, trust, and respect within teams. At its very core, active listening is not merely about hearing words but involves wholly being and understanding the perspectives, feelings, and needs of others. Effective leaders understand that it is the key to creating a supportive and inclusive environment wherein team members can feel heard and respected. They exhibit empathy and compassion in trying to understand the underlying motivations and concerns of their colleagues. A listening where leaders listen in the true sense, without any prejudice, means the support that they provide helps them to deal with a situation. It not only shows them an extension of belongingness and respect that they give them but also helps to avoid acrimonious debates or generalizations.

Moreover, active listening enables leaders to hear issues and needs before they arise as problems or conflicts, in order to address them proactively. By being sensitive to the needs and sentiments of their teams, leaders get involved early enough in issues and seek to resolve them rather than watching them deteriorate into full-fledged conflicts.

With active listening, leaders not only help build rapport within their teams but also promote openness, transparency, and collaboration in the workplace. In this way, team members feel valued and respected, hence increasing engagement, productivity, and ultimate success in the organization. All these underline the method of active listening as a very non-negotiable skill in effective leadership. Active listening is a key to good outcome as it establishes a spirit of unity and a sense of shared purpose in the workplace.

Leading by Example:

Lead by example is the paradigm that characterizes effective leadership, an embodiment of values and principles of what leaders would hope to instill in their teams. It goes beyond mere words or directives to being characterized by action, the behavior and attitudes that define the powerful culture of an organization. Leaders understand that their actions are charged with the power to influence not only the attitudes but also the behavior of their teams. Showing a high work ethic, being transparent in all dealings, or appearing with humility in success and failure, leaders set standards for behavior within their organizations.

Through consistent modeling of desired behaviors, leaders elicit trust, respect, and appreciation from their subordinates. When employees see their leaders living out the values they preach, it is more likely for those employees to internalize such values and institute them in their practices at work.

Furthermore, leading by example trickles down to all levels of employees in the organization to stimulate motivation and efforts towards a better performance. When leaders exhibit a commitment to continuous improvement, innovation, and accountability, they create a culture in which high performance is the norm rather than the exception.

Indeed, leading by example is not a mere act of setting a precedent for others to follow; it's setting a culture of excellence, integrity, and collaboration that affects organizational success. Effective leaders understand that their actions speak louder than words and leverage their behavior as a powerful tool for inspiring and motivating their teams.

Understanding and Adapting to Changing Environments

Change today, the business world operates with a dynamic landscape that can barely take off without it happening. Effective leaders know very well that staying elastic, flexible, and adaptable to its ever-shifting environments is the ticket to all sorts of success.

Market Trends and Industry Shifts:

In a fast-paced and dynamic business environment, staying updated on market trends and changes in the industry is very important to maintain the competitive edge. In fact, intelligent leaders realize that gathering market intelligence and analyzing trends with a foresight approach, in a proactive manner, is not an option but a necessity. By keeping a finger on the pulse of dynamics in markets, anticipation and proactive strategy towards challenges would simply be things that leaders can develop to address the problems before they escalate.

Also, information in regard to emerging market opportunities for growth and innovation emerges while it's up-to-date. Knowing the changing demands and choices within the customers, the organizations can meet the changed patterns of the markets through their products, services, and strategies.

Furthermore, quick reaction to industry changes allows leaders to adjust their business models and processes. Whether it is embracing new technologies, entering new markets, or diversifying the product offerings, companies that are agile and adaptable can position their organizations for long-term success.

In other words, good leaders recognize the value of staying informed and responsive to market trends and industry shifts. They navigate the complexities of the competitive landscape with confidence, agility, and foresight, ultimately positioning their organizations for sustained growth and success.

Agility and Flexibility:

In today's rapidly changing business landscape, full of volatility, uncertainty, complexity, and ambiguity (VUCA), agility and flexibility have become the indispensable qualities for effective leadership. Rather than rigid structures and hierarchical processes, recognition of the limitations that leaders' regimentations impose enables them to be better suited to deal with the dynamic challenges of the modern world. It assists agile leaders to respond fast to emergencies, make quick shifts in the market, and take advantage of new opportunities promptly. Agility and flexibility enable leaders to react and adjust quickly to unforeseen events, market patterns, and emerging opportunities. They create an environment in which experimentation and iteration are essential in driving the philosophy of continuous improvement and adaptation within their organizations.

More so, agility and flexibility breed a culture of innovation, collaboration, and resilience. Empowering employees with ownership of their roles and responsibilities and autonomy in making decisions.

Agile leaders instill an environment where employees take initiative and responsibility.

Such a decentralized approach enables organizations to adapt faster to changes in market conditions and customer requirements, where these organizations will remain competitive in the long run.

In essence, agility and flexibility are not just leadership traits but fundamental organizational values that foster innovation, growth, and adaptability in an ever-evolving business environment. Leaders who value these qualities shape a dynamic, responsive organizational culture capable of flourishing amidst uncertainty and complexity.

Conclusion

In summary, the leadership journey is a journey of continuous learning, growing, and adaptability. In this chapter, we've reviewed the necessity of stepping out of comfort zones, embracing discomfort as a catalyst for growth, and leading by example. Good leadership is all about courage, resilience, and readiness to challenge oneself, and it's also about inspiring others to do the same. Being a leader in an organization is not an isolated effort; instead, it demands engagement, mindfulness, and willingness to be a part of or engaged in the dynamics of organizational life. The trust and collaboration ingredients are fueled by the involvement of the leaders towards their teams. They know that the organizational success revolves around the availability of being aware and responsive to changing situations in the marketplace, and also in terms of industry and environment changes.

Effective leaders pay a lot of attention to active listening, as they know it is a key ingredient for the creation of a nurturing and an inclusive environment, where people feel worth and significance. Leaders who learn to listen attentively and with understanding thereby forge stronger connections, cohesion, and facilitate success within the organization.

More than the organizational goal's achievement, effective leadership is about how the excellence of integrity and collaboration can be created for sustainable growth and success. Leaders who, by embracing calculated risk-taking and learning from failures, have culture resilience and a culture of continuous improvement know that failing is not a sign of weakness but an opportunity to grow and develop. By encouraging risk-taking, experimentation, and innovation, the leaders inspire creativity, in turn supporting innovation, thus positioning their organizations for success in the long run.

In essence, the journey of leadership is dynamic and evolving. To be a leader, you must be brave, flexible, and open to learning throughout the life of your journey. Embrace discomfort, lead by example, and be adaptable to changes in order to inspire your team to the highest level of achievement and reach their full potential.

End of Chapter 7

Chapter 8

Excellence in Execution and Wisdom

The Ramayana is a treasure trove of timeless wisdom, especially in the realms of leadership and management. It is, in that sense, a treasure trove of a classical epic of the Indian literary, full of insights of strategic thinking, effective planning, and the art of execution, exemplified by characters like Hanuman. While observing this aspect of the Ramayana's narrative, a transient but invaluable lesson gets unearthed that leads to timeless guidance offered to managers and leaders to work in complex modernity.

Hanuman, the highly revered devotee of Lord Rama, stands out as a master of strategic acumen and decisive action throughout the epic. His unrelenting commitment to his mission and his remarkable capacity to overcome obstacles seem to be evident of his understanding of the principles of execution. We can then examine Hanuman's doings and emerge with a clearer understanding of the underlying principles of strategic planning, adaptability, teamwork, and disciplined execution that define effective leadership and management.

This exploration attempts to set a connection between ancient wisdom and present practices, equating the experiences of characters in the Ramayana with the problems confronted by the leaders of today in corporate world. What we will do is decipher, from an angle of practical application, the nuances behind strategic planning, adaptability, collaboration, and disciplined execution as reflected in the epic through a lens of practical application.

As this literary odyssey takes us in, it is important to realize how the things that are written now are as relevant as ever to the world of modern management. Although technological tools and means of communicating and having relations with others have undergone changes in the course of evolution, the necessary principles of management remain unchanged. By studying the Ramayana and the lessons, leaders and managers can get the answers to overcoming difficulties in other contexts of life and, more importantly, in their professional environment.

In the chapters following, we shall observe specific episodes from the Ramayana and analyze strategic decisions made by the characters of this narrative and derive actionable lessons that are relevant in today's organizational milieu. From the game-planning of Hanuman to the alliance-building strategy of Rama, every narrative string finds its way to offering invaluable wisdom for doable application.

Finally, our purpose is not simply to have these ancient stories re-told but to condense these into a few keys that can be used as guidance for leaders and managers in all aspects of the art of running organizations. If we can keep in mind the wisdom of the Ramayana, we can envision new perspectives, develop strategic thinking, and chart the path to excellence in leadership and management.

Hanuman's Wisdom in Executing Plans:

Hanuman, Lord Rama's devoted disciple, is characterized by strategic thinking and meticulous planning throughout his journey.

Strategic Planning:

Hanuman's approach to strategic planning has the genius of meticulous preparation and foresight. Before Hanuman embarked on his mission, he had considered the magnitude and complexity of the mission, as it was to search for Sita, Rama's wife, abducted by

Ravanva, into the wilderness. And that is because an assignment of such grandeur and thus magnitude, with other factors considered, required anything but an all-out offensive to keep the uncertainty at bay. Further, Hanuman's planning did not just deal with mere data gathering; it involved the formulation of a comprehensive strategy that would be used when dealing with all types of contingencies and challenges. He anticipated the risks that might be encountered and came up with contingency plans for any risks that might come along. In the current organizational context, the approach of Hanuman towards strategic planning is an illuminating example to all great leaders that the key to success lies in readiness and preparation. A good leader understands the significance of giving time and resources to plan well, knowing that the good old-fashioned plan is what plants success. In emulating Hanuman's strategic acumen and commitment to preparation, leaders can navigate the uncertainty with confidence and steer their organizations towards their goals.

Adaptability and Creativity:

In the face of the vast ocean that Hanuman encountered during his baffling journey, a person would be scared for his life; yet, Hanuman faced this terrifying situation with a mind full of ideas and strategies. The fact that Hanuman had to journey over the ocean to arrive at Lanka, where Sita was held captive, suggested a daunting enough challenge that would have easily discouraged him from embarking. But instead of letting despair take over, he tapped his reservoir of creative thinking. Having enlarged himself to surmount any odds of pursuing the various goals of overcoming the stage of life's trials, Hanuman thus demonstrated adaptability to adapt to an environment and showed resourcefulness. The fact that he thought outside the box illustrates the importance of flexibility and creativity in finding answers to problems, especially in unprecedented or unfamiliar situations.

Amidst the fast-moving world, adaptability and innovativeness have become the cornerstone of organizational success. Managers with this quality of mind and adaptive creativity are more equipped to steer uncertainties and seize opportunities. Such an approach has the potential to foster an environment of creativity, whereby an organization can develop unique abilities, thus presenting it with a competitive edge in the competitive business environment.

Moreover, Hanuman's amazing feat is a source of inspiration, to the effect that not every problem is hopelessly unsolvable. With determination and creativity, a leader can switch any obstacle into an opportunity and create a favorable path for innovation and growth.

Lessons in Strategic Execution from the Ramayana:

Strategic execution shines throughout the Ramayana, offering some valuable leadership and management practices that provide invaluable insights.

Alignment with Long-Term Goals:

The decision of Rama to go into exile, at first perceived as a test of his resolve, ultimately reveals a deeper strategic insight: the alignment of actions with long-term goals and vision. In voluntarily renouncing his rightful claim to the throne and choosing exile instead, Rama demonstrated an admirable combination of selflessness and strategic vision. Having chosen to outlast the immediate success he could have enjoyed, Rama understood he was laying the stage for greater triumphs in the days ahead. This choice substantiated the consistency of Rama's rule and his unrelenting commitment to doing what was right and just. Besides, his exile journey was characterized by personal transformation and preparation for his ultimate status as king. During his exile, Rama perfected his leadership abilities, he was affiliated with allies, and he benefited immensely from his exercises in governance. Each trial and tribulation he faced in this period helped shape him into the best leader he could become as he readied himself for success.

In today's fast-paced and highly competitive business world, it is essential to ensure that the actions one undertakes are geared toward the fulfillment of longer-term goals. Strategic leaders who are able to prioritize the long-term objectives of their organizations in favor of short-term gains are better positioned to steer their companies toward sustainable success. By instilling a culture of strategic thinking and goal alignment, organizations can ensure that every decision and action undertaken will contribute to their long-term vision and mission.

The Power of Collaboration:

The association in the Ramayana between Rama and Sugriva is not just one that stands out as an exceptional testament to the transformative power of collaboration and teamwork. They understood that their unique skills were advantageous and agreed to work together in order to get a common aim—that of saving Sita and defeating the demons, including Ravana.

Each team member fulfilled a specific role that, in sum, contributed to the success of their mission. Rama's strategic leadership and unwavering determination were complemented by Sugriva's intimate knowledge of the terrain and his army's formidable strength. Meanwhile, Hanuman's unmatched courage and intelligence proved useful in gathering intelligence and executing basic tasks.

Such a collaborative effort underlines the importance of building diverse teams by building on respective skill sets and perspectives. By using the specialty of their colleagues, organizations effectively tackle their limitations and attain higher success. Moreover, collaboration provides impetus for innovation, creativity, and resilience, emboldening teams to adapt to flourish in volatile environments.

Besides, the alliance between Rama and Sugriva underlines the imperative of building a culture that is characterized by respect, effective communication, and cooperation in people's lives. Although they had disparities in respect of background and position in society, Rama and Sugriva united on shared values and a common purpose. Indeed, this spirit of camaraderie and unity underwrote their collaborative efforts in conquering various obstacles and realizing objectives.

In this rapidly globalizing and interdependent business environment, the effectiveness of collaboration in generating collective intelligence and the capabilities of teams cannot be denied. Leaders who cherish teamwork and cooperation are more likely to enable better idea generation, increased creativity, and enhanced performance and organizational development. Simply by creating an environment of collaboration and open communication, organizations can unleash the full potential of their resources and deliver the best results.

Achieving Goals Through Focused and Disciplined Execution:

Hanuman's unabating focus and discipline in executing his mission are a motto for modern leaders.

Steadfast Focus:

Hanuman's rigid focus and his uncompromised attitude during his quest to find Sita is a torchlight for leaders facing situations of adversity in today's fast-paced world. Despite different obstacles and distractions that crossed his path, he kept walking resolutely, thus embodying how an obstinate focus helps one achieve their desires.

Hanuman's adventure brought him face-to-face with many obstacles that could have stymied his progress. From scary terrains to tough adversaries, he had to face many tests of his resolution. And yet, from all these, instead of giving up hope and forgetting the objective, he remained very stubborn, focused at the end - finding Sita and delivering Rama's message.

With such firmness of mind and unwavering focus, Hanuman was able to overcome seemingly impossible obstacles with grace and resilience. By holding tight to purpose and minding his vision, he managed to get through adversity in good style and accomplished his task.

In today's dynamic, cut-throat business environment, the example of unwavering focus by Hanuman gives good leadership lessons for leaders. With disciplined thinking and the setting of priorities, the leaders might be able to handle distractions or obstacles more appropriately, so that the staff does not lose focus and more importantly achieves their goals together.

What Hanuman did to show the power of unwavering focus in facing adversity is also on the emphasis on resilience and staying committed to his purposes. Through tough times, leaders could encourage great courage and resilience in their teams, motivating them to plow through challenges and win.

Finally, through this example of being unwavering in the face of difficulties, Hanuman shows that the will to stick to the goal is the secret to all success. Through being firm, and thus leading by example, demonstrating principles like discipline, resilience, and sticking to commitment, the leaders can inspire their teams to climb onto unprecedented heights of performance and success.

Resilience in the Face of Adversity:

Hanuman's capacity to withstand hardship becomes a metaphor for perseverance and commitment for the leaders grappling with the complexity of doing business today. Throughout his odyssey, Hanuman was bombarded with a myriad of several obstacles and challenges that tested his resolve. From the fiercest adversaries to treacherous terrains, he faced setbacks that could easily have demotivated even the most determined individuals. However, instead of succumbing to despair or giving up on his mission, Hanuman stood strong in his dedication and never allowed the chances of failure to win out. His perseverance was no longer just based on personal willpower but also the unquestionable belief he had about the correctness of his cause and the unbreakable faith he had in Lord Rama.

This unshakable sense of purpose and intense dedication to the mission made him stronger; he had the power to conquer even the most arduous tasks with grace and strength. Resilience is a critical trait of leadership in today's volatile and uncertain business environment. Leaders possessing the resilience to persevere through adversity inspire confidence and motivation in their teams, building a culture of resilience and determination.

Emulating Hanuman's example of resilience, leaders can, through this, find the capacity to overcome any obstacle or setback with persistence and improved resilience. In a broad view, Hanuman's unwavering resilience indicates adversity is no longer an insurmountable hurdle but just another opportunity for growth and evolution. With resilience and courage, leaders can find new possibilities and potential victories by taking up challenges fearlessly.

Conclusion

This epic story of the Ramayana translates to a timeless blueprint of wisdom that is all relevant to modern leadership and management practices. Some of the lessons that are gleaned from the characters of the epic include Hanuman, Rama, and Sugriva, whereby strategic planning, adaptability, collaboration, and disciplined execution are further pointed to.

One crucial aspect of the Ramayana is strategic planning and prediction. Hanuman's preparation and risk anticipation depict the value that is place on thorough planning towards organizational outcomes. Leaders in this regard, who reflect strategy within, can move forward in this changing business environment with confidence, knowing the road ahead for success.

Likewise, the epic underscores the importance of adaptability and creativity in finding a way. The way Hanuman could fit any situation to suit the peculiar problem he was facing taught how important innovation is. In this dynamic business world of today, flexible thinking can be seen in those leaders who are ready to address challenges with effective results.

At the same time, the alliance between Rama and Sugriva throws light on the importance of collaboration and teamwork towards achieving common objectives. By working with different teams and developing a culture of cooperation, leaders will further channel the collective intelligence and capacities of teams for success.

Finally, the Ramayana instructs us on focusing on the long term and having goals to match. There is a test of character exhibited by Rama in the decision to go into exile as a measure of his self-constraint, which ultimately prepares the way for his success as a king later on. Leaders who look at long-term objectives rather than short-term gains will lead their organizations towards stable success.

Last but not least, the epic calls for commitment and unwavering resilience in the face of adversity. Hanuman's unyielding dedication to his mission is a powerful example of commitment to leaders faced with obstacles. The leaders who remain focused on their goals and have robust resilience inspire their teams in overcoming the challenges to create great success.

In summary, the Ramayana provides an ultimate repository of timeless wisdom which can help maneuver leaders and managers on how to deal with the complexities of modern business life. Through reflections on these insights and their own management practice, leaders can cultivate a culture of excellence, innovation, and resilience that would finally drive the organization towards overall success within today's dynamic environment.

End of Chapter 8

Chapter 9

Putting a Premium on Values and Ethical Leadership

There is a strong base for good management which is ethical leadership. Not just making choices, but choosing the right ones based on what is morally right. Comprehensively, this chapter will talk about Responsible Leadership.

Basically, ethical leadership means being truthful, fair, and doing what is best for everyone. Integrity-based leaders not only build trust among their employees, but they also make the workplace a place where people feel appreciated and valued. They understand that what they do impacts not only their group but also the totality of existence. That's why responsible leadership is so important: it determines how people behave and how businesses work.

Let us look at an example from a historic tale. Read about Lord Rama. A figure from the Ramayana, an ancient Indian epic. Although it was hard, Rama always did the right thing. It teaches us to always be fair, tell the truth, and fight for what's right.

Today's leaders have to make a lot of tough choices, like how to spend money, treat workers, and protect the environment. These are big problems! Ethical leaders don't avoid them, though. They try to make decisions that are good for everyone, not just themselves or their company's income, by looking at people like Rama.

Setting a moral example at work means making sure everyone is treated with respect and feels safe speaking out. Doing what's right, even if it's hard or not popular, takes courage. This could mean turning down a cash-making opportunity that isn't fair to others.

Leaders who are ethical build trust and respect within and outside of the company. Every choice you make will gradually improve the world. Understanding and using ethical leadership can help us make workplaces where everyone feels appreciated and respected, and where honesty and fairness are the building blocks of success.

Rama as a Symbol of Ethical Leadership

Introduction to Lord Rama:

Lord Rama, a central figure in Hindu mythology's epic Ramayana, personifies ethical leadership through an iron-willed commitment to righteousness and truth. His story begins with humility and sacrifice as he voluntarily forsakes the throne of Ayodhya to maintain his father's word, exemplifying self-denial over personal ambition. Throughout his journey, Rama faces formidable problems such as Sita's abduction by the demon king Ravana. On the other hand, even through the trials and tribulations, Rama stood firm in his adherence to dharma, or righteousness, thus marking his loyalty and perseverance. His exemplary leadership becomes the beacon of inspiration to countless generations, and it serves as the eternal guide to right and honest behavior.

Lessons from Rama's Story:

Lord Rama's history imparts lessons on leadership and moral integrity that have endured time. This is mainly because of the unshakeable devotion of Lord Rama to truth, justice, and duty. To him, the life is guided by the supreme law of karma, from which he did not deviate even for a moment. He showed this by highly revering all the living beings and showing little discriminations from low to high order. In this sense, Lord Rama was an exemplary servant-leader who exhibited compassion and understanding towards people under his care. Besides, Lord Rama's humility and selflessness became apparent in taking advice from elderly sages and listening to his mentors to make his guidance sound. This humility does indicate the importance of openness and collaboration in effective leadership. With this, Lord Rama set an example for leaders to mimic, encouraging them to be true, benign, and humble at all times in the face of hardship.

Applying Rama's Principles to Business:

Implementing Lord Rama's values in the domain of business and management can leave powerful impacts on organizational culture as well as success. Ethical leaders, akin to Rama, act for integrity and honesty in all their dealings and thus set an ethical standard that permeates throughout the organization. By leading in such a way, they inculcate a culture of transparency and trust where employees are esteemed and valued.

Furthermore, they understand that empathy and compassion have greater results in decision-making. They do not consider their choices according to short-term benefit only for shareholders but for employees, customers, and the community at large. As such, they strive to create win-win situations and are not rigid towards securing only short-term advantages over ethical considerations.

Through emulating the virtues of Lord Rama, leaders create trust, loyalty, and respect among their teams, resulting in sustainable success. The ethics of a leader creates an environment where individuals are motivated towards achieving a common goal. This enhances the organisation's resilience towards long term viability.

Balancing Ethical Considerations in Business Decisions

Complexity of Business Decisions:

In this fast-paced world of business, leaders often grapple with complicated ethical decisions. This might encompass a broad spectrum, from resource allocation to competition dynamics and environmental stewardship. Ethical leaders, therefore, must weigh the alternative short-term benefits against the long-term consequences of compromising on quality or safety standards. They know that at any moment, compromising ethical principles can lead to reputational damage and liabilities legally in the future. Similarly, ethical leaders steer clear of the temptation towards unethical practices, like price manipulation and deceitful advertising practices, even with such pressure as harsh competitors do to them. Such people will appreciate the preservation of integrity and trustworthiness for anything and everything they are going to experience within their markets.

Another ethical problem arises when dealing with environmental challenges, and leaders must balance economic interests with environmental responsibilities. Ethical leaders recognize the necessity of sustainability and strive to adopt environmentally friendly practices that will not harm the environment but rather take into account the health of the planet along with that of the company.

Example Scenario:

Imagine a manufacturing company grappling with the decision of outsourcing production to a developing country with relaxed labor laws. While outsourcing promises cost savings and operational efficiency, ethical leaders would take up this quandary with its moral implications. They keep in mind possible worker exploitation in such an outsourcing destination, where the labor laws are very weak, and human rights are violated. Therefore, ethical leaders go over the benefits of outsourcing and its ethical considerations that are given to it and ensure that the outsourcing partner is bound by ethical labor practices, ensuring fair wages, and safe working conditions for his workforce. Ultimately, it is on the level of integrity and social conscience that the ethical leaders make their decisions, making the choices in line with the values of the organization, contributing meaningfully to society, even though it may imply that they let go of the short-term financial gain.

Factors to Consider:

Ethical decision-making must carefully consider the repercussions on all the relevant stakeholders, be it among employees, clients, shareholders, and to the broader community. Ethical leaders are mindful of the welfare of all stakeholders in the realization that sustainable success may only come when there is a harmonious equilibrium of interests among them. In making these deliberations, the ethical leaders contemplate the long-term repercussions that their decisions might bring about. They understand that value creation should go beyond financial benefits and towards societal impact. Hence, they make decisions that generate good outcomes not just for shareholders but for society as a whole.

By taking into consideration the needs and opinions of all stakeholders and adopting a long-term vision, ethical leaders develop trust, loyalty, and sustainability within their organizations. They understand that there should be a balance to decision-making, backed by ethics and social responsibility, for nurturing lasting success and enhancing the contribution towards the common good.

Importance of Long-Term Vision:

Ethical leaders understand the significance of staying true to a long-term viewpoint in their management decisions. They recognize that short-sighted, ethically questionable behavior might yield instant profits, but there are greater consequences. Leaders with integrity in positions of authority reflect ethical principles and values, thereby making it necessary to create a culture of trust and credibility within the organization. Trust, in this case, is therefore the cornerstone of sustainable success. In a way, it promotes respect and confidence among stakeholders, including employees, customers, and shareholders. The trust in this aspect is the starting point that forms an ideal foundation that builds long-lasting relationships and enhances loyalty, together with resilience when it comes to facing difficulties.

Additionally, ethical leaders understand that their actions not only influence immediate profit but also long-term gain. By practicing what they preach and being proactive about ethical behavior, they lay the foundation for an excellent reputation as an organization and help to build the base for success and prosperity in the long term. Thus, ethical leadership does not only mean doing what is right at the time but is about establishing an everlasting legacy of integrity and ethical excellence.

Upholding Core Values During Challenging Times

Challenges in Upholding Values:

At times of crisis or uncertainty, leaders often come under a great deal of pressure to deviate from their core values in search of immediate gain. Economic downturns, industry disruptions, and public scandals may enhance this pressure and convince leaders to forego long-term considerations. Instead of giving in to these pressures, ethical leaders have an unshakeable commitment to their values. They believe that compromising on ethical and integrity issues can lead to huge negative results, such as a downfall of reputation and loss of trust within the stakes. And mistakes in ethics not only shatter organizational credibility but also jeopardize employee morale and customer loyalty. So, ethical leaders understand that keeping up their principles is essential, whether facing challenges that seem invincible.

Ethical leaders are not afraid to maintain their moral compass and display it during critical times. They motivate confidence and resilience within their organization in a way that shows people that they should get the people that have been employed by them from every part of their organization to understand that what is taken during the course of these times is not unimportant. Ethical conduct remains unbiased and uncompromised with values in times of unrest, set a standard to foster trust and stability in the future.

Maintaining Integrity:

During occasions of ethical grayness or undue pressure, ethical leaders hold to uncompromising commitment toward their values and not compromise integrity for the sake of short-term expediencies.

Indeed, their commitment to upholding their ethical principles, preventing them from engaging in risky or fraudulent practices amidst crises, such as the global financial downturn of 2008, indicates the seriousness they bring to adhering to ethics. Some may choose the easy, unethical way out of difficult challenges, but ethical leaders are steadfast in their conviction to protect integrity at all costs. This ethical stance in not only the driving force of organizational credibility but also inspires trust and confidence among stakeholders. Ethical leaders know that maintaining integrity is important, especially in difficult times. This is because by driving integrity, they foster a culture of resilience within their organizations by making clear that ethical behavior is not only a good but important conceptualization of long-term sustainable success.

Transparency and Communication:

In uncertainty or crises, open communication and transparency should be considered crucial pillars in effective leadership by ethical leaders. They are aware that to build trust and credibility, things that are vital for the leadership, the leaders should be truthful and direct in every interaction. Ethical leaders ensure that all interactions are open, realizing the challenges and soliciting input from each member involved. This transparency from ethical leaders reveals their commitment to openness and fairness. Their updates on situations come out regularly, including successes and failures, even with honesty and integrity. By doing so, this transparency kindles a spirit of collaboration and joint effort. They seek input from the stakeholders and value different kinds of viewpoints that help them establish inclusion. When the confidence and reliability are improved, there will be collective resilience as well as solutions by building an environment open and dynamic enough to engage others in the discussion for common purpose.

Learning from Past Mistakes:

Ethical leaders understand that mistakes are an inevitable part of the leadership journey, but they treat them as valuable opportunities for growth and improvement. They do not shy from mistakes but instead openly acknowledge them and take full responsibility for their actions. They realize that transparency and accountability are very important in generating trust and credibility within their teams. Ethical leaders do not shy away from mistakes; they learn from them. They actually proceed to analyze the root causes of the errors and come up with corrective measures to avoid reoccurrence. This not only shows humility but also underscores the commitment to improvement.

Somehow, the ethical leaders benefit from learning from past mistakes and not remaining static and unchanged. They adapt their approach wherever they require in order to overcome challenges or blockades. In this way, the approach of the leaders appears as they meet the challenges and accept the feedback that has been given. Finally, learning and growth that ethical leaders create a culture which enables the organization to survive amidst adversity and uncertainty.

Conclusion

In the realm of management, ethical leadership becomes the bedrock upon which sustainable success and organizational resilience are built. This chapter underpins the meaning and demonstration of ethical leadership, its core principles, and their application across myriad contexts. Ethical leadership is not a matter of decision-making; it consists in making choices guided by moral principles, integrity, and a commitment to do what is right. It is thus a matter of commitment to honesty, fairness, and well-being for all stakeholders, including in uncomfortable situations or temptation.

The story of Lord Rama, a symbol that has timelessly depicted the essence of ethical leadership, is a testament to the enduring significance of righteousness, humility, and selflessness in leadership. His dedication to truth and justice, which encourages the individuals of this organization, is going to inspire the people to maintain ethics and principles no matter what the circumstances may be.

By living by the principles of Lord Rama, business leaders can create a culture where there is honesty, transparency, and a capacity for empathy. There will be no compromises with ethics and integrity, understanding that success is more sustainable in the long run, and the needs of all members of the organization have to be balanced with others.

In this chapter, we have examined the complexities of ethical decision-making, the importance of maintaining integrity, and the necessity of transparency and communication to foster trust and credibility. We have also looked into the importance of learning from past mistakes and adopting a growth mindset to foster continuous improvement and adaptability.

Finally, in this chapter, ethical leadership is not merely a desirable trait but an essential component of effective management. In this regard, by exercising the principles of ethical leadership, they can inspire trust, loyalty, and respect among their teams; such loyalty cannot occur without enduring success, and can allow meaningful contributions to a bigger sphere. As we navigate the complexities and uncertainties of this modern era, let us draw from the timeless wisdom of ethical leadership in leading with integrity, compassion, and humility towards all that we encounter on this journey.

End of Chapter 9

Chapter 10

Leadership Skills

Holding a position of authority is the beginning point of the world of leadership. To be a leader is to ignite inspiration and guide others towards collective excellence. In the pages of this chapter, we embark on a journey through the ancient epic Ramayana to uncover profound insights on leadership etched in its timeless tapestry. These invaluable lessons, distilled from the lives of revered characters, resonate with the essence of leadership in today's corporate landscape.

In the Ramayana lies a treasure trove of wisdom, where the heroic exploits of Lord Rama and his companions illuminate the path to effective leadership. Through their trials, triumphs, and tribulations, we glean timeless principles that transcend the boundaries of time and culture, offering guidance to leaders in every sphere of influence.

As we move through the pages of this epic narrative, we shall unravel the essence of leadership manifested in Lord Rama's unwavering integrity, boundless courage, and profound compassion. We shall draw inspiration from Sita's unwavering loyalty, Hanuman's selfless devotion, and Lakshmana's steadfast sacrifice. And in the shadows of Ravana's downfall, we shall heed the cautionary tale of unchecked ambition and hubris.

But our journey does not end within the realms of mythology; it extends into the modern-day corporate arena. Here, we shall bridge the gap between ancient wisdom and contemporary challenges, translating the timeless teachings of the Ramayana into actionable insights for today's leaders.

Through introspection and exploration, we shall uncover how integrity, courage, compassion, wisdom, and humility—epitomized by the characters of the Ramayana—serve as guiding beacons in the tumultuous seas of corporate leadership. We shall discover how the principles of ethical decision-making, strategic foresight, and inclusive leadership find resonance in the timeless narratives of ancient lore.

As we embark on this odyssey through the annals of mythology and business, let us open our minds to the profound truths awaiting discovery. Let us glean inspiration from the timeless wisdom of the Ramayana, drawing strength from its timeless teachings to navigate the complexities of leadership in the modern world.

For in the stories of gods and mortals, heroes and villains, lie the keys to unlocking the true potential of leadership—a journey that transcends time and space, guiding us towards the pinnacle of excellence and achievement.

Analyzing Ram's Leadership Qualities in Depth

Lord Rama, the central figure in the Ramayana, epitomizes exemplary leadership qualities that have inspired generations. Let us now delve into the depths of his character and unravel the key attributes that make him such a revered leader:

Integrity:

In fact, Rama's integrity was not some attribute but rather the very essence of his being, a guiding light that illuminated his path through the darkest times. His commitment to truth and righteousness became an inspiration for leaders across generations. Whether facing the heart-wrenching exile from his kingdom or facing the formidable demon king Ravana, Rama has never wavered from his principles. He has never compromised, even when there was the tantalizing allure of personal gain or convenience. Rama's integrity is not just a virtue but a testimony to the power of conviction and the unwavering resolve to stand for what is right, regardless of the challenges that may arise. Rama's example, therefore, illuminates the present moral and ethical ambiguities in our world with the truth of true leadership grounded in integrity, paving the way for trust, respect, and enduring success.

Courage:

Rama's courage is not a display of bravado, but a manifestation of inner strength and conviction. He continually faces trials and tribulations on his epic journey, each demanding immense courage and fortitude. Whether it's battling with the awesome demon king Ravana or making his way through the toughest jungles of Dandaka, Rama's unyielding determination captures one's attention. His unwavering courage inspires those around him and brings along courage and self-assurance to his allies. At the same time, his adversaries are instilled with fear and panic by his unyielding courage. But Rama's courage is not just physical; it is also a reflection of moral courage. He stands firm in his principles and does not waver, even with a hurdle so big that a lesser soul would be, by then, already dead and broken. The willingness of Rama to take risks and face challenges head-on therefore demonstrates the transformative power of fearless leadership. The example of Rama is such that true leadership requires not only physical courage but moral courage to stand up to what is just and righteous, even against adverse conditions.

Compassion:

Rama's compassion is a defining trait that sets him apart as a leader of exceptional caliber. Despite the warrior status that he holds and the challenges that come with it, Rama's heart brims with empathy and kindness towards all beings. He extends compassion not only to his loved ones but also to the other strangers and even his enemies, recognizing the inherent worth and dignity in every person. Rama's capacity for compassion can be seen in his relationships with people around him. Whenever he consoles his beloved wife, Sita, during the hard times or exhibits his enlarged heart in favoring his foes, Rama gets through as an empathetic person. His approach shows this compassion in the environment he cultivates. People are taken by a sense of care and kind regards in the culture that the leaders who emulate Rama's example create. Leaders are beginning to understand that while doing so, empathy is not a weakness but a strength for understanding, ascertaining, and generating the trust of those around them through empowerment. Prioritizing empathy and kind-heartedness in their leadership approach, they actively build an inclusive and supportive environment where all feel valued and respected.

Wisdom:

The move of empathy is paramount in Rama, thus making him a leader of great quality. Being a warrior, but also facing obstacles, Rama shows empathy and love for all other people. He radiates kindness, love, and compassion not only towards his loved ones but also towards strangers and even his foes. Rama understands that each person is a creation with a unique worth and dignity. In his relationships with people around him, he shows he has compassion. He is always consoling his beloved wife, Sita, in moments of distress or showing mercy to his enemies after a battle, which he personifies as wisdom. Rama symbolizes humane leadership where compassion prevails as the style of communication, embodied in people. Leaders who emulate such an example have come to appreciate the fact that compassion is not a weakness but a means to foster trust, commitment, and cooperation among team members. Compassionate leaders raise an inclusive environment where each person feels valued and appreciated.

Humility:

One characteristic, defining Rama's leadership, is his humility, which places him among exceptional integrity and grace. Despite the grandeur of his lineage and the fact that he eventually ascends to the throne, Rama adopts a modest and humble attitude in everything he does. He does not seek any accolades or praise for his actions but instead leads by example, through his humility and selflessness in all his dealings.

Humility of Rama is visible in everything that he does to his fellow people, regardless of their place and status. He shows reverence to all beings with absolutely no preference to their social rank, setting his leaders as ones with great ability to be humble. His humble approach wins him hearts in the eyes of all those people he respects and to whom he extends kind regards, inspiring group spirit and fellowship among his colleagues.

In fact, there are many leaders that imitate his humility by recognizing it is not a weakness, but an opportunity to engender confidence and togetherness in any group. By humility and grace, those people foster an environment where everybody feels okay to share his opinion while being assured of a friendly and cooperative working environment.

Translating Leadership Skills from the Ramayana to the Corporate World

Ramayana is not one for ancient mythology that could not translate into the modern corporate world; it is important, for this day, the timeless lessons that were learned still are relevant in today's business environment. Let's dive in to see how these ageless teachings can be applied in today's business environment:

Integrity in Business:

Just as Rama remains undeterred in his faithfulness to what he perceives to be right, corporate leaders need to uphold those same standards of integrity. Integrity in business involves much more than merely following the rules; it embodies an unwavering commitment to moral principles, honesty, and transparency in all dealings. Just like Rama, leaders who are honest and ethical are often very trustworthy and reliable. His strict adherence to ethical norms inspires confidence among employees, customers, and stakeholders in creating a culture of respect and loyalty within an organization.

More so, leaders who promote integrity help employees to emulate this behavior, encouraging ethics across all the corporate organization. It also sets a model for accountability that leaders want to see come out of the team. With these approaches, leaders minimize risk through examples of ethical behavior in ensuring that their team delivers on objective expectations. A culture that fosters integrity establishes the foundation for a better world of corporate success and lasting corporate image.

Courage to Innovate:

As Rama took on courageous battles, so do leaders in this world take up courage in the new times, bravely innovating and positively suggesting risks to take. In this fast-evolving business setting, where most companies are continually adapting to changing technological trends and shifting market tastes, innovative organizations have become superior in seizing their opportunities. Courage in innovating entails not only thoughts and visions but also the courage to implement them despite the inherent uncertainties and risks present in the process. The leaders with a culture of innovation allow their team to create, think, and innovate, ensuring employees have openness in making new proposals and improving them.

The courage to innovate empowers leaders to adapt to changing environments and benefit from opportunities for growth. Posing a mindset of continuous growth and embracing change, leaders can position their organizations as pioneers in their industries, driving sustainable success and resilience in the face of uncertainty. In this vein, it is like daring Rama's exploits in turning to new horizons of achievement and prosperity.

Compassionate Leadership:

A powerful, compassionate leadership style that Rama exhibits is an empathetic one to all living beings, and it creates positivity and nurtures the development of a positive and work-friendly environment. Leaders by value, who would place compassion before all else, exhibit a genuine interest in taking care of their workforce by going beyond being just leaders to being considered as real people with their own vulnerabilities and life experiences. Such compassionate leading establishes an empathetic and nurturing environment whereby team members are treated as valued, understood, and feel empowered to bring their whole selves to work. These leaders actively listen to their team, provide encouragement, and support them during both the good times and the down times. In addition, a compassionate leadership style strengthens trust and loyalty, motivating team members to collaborate and work together towards the goals of the organization. Employees in such workplaces who feel valued and are taken care of by their leaders are more likely to be engaged, motivated, and committed to making the organization great. In essence, compassionate leadership promotes employee well-being and organizational success by fostering a positive and inclusive work environment where everyone can thrive and contribute their best.

Wisdom in Decision-Making:

In the arena of decision-making, akin to Rama's insightful approach to dealing with perplexing circumstances, wise leaders establish prudence and deliberation in their choices. Wise leaders are aware that the decisions they make could create far-reaching implications for their organizations, stakeholders, and the wider community. With an assortment of knowledge and experience to draw upon, wise leaders, therefore, embark upon a comprehensive analysis and make all relevant factors carefully. They welcome diversified perspectives by opening doors for open dialogue and ensuring harmony among team members. Wise leaders also seek the counsel of subject matter experts and confidants in making informed, strategic decisions in line with the organization's vision and goals. With a wise like approach to decision-making, leaders can navigate risks, capitalize on opportunities, and lead their organizations toward sustainable success. Wise choices establish the foundation of ongoing growth and adaptability, a reflection of leadership's dedication to ethical stewardship and strategic vision.

Humility in Leadership:

Humble leadership, embodying Rama's modest demeanor despite his exalted status, enhances an environment of trust, collaboration, and mutual respect within organizations. Humble leaders realize that they are not always correct and would sincerely admit to their limitations and accept criticism, being fair, as they work through their team's prospective solutions. By being a humble leader, he would create a culture where all the team members are valued and recognized for their contribution. He encourages free communication and conversation with all people working in the organization, also inviting a different point of view from different levels. In doing so, humble leaders inspire a spirit of ownership and commitment amongst their team members, inspiring them to bring in their best selves for work every day. Further, a humble leader will prioritize the success of a team over personal accolades or recognition; he celebrates others' success, sharing credit for accomplishments. This approach of selflessness in leadership builds trust and loyalty amongst team members, driving organizational success through collaboration, innovation, and a shared sense of purpose.

Leadership Lessons from Various Characters in the Epic

The Ramayana is replete with characters whose actions and decisions offer valuable insights into effective leadership. Let's explore some key lessons from these iconic figures:

Sita:

Sita, through all her tests and struggles, came up with strength and steadfastness in her loyalty to Rama. Though she has been punished many times—from the position that took her from her kingly seat to some very unfriendly places, and finally abducted by the king of demons Ravana—it never helped her waver from being devoted to Rama. Her loyalty to her husband is exemplified with such vividness. The willingness of Sita to go through hardships, which have the power to shake even the strongest human, showcases her deep personal connection to Rama. Her courage amid adversity inspires her husband and teaches others of us the virtue of remaining committed even in the worst of circumstances. Sita's character points to the fact that real leadership requires courage, stamina, and unwavering loyalty and commitment to whoever stands by her. Her unwavering faith in Rama and her commitment to him during trying times prove a timeless testament to how profound the bond of trust and mutual respect can be.

Hanuman:

Serving as the epitome of devotion and self-denial in the Ramayana, Hanuman embodies leadership characteristics in his unrelenting dedication to serving others, humbling himself to the core in the process. Driven by his unique abilities and strength, he uses his energies to cater for the needs of others, exhibiting the virtue of servant leadership. This unyielding commitment to the mission of finding Sita, wife of Rama, illustrates dedication to the pursuit of noble objectives, even in the face of formidable challenges. Hanuman's miraculous feats of strength and courage, leaping across oceans and battling enemies, provide inspiration for leaders to overcome obstacles with fortitude and doggedness. Further, the selflessness and humility in service to Rama and his mission demonstrate the centrality of these qualities to leadership. To serve with dedication and humility is something that he does through his self-sacrifice of personal glory that stresses the transformative nature of servant leadership in which leaders put the needs of others above themselves and work tirelessly to fulfill common goals.

Lakshmana:

Lakshmana, the epitome of loyalty and commitment, is a constant in the Ramayana, one who showcases some very quintessential leadership qualities of the stable character and the selfless man. True to its literal meaning, Lakshmana remains committed to the older brother, Rama, and hence exhibits a bond of unwavering loyalty and support. An unbreakable flow of loyalty to his brother is perceived through his constant readiness to make personal sacrifice for the greater good. Lakshmana maintains loyal to his brother's cause irrespective of the myriad challenges and adversities he faces along the way. His willingness to put his own self-interest aside for the good of his brother's mission shows the importance of selflessness in leadership.

Through his character, Lakshmana gives us an understanding of what true leadership comprises, not only in loyalty but also in dedication to one's ideals, to the cause one supports, to anything for the sake of the people. He is a perfect example of how the selfless devotion and sacrifice can turn a mere person into a leader.

Ravana:

Ravana, the antagonist in the Ramayana, functions as a cautionary example for leaders of the dangers of pride and ethical corruption. He eventually meets his undoing, despite all his cunning and strength, as a result of his unstoppable ambition, including the disregard for ethical principles. His arrogance blinded him to the consequences of his actions, and he made decisions about this or that merely according to his own desires and ambitions. He is thoroughly consumed by the lust for power, which propels him to commit major injustices, among them the abduction of Sita and the war against Rama. However, his downfall serves as a morbid reminder of the shallow results that come from success that is bought by way of immorality. He meets his end handsomely and earnestly in the face of Rama, who thumped him in his good eye. This defeats the very core of character; leaders may learn from Ravana's blunder by prioritizing humility, integrity, and ethical conduct in leadership. By just remaining normal the leaders can avoid the pitfalls of arrogance and hubris to raise a culture of integrity and accountability within organizations.

Conclusion

In the vast landscape of the Ramayana, we journeyed through timeless teachings on leadership, intricately woven into the lives of the characters of this revered epic. From Lord Rama's unwavering integrity to Sita's steadfast loyalty, Hanuman's selfless devotion to

Lakshmana's unwavering sacrifice, and even the cautionary tale of Ravana's downfall—each character embodies profound lessons that transcend the boundaries of time and culture.

As we pull the curtains down on this chapter, we are standing at the crossroads of ancient wisdom and modern leadership challenges. The epic narration of the Ramayana serves not just as a lookback of mythology but as a timeless reservoir of guidance for leaders today.

Examining the virtues of integrity, courage, compassion, wisdom, and humility of the characters in the Ramayana, we are confronted with some great truths about leadership. These virtues, given the character from heroes to villains, constitute a code of behavior guiding leaders on the winding paths of a modern corporate world.

Translating such ageless principles into actionable insights for today's leaders, we emphasize upholding ethics, innovation, compassion, making good decisions, and humility. These attributes can create inclusive and supportive environments where there is trust, partnership, and mutual respect.

As the epic saga of the Ramayana comes to an end, while placing us in the contemporary realm of modern-day leadership, let us carry with us the wisdom gleaned from its pages. Let us heed the lessons of integrity, courage, compassion, wisdom, and humility to enable us to implement them in our role as leaders, so that we inspire greatness, guide others toward collective excellence, and chart a course towards lasting success and fulfillment.

For, in the stories of gods and mortals, heroes and villains, we find the keys to unlocking the full potential of leadership—a journey transcending time and space, guiding us towards the pinnacle of excellence and achievement.

End of Chapter 10

Chapter 11

Delegation of Responsibility and Effective Task Assignment

Delegation is the bedrock of successful management, enabling the fair distribution of work, development of team empowerment, and achievement of organizational objectives with absolute efficiency. A leader can delegate responsibilities, bring out collaboration, and create levels of productivity and creativity among team players. For a specific guide on delegation, there stands a timeless epic, the Ramayana, that has much wisdom to share and greatly qualifies the work of a leader across cultures and ages. The Ramayana, an ancient Indian epic, is thus a valuable source that captures wisdom about life, morality, and leadership. For example, within the lengthy scope of the narrative lies a wealth of lessons on delegation, as exemplified by the actions of its central characters. From the noble endeavors of Lord Rama to the steadfast loyalty of his allies, the epic provides a vivid canvas upon which the art of effective delegation is painted with strokes of clarity, trust, and empowerment.

Accordingly, at the heart of efficient delegation lies clear communication, ensuring that tasks are assigned with clarity and purpose. Just as Lord Rama gave precise instructions to his reliable allies, so too, do modern-day organization leaders impart clear objectives, expectations, and timelines with clarity and coherence. Leaders provide a roadmap for success, guiding their team members on how to handle challenges with confidence and clarity.

Moreover, trust is the essence of delegation—the belief in one's team members that they will complete tasks competently and with dedication. The statement to this effect of Lord Rama's unwavering confidence in the skills and talents of Hanuman, Sugriva, and others testifies to the importance of trust in delegation. In a fast-paced business environment, trust serves as the backbone for productive teamwork, fostering collaboration, innovation, and mutual respect among peers.

Furthermore, the proper manner of conducting delegation entails ensuring that one supports and advises team members regarding the tasks assigned to them. Just as Lord Rama stood by the side of Hanuman during his quest to rescue Sita, so did the leadership provide support, resources, and mentorship that enabled their team members to succeed. By enabling a culture of support and collaboration, leaders will improve the ability of their team members to surmount obstacles and have their objectives met.

Concerning the sphere of delegation, one point that has become critical in personnel selection. An example of the same may be seen in Lord Rama assigning jobs in such a manner so that complementary skills and abilities could be adequately used. In today's dynamic work setting, leaders have to leverage the exclusive talents and competencies of their team members for maximum productivity and efficiency.

Furthermore, effective delegation entails drawing a fine line between assigning tasks to the members and exercising powers, which makes it important. Lord Rama entrusted his allies with the autonomy to make decisions within the scope of the tasks assigned to them, much like modern-day leaders do. Effective delegation helps the leader empower the team members while still retaining accountability and oversight. Establishing clear limits and channels of communication would be the best avenue toward cultivating an environment of accountability, ownership, and innovation in their organizations.

Delegation stands as the epitome of effective leadership, the pathway to shared success and collective achievement. The timeless wisdom of the Ramayana could even provide a pathway for leaders to glean invaluable insights into the art of delegation, empowering their teams to take off in the complex and ever-evolving world of business. Through clarity, trust, empowerment, and accountability, leaders unlock the full potential of their teams and push their organizations toward excellence and prosperity.

The Art of Effective Delegation:

The art of effective delegation is to handle a single stroke of guidance, which creates the masterpiece itself. Lord Rama, the protagonist of the Ramayana, is a great example of this art through the delegation of tasks to his allies. He instructs his students to concentrate on forming their consciousness, being willing to share his view as well as to interact with them and support them in case of failure. His actions teach us invaluable lessons:

Clear Instructions:

Clear instructions are the cornerstone of effective delegation, serving as the guiding light that illuminates the path to success. Just as Lord Rama meticulously imparted clear instructions to Hanuman before sending him to find Sita, modern leaders must articulate a vision of tasks with precision to their teams. This will entail stating the specific objective to be achieved, outlining the goals to be met, setting realistic deadlines, and delineating available resources. By providing a complete roadmap for action, leaders will enable their team members to approach challenges confidently and clearly. Additionally, clear instructions enhance agreement and coherence across the team, ensuring that everyone aims at the same goal. Whether in a corporate setting or within a project team, clarity of instruction forms the pillars upon which effective delegation is built, providing a foundation for achievement and excellence.

Trust:

Confidence is inborn from trust. In the case of Hanuman's talents, such trust is exemplified by Lord Rama's unwavering confidence in him. When leaders trust in the abilities of the people under their command, they instill a sense of confidence and empowerment that fires motivation and fosters a culture of ownership. By entrusting them with work, leaders speak of trust in their skills, knowledge, and dedication to doing excellent work. This trust spurs personal growth as well as collective development; team members push beyond their limits to reach a standard of perfection. Further, trust helps to establish open communication, bring team members together, and show mutual respect between the leader and his team. In essence, trust is not just a belief in others' abilities but also a testament to the leader's confidence in the collective potential of the team to realize common goals.

Support:

Support is the cornerstone of effective delegation, mirroring Lord Rama's unwavering support of Hanuman in the Ramayana. Supporting Hanuman's confidence and offering support at times required of him were the prime tenets of Rama. Leaders must equip their team members with the required support, resources, and encouragement to enhance their performance. The leader should offer support to help them out whenever they need to set difficulties into perspective. To become efficient in problem-solving, each team should support its colleagues in working toward a shared goal. With such support and cooperation, the team can break each obstacle and comfortably reach their goals, both of which contribute to the confidence with which they handle challenges. Support should provide trust and strengthen the ties between leaders and their teams, creating a sense of camaraderie and mutual respect. Regarding the effective delegation, it is not only about assigning tasks; it includes delivering the necessary support and direction to ensure success and growth.

Feedback:

Feedback plays a crucial role in effective delegation, where Lord Rama listens carefully to Hanuman's return and gives feedback with a positive approach to his successful mission. In contemporary leadership contexts, offering timely and meaningful feedback is critical to developing sustainable improvement and synergy with expectations. With such regular visits to check the status of delegated tasks, leaders learn about progress, discuss areas that need improvement, and achieve both individual and collective accomplishments. Constructive feedback acts as a catalyst for growth, which enables team members to refine their skills, overcome challenges, and even perform more effectively. In addition, feedback enhances a culture of transparency and accountability across the team by facilitating open communication and the building of trust in the team. Providing feedback consistently and mindfully inculcates a sense of confidence among the team and drives performance. Such an approach nurtures a culture of excellence and continuous learning within organizations.

Selecting the Right People for Specific Tasks:

In choosing the right people for specific tasks, delegation will have the best results, just as Rama entrusted specific tasks to individuals according to their strengths and capacities.

Skills and Strengths:

Allocating tasks to an individual's skills and capabilities in the workplace is akin to piecing together the puzzle into a picture of productivity and success. Just as Lord Rama assigned each of his allie's duties that required their unique skills and abilities in the Ramayana, so, too, must modern leaders carefully consider what tasks to assign to each team member based on their expertise, experience, and preferences. Tailoring tasks to individuals' capabilities will enable leaders to maximize efficiency and productivity and, therefore, boost motivation and job satisfaction. When team members are put into tasks that match their skills and strengths, they are more likely to feel a sense of fulfillment and purpose in what they do. Besides, matching tasks to an individual's strengths sets an environment of collaboration and support, where each team member can work on the goal, towards maximum productivity. In other words, by bringing out the skills and strengths of team members, one ensures optimal performance and a culture of excellence in the organization.

Interest:

By the same token, for every individual, his interest in the task becomes his motivation, steering him toward success. Hence, just like Lord Rama entrusted tasks to his allies that resonated with their passions and interests in the Ramayana, modern leaders must recognize the importance of aligning assignments with individual passions of their team. When individuals are engaged in tasks that align with their interests, one would expect them to demonstrate enthusiasm, creativity, and dedication towards their work. This sense of engagement translates into better productivity and higher quality of output. Encouraging open dialogue on what a person would want to do and what he finds interesting helps lead a self-determining team. Tailoring work to an individual's preferences helps to maximize their capabilities and generates a culture of trust and empowerment. When work is done on something that a person likes, the chances of them taking it seriously are very high. Therefore, it is the individual who steers the ship to success by doing work that he likes.

Availability:

Measuring people's availability and workload is like engaging in a delicate balance of productivity and well-being. Just like how Lord Rama assessed the circumstances and limitations of his allies and so gave out the tasks in the Ramayana, modern leaders should consider the well-being of their team members while assigning responsibilities. Assessing availability gives the leader a way to mitigate overloading and get the tasks done just in time. To allocate tasks such that they give a return to a work environment that satisfies the needs of every individual has to be approved in a manner that ensures timely and efficient execution with team members. Workload management also involves good time management and balancing effort on every single person involved. Effective effort management and workload balancing is required for the proper order of priorities to help ensure that everyone in an organization can thrive. By proactively handling workloads and respecting the person's time constraints, a leader conveys empathy and support to his team members, nurturing a very positive and sustainable work environment where everyone feels good. In other words, the appreciation of availability and efficient management of the workload enhance the morale, engagement, and overall performance of the organization.

Development Opportunities:

Delegation is a fertile ground for growth and professional development within a team, just as Lord Rama entrusted his allies with tasks challenging their abilities and expanding their horizons in the Ramayana. Today's leaders are in a position to capitalize on the effect of delegation to empower their team members, enabling them to grow in terms of skill and competence. Entrusting challenging tasks to individuals propels them to their limits and pushes them into new terrain, thereby imbuing them with fresh challenges and valuable experience. Moreover, leaders can create a learning culture through the provision of training opportunities, mentorship, and skills improvement. It shows to his subordinates the commitment of a leader to their development and, by extension, to their success. When those people find confidence in their abilities and their resilience increases by accepting new responsibilities, it leads to building a sense of ownership and accountability. Ultimately, delegating as an agent of development nurtures a dynamic and agile workforce, which can meet the continuously changing demands of the modern workplace.

Balancing Responsibility and Authority in Delegation:

Delegation means trusting responsibility while staying near power. Achieving this balance requires careful consideration and communication.

Clear Boundaries:

Simple, clear boundaries serve as the guardrails that define and bind the delegation process in such a manner that clarity, accountability, and alignment with organizational objectives are apparent. Just as Lord Rama delineated the boundaries of authority and responsibility for his allies in the Ramayana, modern leaders should define clear expectations and parameters while delegating tasks. By defining the scope of delegated authority, decision-making parameters, and reporting structures, leaders outline the roadmap for action and establish the framework for accountability. Clear boundaries give team members the chance to be independent under defined bounds, yet with ownership of the work. In this regard, setting boundaries reduces uncertainty or any misinterpretation in the work procedure for effective collaboration. Through fostering transparency and openness, leaders create an environment where all team members are aware of roles and responsibilities that eventually lead to higher productivity, better efficiency, and organizational success.

Empowerment:

The deep root of successful delegation lies in empowerment, which allows for people's autonomy and authority in making choices and decisions that help to make progress, not only for an individual but also for the institution. Just as Lord Rama entrusted his allies with the freedom to exercise judgment and take ownership of their task in the Ramayana, present-day leaders should grant members of their team the freedom to tackle challenges and take advantage of opportunities. The mere act of granting people autonomy has instilled confidence and empowered them to contribute ideas and participate more effectively. Team members, therefore, are motivated, creative, and proactive in solving problems because they have a personal interest in the success of their work. In addition, empowerment creates a culture of accountability and collaboration, whereby individuals take responsibility for their tasks and contribute effectively to the achievement of common goals. When empowering their employees, leaders unleash their full potential to drive organizational success and growth.

Accountability:

Accountability can thus be seen as the bedrock upon which effective delegation stands since it ensures that individuals are held responsible for the outcomes of their delegated tasks, just as Lord Rama held his allies accountable for their assigned duties in the Ramayana. Modern leaders should establish clear expectations and mechanisms for tracking progress and evaluating performance. By holding individuals accountable, leaders inspire transparency and responsibility throughout the team, resulting in a culture of trust and integrity. Mechanisms for progress monitoring enable the leader to keep track of the performance of delegated tasks and to be able to intervene in time if there are any issues. On the other hand, accountability fosters continuous improvement since team members get motivated to learn from successes and setbacks. A culture of accountability breeds a sense of ownership and commitment among team members, which enhances the efficiency, productivity, and success of the organization.

Communication:

Effective communication is the soul of accomplishing successful delegation, and maintaining clarity, alignment, and cooperation between team members. Like how Lord Rama kept the channels of communication with his allies moving during their missions in the Ramayana, modern leaders must prioritize transparent and regular communication when delegating tasks. In this manner, leaders will facilitate opportunities for guidance, address concerns, and share feedback on time. Encouraging people to seek clarification, raise questions, and report their progress updates will ensure a culture of open communication and responsibility within the team. Communicating effectively not only builds trust and relationships but also reduces misunderstandings and conflicts. Fostering a culture of open communication not only helps team members collaborate effectively, share ideas, and work towards common goals, but it is also essential for achieving clarity, alignment, and success in the delegation process.

Conclusion:

In conclusion, a successful manager or leader has to have some understanding of the assignment of responsibilities that is most effective; this paper will do an invaluable exploration of the art of delegation by drawing insights from a timeless epic, the Ramayana. To that effect, from Lord Rama's instructions to Hanuman and the fact that Lord Rama honored his allies, nothing ever went unanswered, and the moment he delegated his tasks to Sita, there was no, in the external world, need for people to come and celebrate the victory of Rama over the demon king Ravana. He availed his team members with the necessary support and empowered them with confidence. The epic provides an overall range of excellent lessons to be transferred to modern business environments. What eventually emerges as the cornerstone for effective delegation is effective communication in providing a roadmap towards success and alignment of the team. The trust serves as the bedrock on which delegation stands and empowers the team members toward collaboration and innovation. Supportive leadership ensures the team members with the resources and guidance needed for achieving success, and feedback fuels continuous improvement and growth.

Task matching with individuals' skills, strengths, and interests is very crucial to maximize productivity and engagement. Clear delineation of boundaries and empowerment within the task allows the team member to lead the given responsibility while retaining accountability. This assures that the individuals shall be held accountable for the outcomes of their delegated tasks and hence transparency and continuous improvement.

Communication is the backbone of successful delegation, facilitating clarity, alignment, and collaboration within the team. Effective communication underpins successful delegation in its facilitation of clarity, alignment, and collaboration within the team.

Essentially, effective delegation serves as a vital skill for leaders who aspire to achieve greatness and impact while navigating through the complexities of the present-day business landscape. Through transparency, accountability, and collaboration, leaders can raise a culture and team environment that demands excellence and innovation.

By echoing these principles of effective delegation in the spirit of the Ramayana, let us remember that what is effective with respect to delegating responsibility is not limited to task distribution alone but also that it supports individuals to be empowered, collaboration to be fostered, and an ethos of accomplishing greatness in the journey of shared goals and visions. Through effective leadership's exercise of this principle, leaders can mold high-performing teams that would pull the organization along a path to success and have an impact on the betterment of people and the world.

Reflecting on the lessons derived from the Ramayana, let us remember that effective delegation is not just assigning tasks but empowering individuals, fostering collaboration, and a culture of excellence and innovation. Under the guise of effective delegation, leaders have been able to build and train high-performing teams that they could have pulled their organizations across to be able to achieve great successes and leave an indelible impact on the world.

End of Chapter 11

Chapter 12

Teamwork and Collaboration

In achieving goals together in any organization, and in accomplishing so much in today's world, teamwork and collaboration present the pillars of achieving greatness. They become the springboards that motivate people toward success and the driving force behind innovation. When individuals come together as a team, combining their unique talents, skills, and efforts towards a shared goal, they have the potential to achieve extraordinary results that go beyond individual capabilities. In the dynamic contemporary landscape of modern management, utilizing the wisdom embedded in timeless stories such as the Ramayana provides profound insights for fostering a culture of collaboration and realizing collective success.

This epic narrative, an ancient Indian epic regarded for its moral teachings and profound wisdom, stands as a treasure trove of ancient sources of inspiration for the modern manager in the complexities of today's business world. In the verses lie profound lessons on leadership, teamwork, and the power of collective effort. When we look at the epic narrative, then we come to know the principles and practices that underpin effective collaboration and enable organizational success.

Indeed, we visit one rich tapestry of characters and narratives in the Ramayana that illustrates the transformative potential of teamwork and collaboration. From the noble endurance of Lord Rama and his co-ops to the strategic alliances sought in the pursuit of righteousness, the Ramayana provides a treasure trove of real-life lessons that resonate across cultures and generations. When we draw the parallels between the challenges the characters in the epic faced and the realities of modern organizational dynamics, leaders glean some actionable strategies for creating a collaborative culture and achieving collective success.

In the following chapters, we shall journey through the ancient wisdom of the Ramayana and unravel the key principles and practices that underpin effective teamwork and collaboration. We will explore communication, trust, and shared vision towards aligning individual efforts toward the achievement of common goals. Additionally, we will explore leadership in the cultivation of a culture of collaboration and obstacle-overcoming strategies in the face of diverse teams.

By the light of the Ramayana, we will gain a deeper understanding of the dynamics of teamwork and collaboration, thus identifying usable insights that can be adapted in real-life organizational contexts. With the help of this ancient epic, leaders can inspire their teams to work together and overcome challenges to achieve collective success.

Together, as leaders, fostering collaboration, and together we will unleash a collaborative potential and stroll towards a brighter future for teams and individuals.

Lessons in Collaboration from Building the Ram Setu Bridge:

Thus, the construction of the Ram Setu bridge in the Ramayana sets a poignant example of effective collaboration. According to the legend, the army of monkeys and bears under the guidance of Lord Rama built the bridge that connected India with Sri Lanka, allowing Rama's army to pass over and retrieve his abducted wife, Sita. Within the epic tale lie several crucial lessons on collaboration, as follows:

Unity in Diversity:

This is very well put forth in the narration of building the bridge in the Ramayana through the idea of "Unity in Diversity" where the strength of collaboration overrides varied backgrounds and abilities. The army assembled for the monumental task, had diversity not as some form of acceptance but as a source of strength. Each member of the team, whether it was a monkey or a bear, was known for their unique set of skills, strengths, and characters that were valuable towards the general objective of the team.

This diversity proved very instrumental in overcoming the challenges of constructing the bridge. The monkeys are known for their agility and dexterity, while the bears are known for their strength and resilience. This diversity was hence complemented towards filling in gaps and using the different strengths collectively to complete their common purpose.

In an organizational context of modern settings, the relevance of the issue of diversity lies in embracing diversity. By ensuring an environment where each individual feels valued and respected from various backgrounds and cultures, organizations can bring the best out of all their collective contributions. This is how embracing diversity will facilitate creativity, innovation, and adaptability to meet complex problems.

Moreover, embracing diversity fosters a culture of inclusion and belonging, where the identity of every team member is granted a sense of empowerment to contribute with their special talents and ideas. This inclusivity facilitates collaboration, sharing, and a mutual appreciation for things to be delivered by any team member. Therefore, it sets the groundwork for high-performance teams and organizations in good standing.

Finally, this lesson of "Unity in Diversity," from the Ramayana's army of monkeys and bears, illustrates the transformative power of collaboration despite differences. When diversity is embraced with which each person gets accepted in his individuality and values, organizations may get the best of both worlds out of their teams and gain great achievements.

Effective Communication and Coordination:

It was marked by effective communication and coordination among the diverse team of monkeys and bears, and the success in the construction of the bridge was mostly built. There was a unified understanding of roles and responsibilities amongst the team members, hence avoiding any confusion. There was a very clear, open pathway for communication and feedback between team members; coordination was also very good, allowing team members to go in sync with the main plan. Organizations can learn from this illustration by giving more priority to communication clarity and coordination within teams. In case clear roles and responsibilities, as well as the channels of communication, are defined and clear-cut, teams will be able to work much more efficiently, reducing misunderstandings, and reacting with flexibility towards challenges. Teams working together in such a manner encourage a culture of collaboration and transparency, in a way that helps organizations harness their collective strengths and provide stunning results.

Shared Vision and Goals:

The common vision and purpose for an individual to a shared project, evidenced by the construction of the Ram Setu bridge, showcase how it serves to drive collective action toward a common goal. Every team member, be it a monkey or a bear, unites with one collective purpose: the reunion of Lord Rama with his beloved wife, Sita. This shared vision instilled in this project meaning and significance that sparked a sense of purpose and commitment in each team member. With a strong appreciation for the contribution that they are making to the organization, the monkeys and bears worked tenaciously and, in effect, with a determined conviction that each one is making an actual contribution towards the achievement of this fundamental goal. Thus, when the duty of the individuals was coordinated with the overall mission of the organization, it enabled every action to form a part of the big goal of constructing the bridge.

In modern organizational contexts, the idea of shared vision and goals should prove invaluable. A meaningful vision and well-defined goals help align individual contributions toward the common mission. When employees know why they work and how the same contribution they offer helps in realizing the goal of the organization, they become more motivated, engaged, and committed to delivering good results. That, therefore, makes it extremely beneficial for creating a sense of unity and purpose in teams that would in turn create excellence and accomplishment.

Fostering a Culture of Teamwork Within An Organization:

These are strategies for building a culture of teamwork: Deliberate effort and commitment, both from leaders and team members.

Clear Vision and Goals:

Clear vision and clearly defined goals help to demarcate the leadership path, guiding stakeholders along a road towards success and teamwork. A compelling vision that sets forth an organization's purpose and direction could be conveyed by the leaders, and employees may relate to them in the sense of how this organization leads to and realizes its goals. The knowledge of how your actions support a common vision brings up an internal sense of participation and a goal to be amongst others who also share similar objectives towards a common goal.

Furthermore, detailed goals lay a path to the realization of success through concrete action, orienting what the vision defines. By breaking down the visions the actionable steps that define such a mission, employees may relate better in realizing their roles within the broader scheme and how their actions will help in the realization of organizational objectives.

Where vision and goals are clearly understood and expressed within the organization's culture, employees get motivated to work together effectively, pooling individual strengths, perspectives, and experiences with confidence in each other to deal with problems and innovate. This way, collaboration among groups can be a remarkable group of workers who are keen and committed to working together to reach common goals and, in doing so, contribute to the general growth of the organization as a whole. Hence, in this case, a clear vision and goals become the foundation of a culture of teamwork, endorsing sustainable growth and success within an organization.

Leadership by Example:

Leadership by example could make a powerful catalyst in fostering teamwork and collaboration within an organization. When a leader exposes collaborative behavior through his or her example, he or she not only sets a standard for others to follow but also instills trust, respect, and camaraderie within the team. Leaders who take part in collaborative efforts personally demonstrate their commitment to ensuring that the team should succeed and reinforce the importance of working together towards common goals. In addition, by engaging in open communication, transparency, and inclusivity during their interactions with the team members, leaders would inspire openness, trust, and collaboration among team members. They promote openness, trust, and a culture of psychological safety whereby the employees would be more prone to contribute their knowledge, seek feedback, and collaborate in a more effective and team-based approach without feeling the fear of judgment or punishment.

Moreover, leading by example in the spirit of collaboration, leaders push accountability and ownership onto team members. When the team sees its leaders actively collaborating with others and taking collective responsibility for outcomes, then they get motivated to do the same. This gives a culture of responsibility and ownership of the people on the team so that everyone is vested in the success of the team and works with others to ensure that everyone achieves his or her goal.

In essence, therefore, leadership by example is not what has been said but rather the deeds of the leader. When leaders internalize the values of teamwork, communication, and mutual respect in their behavior every day, they inspire others to do the same, resulting in positive change within the organization. Through modeling collaborative behaviors, leaders can foster teamwork that generates innovation, productivity, and success in the organization.

Team Building Activities:

Team-building activities are indispensable tools in promoting collaboration, developing stronger bonds, and promoting a sense of unity among team members. These activities offer a platform whereby individuals can interact in an informal and relaxed setting to get to know each other better and build deeper connections than just professional links. Through team-building exercises and workshops, organizations will offer structured opportunities to develop interpersonal skills, such as communicating and working together. These activities often present participants with tasks or assignments that require cooperation and teamwork achieve a common objective. As members move through these activities, they learn to trust the ability of their colleagues, communicate sufficiently, and rely on each other's strengths to make them stronger collectively. In addition to off-site retreats and social events, creating an off-beat environment with relaxation and socialization, encouraging team members to get along and experience together. It can be a team-building retreat in a natural setting or a relaxed social gathering after work that has been providing such opportunities for shared activities, an opportunity to build camaraderie and share experiences together that result in memorable times.

Thus, through team-building activities, it pays to solidify the experience of an interesting workforce where collaboration and teamwork go in hand. Such activities enhance the collective bond of the team and create a vibrant atmosphere within the team, making the team more enthusiastic about its work. In the end, by constructing strong relationships and creating a feeling of belonging, team-building activities lay the groundwork for enhanced collaboration and collective success within the organization.

Achieving Collective Success Through Effective Collaboration:

Effective collaboration is quite a determinant in making organizations successful. Some key principles to foster effective collaboration are:

Trust and Psychological Safety:

Trust and psychological safety are the two fundamental elements of effective collaboration in teams. In a situation where team members feel safe in expressing their ideas, opinions, and concerns without any risk of it's consequences, they will have a predisposition to take part actively in discussions and to contribute toward the team's goals. In a psychologically safe place, one would feel valued and respected, knowing their contribution is relevant, and they are never ridiculed or criticized for speaking up. This encourages an open environment, where team members feel empowered to present their viewpoints, contribute ideas for creative solutions, and challenge the standard without fear of judgment or retribution.

Furthermore, trust sets the foundation for strong team dynamics. If there is a high level of trust between team members, they will be more willing to collaborate, openly communicate, and support each other. Trust helps teams handle problems and conflict with adaptability and resilience because it knows that someone will be there to help work together to reach common objectives.

Promoting a culture of trust and safety psyche will lead to an environment where innovations and creativity flourish. Teams feel inspired and empowered to take risks, share ideas, and collaborate effectively, hence overall better performance and collective success. All in all, trust and psychological safety underpin strong team cohesion, high morale, and a positive work culture.

Shared Understanding of Goals and Roles:

A common understanding of goals and roles helps initiate good teamwork. In case a team member understands the overall goals and objectives of a project or initiative that the team is working on, he or she will know where to direct his or her efforts and will be working for a common purpose. Defining goals is critical in that with this clarity, the team will avoid ambiguity and ensure all members are working towards the same results. This sets up anticipation where team members do not just guess their expectations or roles but are aware of what is expected of them and how the contribution they make supports the goal.

Moreover, one of the most important things to define in teams is the role of every member of a team. To be able to focus your attention on an area of expertise and ability, each team member should know his or her exact role and responsibilities that he or she has. Team members contribute more effectively within this realm of accountability and productivity.

Furthermore, the identification of goals and roles fosters unity and cohesion among team members. When the team has a commonality of purpose and is aware of the individual contributions that have to be performed, this energy gives more drive to work together to achieve common goals.

In a nutshell, creating a shared understanding of goals and roles provides a platform for effective collaboration, coordination, and communication between teams. This allows teams to effectively pool their strength and resources towards a given end, resulting in productivity and realization of the objectives in pursuance of the set goals.

Commitment to Continuous Improvement:

Commitment to continuous improvement becomes essential in fostering effective collaboration within teams. The teams that foster this commitment towards having a constant attitude of lifelong learning will be better prepared to meet changing circumstances and overcome challenges that might have hindered their success. This can include conducting regular evaluations of their processes and results and calling for feedback from team members, stakeholders, or an outside party to get insights into areas that need refining or adjustments. If the team embraces feedback as an opportunity for growth rather than criticism, they can promote a culture of openness and transparency that fosters collaboration and innovation.

In addition, the teams committed to the culture of continuous improvement actively seek out opportunities for learning from their experiences and applying lessons learned in future endeavors. This may involve conducting post-project reviews or debriefings to reflect on successes and challenges, celebrate achievements, and identify areas for improvement. By bringing these insights to practice, teams can continually fine-tune their approach and excel in their mission over time.

An environment of continuous improvement also holds experimentation and innovation within teams. Organizations that encourage team members to explore new ideas, technologies, or methodologies come out with stimulated creativity and positive change. This willingness to embrace change and embrace new ideas creates adaptability and resourcefulness within teams to enable them to succeed in dynamic and unpredictable environments.

In a nutshell, a commitment to continuous improvement is vital in the promotion of collaboration within teams. It is through the harnessing of learning opportunities, adoption of feedback, and a thrust for excellence that teams can enhance the quality of their output, foster creativity and innovation, and hence achieve greater success together.

Conclusion

In conclusion, the principles and practices of teamwork and collaboration inspired by the timeless wisdom of the Ramayana reveal valuable insights for modern organizational leaders. We have covered the importance of unity in diversity, effective communication, shared vision, and goals; leading with leadership, team-building activities, trust, and continuous improvement in inspiring a collaborative culture. From the construction of the Ram Setu bridge to the intricacies of diverse team performance, the epic narrative gives a vivid portrait of the timeless lessons that find resonance across cultures and generations. A comparative analysis of the experiences of the characters in the epic with the realities of modern organizational dynamics is a great source of actionable strategies for leaders in attempting to establish collaborative cultures and collectively succeed.

Moving forward, leaders need to embrace diversity to encourage clarity in the development of the communication path, by developing a shared sense of purpose amongst their teams. From inspiration by example and through the conscious design of trust and the psychological safety environment, leaders can inspire their teams to collaborate effectively to face any challenges together.

Additionally, investing in team-building activities and continuous improvement will help nurture stronger team relations and spur innovation within organizations. Through the development of an environment where everyone feels valued and respected to contribute his unique talents and ideas, organizations can tap into the high potential of their teams for great results.

Essentially, the journey to greatness through teamwork and collaboration is full of dedication, perseverance, and a commitment to promoting a culture of collaboration. By implementing the lessons learned from the Ramayana and operationalizing them within real-life organizational contexts, leaders can inspire their teams to work together towards shared goals, thus creating a brighter future for both teams and individuals alike.

With gratitude, we urge our clients and friends to continue to release their collaborative potential in an environment imbued with this spirit of collaboration. Together, as leaders, let us keep pushing the boundaries of what is possible through our collective efforts and make a lasting impact on society.

End of Chapter 12

Chapter 13

Ethics and Righteous Decision-Making

Ethics and making sound decisions become guiding lights in life, much like a compass leading a ship through the tumultuous seas. As we embark on this chapter's journey, we shall delve into profound insights offered by the timeless epic of the Ramayana, discovering how its ancient wisdom can illuminate the path to ethical decision-making and principled leadership in today's dynamic business landscape. The Ramayana, one of the most venerated texts in Hindu mythology, is a narrative rich in moral teachings and profound philosophical truths. At its core lies the story of Rama, the embodiment of virtue and righteousness, whose life serves as a beacon of inspiration for generations to come. Through Rama's trials and triumphs, we glean invaluable lessons on integrity, honor, and the unwavering pursuit of truth.

In the contemporary arena of business, steeped in ethical dilemmas and moral compasses so often tested, the ancient wisdom of the Ramayana proves invaluable in providing guidance. Drawing parallels between the moral considerations of Rama and the contemporary business challenges, we uncover timeless principles that transcend the boundaries of time and culture. Rama's unwavering commitment to the dharma, or righteousness, and the sacrifices he had to make to uphold principles of integrity and honor, underpin the blueprint for modern-day business dilemmas. Across the pages of the Ramayana, we can find guidelines on decision-making that are still valid today, in the wake of competing interests and moral complexities.

We will investigate how contemporary business situations may be influenced by righteous principles, and further elaborate on how leaders can prioritize ethical issues in their business decisions, keeping in mind their choices for greater profits and competitive market environments. Through this episode of Rama, a means will be discovered to develop ethical visions and pledge loyalty to values such as fairness, transparency, and social responsibility, even amidst adversity.

We shall explore how a culture of integrity and ethics can be cultivated in organizations, whereby leaders model the behavior they wish their teams to learn from and enable them to make sound choices. Properly rewarding ethical conduct, open communication, and developing clear expectations are ways in which organizations can create an environment where fairness prevails and principles of right-doing are not merely prerequisites but become a part of the fabric of daily operations.

In essence, the Ramayana stands as a timeless guidebook to ethical leadership and righteous decision-making, offering profound insights that resonate across generations and cultures. By embracing the wisdom of this ancient epic, leaders can navigate the complexities of modern business with integrity, honor, and an unwavering commitment to doing what is right.

Rama's Ethical Considerations in Decision-Making

And now, going back to the days of Prince Rama, when he was put through an unfathomable number of tough decisions. Rama was a prince known for his unrelenting commitment to the noble, despite the dilemmas he had to confront. One of them was where he had to leave his kingdom and go into exile for 14 years, to honor his father's word.

Rama's Loyalty to Dharma

In making ethical decisions in the life of Rama, the Ramayana affirms his loyal adherence to dharma as the path of righteousness and duty. Dharma denotes duty, morality, and righteousness that one does follow in life. Rama represented these ideals by portraying himself through his life with a high sense of integrity and selflessness. When he was beset with the dilemma to honor] his father's words and agree to be exiled because of this, on the other hand, Rama's dedication to duty showed through unmatched preference to accept exile and suffer. Though it meant the risk of personal sacrifices, Rama kept in mind the welfare of the kingdom before any of his desires, a clear indication of how a commitment to the greater good should take priority in decision-making. His unwavering adherence to dharma not only brings out his character but at the same time serves as the timeless exemplar of ethical leadership and moral courage for future generations.

Rama's Sacrifice for Principles

Rama's sacrifice for principles denotes the profound importance of integrity in leadership. Despite suffering personal costs and innumerable challenges, Rama did not waver from upholding his word, and standing by the principles that he held shows resolute dedication. He proved himself to be selfless, resilient leader who is dedicated to upholding righteousness by willingly forfeiting his claim to the throne and having to endure the difficulties of living in the forest. Thus, the personal cost, rather than any negative public opinion, motivated Rama's noble deed. His self-pronounced sacrifice for his principles put a great example before both ordinary humans and celestial beings, who responded with universal approbation and praise. After all, the unwavering commitment to truth and righteousness has gotten Rama an unbelievable amount of trust and respect. His example sets the contemporary leaders as well as the succeeding generations on how to remain firmly committed to doing the right thing, but accept what comes with it. With the ending power of integrity, it remains a reminder about true leadership that involves personal sacrifice for the greater good, along with unwavering dedication to moral principles, even in the face of adversity.

Applying Righteous Principles to Contemporary Business Dilemmas

Now, let's bring Rama's principles into the modern-day boardroom. In today's business world, leaders often have to grapple with complex dilemmas where ethical considerations clash with financial interests or market pressures.

Product Safety Vs. Profit Maximization

Rama's principles bring out quite clearly the imperative for placing more importance on product safety than on maximizing profits. Ethical leaders are aware that denying product safety not only jeopardizes customers' health and safety but also weakens the credibility and reputation of the firm. Rather than succumbing to the temptation of short-term financial gains, ethical leaders look ahead and prioritize investing in quality control measures and ensuring their products meet the highest safety standards. Through this commitment to consumer welfare, a company builds trust and creates loyalty among its customer base, promoting a long-term relationship, and therefore sustainable success. This adherence to Rama's principles in decision-making ensures ethical conduct while ensuring overall prosperity and reputation in the marketplace.

Fair Labor Practices and Corporate Social Responsibility

Rama's preference for justice and fairness is an enduring guide for the ethics of the leaders in terms of consideration given to business decisions involving workers and communities. In this modern era, issues such as worker exploitation and environmental degradation are prevalent, and ethical leaders recognize the importance of upholding human rights, labor standards, and environmental stewardship in their operations. By placing an emphasis on fair labor practices and embracing corporate social responsibility (CSR) initiatives, companies display their ethical conduct and positively impact society.

Incorporating fair treatment towards employees, including the provision of fair wages, safe working conditions, and opportunities for professional growth, leads to greater employee satisfaction and loyalty and reflects well on the company's reputation and brand value. Furthermore, by implementing sustainable business practices and minimizing the environmental impact, ethical leaders can act as flag bearers for preserving natural resources and promoting environmental sustainability for future generations.

Building a Culture of Integrity and Ethics Within an Organization

However, ethics is not just about individual decisions; it's also about the culture we create within our organizations. Just as Rama upheld righteousness in his kingdom, leaders should foster a culture of integrity and ethics within their teams.

Setting Clear Ethical Expectations

The culture of integrity is what organizations value and cherish for a well-situated journey, where clear expectations need to be set. Leaders lead in setting these expectations as they outline the core values of the company such as truth, integrity, and accountability. Clearly articulating the values and expectations to the employees creates a shared understanding of what ethical conduct constitutes in the work environment. This makes it clear what the employees have to follow to make decisions that are right and ethical. Organizations can promote these expectations through various means, such as developing and enforcing policies, codes of conduct, and training programs. These initiatives are aimed at helping to educate employees on ethical standards and, in a more defined way, help to institutionalize ethical behavior within the corporate culture. Leaders, through consistently promoting and sustaining expectations, set a standard of conduct that encourages trust, respect, and accountability that helps in the general development of the organization for a long duration.

Leading by Example

One of the very epitomes of effective leadership is leading by example, especially where ethical behavior within an organization is concerned. Leaders who foster honesty, transparency, and fairness have created a corporate culture for sound ethics to thrive. By consistently exhibiting these values in all their dealings with employees, clients, and stakeholders, leaders create a positive influence on the whole organization. As long as leaders show ethics by example through recognition of mistakes, keeping commitments, and doing ethical things, they instill respect in their people. Ethical behavior promoted by leaders who model the same and portray this behavior to their subordinates will often be mirrored by employees. A leader who sets an example by having integrity in their acts makes more people feel secure and more respectful of their leaders, which enhances the business's culture of trust and accountability. Moreover, when leaders lead by example, they reinforce the importance of ethical behavior and create a standard of conduct that permeates throughout the organization. That would not only make the organization reputation-friendly but also create a sense of pride and commitment in the employees, hence leading to success with increased productivity.

Recognizing and Rewarding Ethical Behavior

Reinforcing integrity and cultivating a culture of ethical conduct within organizations will involve recognizing and rewarding ethical behavior. Rewarding leaders will send a clear signal to employees that the organization holds firm to its values and expectations. Some approaches for doing this include formal recognition programs, performance evaluations, and promotions. Coupling ethical considerations with career advancement and rewards puts the organization on the right side by showing that integrity is a value that pays.

Moreover, celebrating ethical achievements emphasizes the tremendous impact that principled conduct has on the organization and its stakeholders. This motivates employees further to continually adhere to ethical norms, and it also motivates others to do the same.

Leaders, therefore, underline the message that integrity is not just a personal virtue but an integral component of organizational culture. This way, it helps to create an environment where ethical conduct is the norm, which finally translates to the long-term success and sustainability of the organization.

Conclusion

This journey through the principles of ethics and righteous decision-making, entwining the great epic of the Ramayana, has enlightened our path to ethical leadership and principled conduct in today's dynamic business landscape. The Ramayana, rich in moral teachings and philosophical perceptions, indeed stands as a guiding light for modern leaders to maneuver the intricacies of today's business landscape with the standards of integrity, honor, and the determination to seek truth. When we follow the lesson of the unwavering commitment of Rama to righteousness and his sacrifices for principles, we see the timeless relevance of ethical leadership in the making of decisions. The fidelity of Rama to dharma, loyalty toward duties and righteousness, and sacrifice of personal interest for public welfare stand as enduring examples of ethical conduct for leaders throughout generations.

Consequently, establishing parallels between Rama's ethical considerations and today's business dilemmas has helped us understand how leaders can apply those principles to current business conflicts, even in the presence of competing interests and moral complexities. Embodying a culture of ethics and integrity within their organization can provide leaders the opportunity to create a world where transparency is second nature, and the principles of right-doing are part of the organizational culture.

Besides, by demonstrating ethical behavior and developing a process to identify, reward, and honor good ethical conduct, leaders can encourage their staff members to follow ethical values by celebrating ethical victories and exhibiting the positive outcomes of having an ethical character, such as having ethical organizational cultures.

In other words, it serves as the eternal guide, the Ramayana, which at first glance, would seem to be full of wisdom and stories that are applicable, cutting across cultures and ages. Embracing this ancient epic, in its wisdom, allows leaders to perform under great pressure, with integrity, honor, and commitment to doing what is right. As we continue on this journey, let us heed the lessons of Rama's ethical principles and strive to uphold the highest standards of integrity and righteousness in all our endeavors. Through our collective efforts, we can build organizations and societies where ethics and righteous decision-making are not just ideals but lived realities, ensuring a better and sustainable future for all.

End of Chapter 13

Chapter 14

Time Management and Planning

Time management and planning are not simply administrative deeds but rather prerequisites for effective leadership and organizational success. In the competitive business dynamics of today, the ability to harness time judiciously and chart a strategic course is not optional, but a must-have. Through history, in all its richness and complexity, which provides narratives and epics that are repositories of ideas and lessons that go beyond the boundaries of time and culture, can be understood. This chapter is a navigational effort through the hallowed pages of the Ramayana, where the saga of Ram's 14-year exile unfolds profound insights into the art of strategic planning and time management.

While we navigate through the annals of the Ramayana, we discover a tapestry of strategically planned lessons woven into the fabric of Ram's exile. The unwavering commitment to his father's word and the righteousness of the path, though fraught with hardship, becomes a source of inspiration for leaders who must struggle against the tides of tribulation. Through his journey, we see how to set goals, adapt to change, and the significance of long-term perspective for organizational objectives.

We then delve into the arena of timely production and delivery in the corporate world. Just as carefully Ram planned everything during his exile, organizations can achieve the rigors of a fast-paced market by optimizing their resources and processes. He draws parallels between ancient wisdom and the present-day challenges. From efficient resource allocation to effective time management, the Ramayana holds insights that ring true of the requirements of modern business operations.

Central to our exploration is a realization of the indispensable role played by time management in shaping organizational destiny. In the highly competitive organization of the present, therefore, time is the most precious resource which must be handled with care. Through the prism of the Ramayana, we unravel the complexities of this art and explore strategies for prioritization, delegation, and optimization that serve as the bedrock for sustainable success.

Honing, therefore, the lessons of the Ramayana, leaders can instill timeless principles that transcend the ephemeral fluctuations of the business world. In strategic planning, timely execution, and prudent management of resources, organizations can effectively navigate the currents of change and emerge triumphant and stronger.

Strategic Planning Lessons from Ram's 14-Year Exile:

Ram's 14-year exile from Ayodhya becomes a great example of strategic planning amidst adversity. Against a background of unforeseen circumstances, Ram took an approach to his exile that was organized and firm-set, always mindful of the principle to be upheld. Here are some key lessons we can learn:

Setting Clear Goals:

Ram's exile from Ayodhya did not come out of a random act; rather, it was an intentional and considerate act done out of a duty to fulfill his father's word and to live up to the virtues of righteousness. In such a case, Ram's accepting exile was just a display of proper notions of target. The parallel course of events in the lines of business is finding the right setting of objectives for the organization that needs to be run. Such goals give a sense of direction to actions taken by offering a clear and noble set of objectives. They unite efforts, aligning individuals and teams towards a common goal. Just as Ram's exile had a message of sacrifice in adherence to the principles of righteousness and dharma, clear goals have a message of excellence in honing and maintaining organizational values, even in times of challenge.

Adapting to Change:

Ram's exile from Ayodhya did not come out of a random act; rather, it was an intentional and considerate act done out of duty to fulfill his father's word and to live up to the virtues of righteousness. In such a case, Ram's accepting exile was just a display of proper notions of target. The parallel course of events in the lines of business is finding the right setting of objectives for the organization that needs to be run. Such goals give a sense of direction to actions taken by offering a clear and noble set of objectives. They unite efforts, aligning individuals and teams towards a common goal. Just as Ram's exile had a message of sacrifice in adherence to the principles of righteousness and dharma, clear goals have a message of excellence in honing and maintaining organizational values, even in times of challenge.

Long-Term Perspective:

Ram's unwavering focus on the greater good and his eventual return to Ayodhya exemplify the power of maintaining a long-term perspective even when facing temporary setbacks. Such a principle should also apply within the borders of organizational leadership, having all the time a forward-looking approach that goes beyond short-term gains. Leaders should lead by focusing on the effect that decisions and actions of today can have in the future, considering that often , decisions made in the moment of rush may have long-lasting effects that sometimes outweigh short-term gains. While developing strategies for organizations, a forward-thinking vision is called for to integrate the short term with the long term in planning, rather than disregard the latter. In this way, the principle of this approach not only encourages organizations to develop their initiatives under overarching goals but also nourish resilience and flexibility in times of uncertainty. This strategic foresight helps leaders anticipate challenges, identify areas for growth, and cultivate a culture of innovation and continuous improvement. Just as Ram stood firm in his belief in dharma throughout his exile, a long-term perspective empowers leaders to navigate complexities with clarity, purpose, and conviction, thus driving sustainable success and the longevity of the organization.

Timely Production and Delivery in a Corporate Context:

In the corporate world, timely production and delivery are essential to keep up with a competitive edge and to meet the expectations of the customer. Let us see how one could apply lessons from the Ramayana to ensure timely execution:

Efficient Resource Allocation:

Ram's exile illustrates the importance of judicious usage of resources in getting things done efficiently despite constraints. Through intellect, physical strength, and allies, Ram negotiated the challenges of exile, demonstrating tenacity and purpose. Similar to this, in the corporate world, efficient resource allocation is of utmost importance in ensuring productivity and minimizing wastage. This boils down to planning activities such that they make the most sense in terms of a good return on investment in time, financial resources, and human capital. The leader must prioritize projects and initiatives that align with the general objectives of the organization and value creation opportunities. By utilizing resources effectively, firms can increase operational efficiencies, manage risks, and tap into growth opportunities and innovations. Just as Ram's resourcefulness enabled him to overcome hurdles during his exile, efficient resource allocation empowers an organization to adapt to dynamic environments and achieve sustainable success in the long run.

Effective Time Management:

His skillful time management during exile makes one note the critical importance that time management has in relation to organizational objectives. Just like Ram, he must work out all the tasks and responsibilities he is supposed to go through in the corporate world. An effective time management strategy must involve strategically prioritizing tasks based on their importance and urgency. With these deadlines and milestones in place, this infuse accountability and urgency into the team, driving productivity and progress. Besides, dealing with procrastination demands the biggest cut in task progress. Project timelines must be met, and everything is done according to the plan to maintain some trajectory. Leaders must also realize the importance of delegation, where team members can take up certain tasks and contribute towards realizing organizational goals. This can be translated into effectively ordering efficient and effective processes that finally steer the company toward lasting success. Just like Ram's strategic use of time while in exile, smart time management empowers leaders to manage their business affairs through clear and purposeful decision-making.

Continuous Improvement:

During his exile, Ram's dedication to the continuous improvement of himself and learning serves as a reminder of the transformative power of embracing a culture of continuous improvement. Just like Ram sought to refine his abilities and expand his knowledge amidst the challenges of exile, businesses must foster an environment where innovation and growth are core principles. Continuous improvement involves the regular evaluation and optimization of processes to increase productivity and efficiency. Through active feedback, idea generation, and iterative change implementation, organizations can identify and tackle the bottlenecks as an outcome. Moreover, one fosters a culture of continuous improvement to promote a mindset of adaptability and innovation that helps empower employees to challenge the status quo and seek innovative solutions for complex problems. Here, through this unyielding quest for excellence, a business can remain agile, reactive, and competitive in an ever-changing marketplace. Just like Ram's journey through exile was marked with a commitment to self-betterment, embracing continuous improvement enables organizations to embark on a journey of perpetual growth and evolution.

The Importance of Time Management in Achieving Organizational Goals:

Time management becomes the cornerstone of organizational success, with the productive, efficient, and, ultimately, profitable perspective in mind which is why it's crucial:

Maximizing Productivity:

Effective time management is, in fact, the lynchpin of maximizing productivity within individuals and teams. Organizations, under such rigorous time dedication to the most pressing tasks, can attain absolute plenitude, with unnecessary distractions minimized. Organizations, as it is an orchestra of a skilled conductor, will apply every minute in purposeful movements, which will add to the collective harmony of organizational goals. They can pick the tasks that would hold the most impact and focus their efforts on them, making it count. Besides, if such organizations continue to guard themselves against some of the most common time thieves, such as too many meetings, interruptions that are not wanted, and procrastination, they could reclaim valuable hours to redirect towards something that will deliver results that are real and tangible. By building a culture of discipline and accountability on time management, businesses can develop a team that runs at maximum efficiency and achieves much more than is possible with a good team. In essence, effective time management is the cornerstone upon which organizational productivity thrives, enabling people and teams to reach their full potential and achieve greatness.

Meeting Deadlines:

Meeting deadlines is essential in today's intensely competitive business environment, where success often comes at the end of deliverables done promptly and, therefore, reliably. Effective time management plays a crucial role in ensuring the timely completion of tasks to enable organizations to fulfill their promises and meet customer expectations. By adhering to deadlines, businesses display reliability and professionalism, which increases trust and confidence among clients and stakeholders. The timely delivery goes a long way in ensuring that customers are satisfied with the product or service when needed; thus, loyalty is increased, and frequent business is sustained. Further, meeting deadlines offers an advantage in competition since only companies that meet deadlines can place themselves ahead of rivals and take advantage of market opportunities. Streamlined workflows, resource management, and proactive management of processes enable businesses to meet deadlines repeatedly to position themselves as industry leaders. Essentially, proper time management not only facilitates timely task completion but also creates the foundation for organizational success, embodying customer satisfaction, competitiveness, and longevity.

Reducing Stress and Burnout:

Poor time management brings immense costs to the employee, as it may involve stress, burnout, and decline in morale. When workers are caught up in the dilemma of relentless deadlines and an avalanche of work, it may negatively impact not just their physical but also their mental health; hence, there is an increase in the absenteeism rate, a decrease in productivity, and an increase in turnover rates. In this respect, a culture that prioritizes work-life balance and supports employees' holistic well-being can mitigate the adverse effects of poor time management. Providing flexible work arrangements, offering wellness programs, and encouraging regular breaks will help employees recharge and replenish their energy reserves. But, by giving workers tools and resources to manage their time more effectively, organizations also empower individuals to manage their workload and navigate challenges with resilience. Such investment in employee well-being not only fosters a healthier, more engaged workforce but also begets advantages in the forms of improved morale, heightened productivity, and better retention rates. This way, by keeping the well-being of the employees in mind, the organization develops a sustainable and healthy culture in the workplace.

Conclusion:

The tour through the timeless wisdom and principles of time management and planning, drawn from the Ramayana, has led us to a rich landscape of depth. From strategic planning and the realization it showed from Ram's 14-year exile to meeting deadlines and reducing stress and burnout, all that can be said about these facets is: that they pinpoint how sound time management translates into organizational success. Reflecting on the parallels to the problems that Ram faced during his exile and those that are currently present within the world of business, there is no question about the universality and timeless nature of these lessons in strategic planning and time management. Ram moved through the exile complexities, with determination and foresight, just as any modern-day leader has to take over an organization with the same qualities and lead it through the changing waters of the business environment.

Lessons drawn from the journey of Ram are universal and eternal guiding lights for leaders who want to navigate the complexities of the modern business world. Clear goals, adapting to change, and long-term vision—all these together form the mindset for achieving durable success in an organization, anchored with principles of integrity and purpose. It is time to consider the importance of timely production and delivery, which will enable efficient resource allocation and proper time management toward ensuring productivity, growth, and effective utilization of the resources. For effective implementation, strategic planning and disciplined execution are necessary. This will go a long way in optimizing operations, customer satisfaction, and maintaining a competitive edge in the market.

The journey traversed does not rob individuals of work-life balance. On the contrary, efficient leaders will mobilize resources to provide excellent conditions to enable staff members to work with vigor, devotion, and balance life. The employees must be healthy, focused, and happy so that their organization may prosper and sustain its growth and success in the long run.

Conclusively, the journey towards time management and planning, spruced up by the timeless wisdom of the Ramayana, underlines the enduring relevance of these principles to the pursuit of excellence by organizations. Leaders, once they incorporate these ideas in terms of culture within their organizations, have less trouble deploying and executing their organizational mandates with clarity, purpose, and fortitude that sustain success and flourishing of their organizations.

End of Chapter 14

Chapter 15

Decision-Making and Quick Thinking

In the swiftly evolving management landscape, the skill of making quick decisions in rapidly changing situations makes the difference. This chapter not only presents the compass for the frenetic contemporary world but also empowers leaders to maneuver through the intricacies of the ever-changing business environment. On this path, the mighty Hanuman sets an example with his legendary agility of mind, serving as a source of inspiration for leaders across the world. From Hanuman's timeless wisdom, we'll unpack strategies to overcome the challenges in decision-making and be able to thrive in the chaotic pace of today's business world. The art of quick decision-making is not an inborn talent but one that can be nurtured and enhanced with time. The modern business world demands quick and firm decision-making, yet it does not arise in the first place. There will be times when leaders must make swift decisions that impact the business as it is, given the dynamic nature of modern business. We will then delve into the minute point of decision-making that is required and point out the different techniques and approaches that one can apply to become a leader with quick decision-making skills and working under pressure in challenging conditions.

Hanuman, the revered hero of the epic Ramayana, illustrates the very essence of swiftness of thinking and resourcefulness. His adventures bring forward knowledge that never passes time and still holds an invaluable worth, even today. The story of Hanuman's legendary heroics is a guide for solving today's difficult business problems. In drawing parallels between Hanuman's remarkable deeds and real-life business scenarios, we will dig out practical actionable strategies that will assist leaders in sorting out the complexities in modern decision-making.

Quick and sound decision-making is about decisions that do not merely seem the right ones but are indeed the best that need to be made at the right time. We will discuss the significance of gathering the right information, trusting your instincts, and committing yourself to the setting up of clear objectives that will enable a leader to come up with a good judgment of the situation to make a viable decision. With visualized concepts and case studies, we will not only show leaders the development of a decisive mindset but also how they should make informed decisions that could help push the organization to new horizons.

We will also dive into the concept of quick thinking and its application in modern business. Hanuman's capability to adapt to changing circumstances and to find new solutions demonstrates how leaders facing uncertainty and ambiguity can draw inspiration from this beacon of inspiration. We'll decode Hanuman's process and examine how leaders can apply the same principles to overcome setbacks and seize opportunities in the fast-changing world of modern business.

Real-world business decision-making, and hence most strategic management decisions, are not a solitary case of speed but agility, resilience, and strategic thinking. We will provide an analysis of strategies that can be employed to overcome the most common challenges faced by leaders in decision-making, ranging from analysis paralysis to fear of failure, and enable leaders to make strong and courageous decisions that can influence the growth of their organizations.

Ultimately, it is an eye-opener to the relevance of Hanuman's wisdom in this era of modern management. By drawing on his legendary exploits and timeless principles that are applicable to the real-world business situation, leaders can instill the skills and mindset required to succeed in today's fast-paced environment. So, join us in this journey as we look at the secrets of quick decision-making and unleash the power of rapid thinking to make success possible in the chaotic world of modern business.

Developing Quick Decision-Making Skills in Leadership

Effective leadership lies within the ability to make timely and well-informed decisions. However, mastering the art of quick decision-making requires practice and strategic thinking. Listed here are some key strategies for cultivating this crucial skill.

Gathering Information:

The essence of effective decision-making in any context is gathering information. It is a thorough examination of pertinent data, insights from subject matter experts, and in-depth research of all aspects that would be relevant to the situation. This process would allow leaders to gather a sophisticated understanding of the challenges and opportunities they face, facilitating informed choices that are optimized for both immediate gains and long-term, overarching goals and objectives of the organization. By spending time and effort on information gathering, leaders can reduce the chance of risk or be cautious of any probable pitfalls and capitalize on emerging trends or opportunities. In the end, a thorough information-gathering process places the foundation of sound decision-making, so that a leader can face complex scenarios with confidence and clarity.

Trusting Your Instincts:

In many instances, trusted instincts are very much akin to tapping into your subconscious knowledge and past experiences—the kind that you can often instinctively do, and in cases where time may be short, it can be a guide post for making quick decisions. In other situations, intuition acts as a much quicker guidepost for fast decisions that one may not have in a circumstance where time is at a premium. Intuition may offer a unique perspective that may not immediately come up from rational analysis alone, enabling leaders to make the most of their chance to seize opportunities or avoid potential risks. However, it should not be emphasized too much that intuition should not surpass rationality. Data-driven analysis, on the other hand, should help to develop a well-thought-out decision rather than just using instinct. Combining these two, intuition and rationality, helps in making quick decisions that not only seem good but also are sound and based on solid evidence, even when time is of the essence and the situation is high-pressure.

Setting Clear Goals:

Clear goals serve as a north star for decision-making, giving direction and purpose. Leaders setting these clear goals and objectives articulate a road map that would guide them in their decision-making processes. With a clear roadmap of what is desired to be attained, the decision-making process becomes more straightforward and helps leaders in choosing what course to take. This clarity helps leaders determine which tasks are a priority, resource allocation to ensure an effectual expenditure, and which decisions align with a wider scope of activities the organization is looking at to achieve its overall objective. More than that, establishing clear goals helps to ensure that the whole team, if working together, will strive towards one common purpose. When making choices based on well-defined goals, decision leaders will be able to navigate the complexities and uncertainties more confidently since they will know that all their choices are leading toward the fulfillment of the overarching goals of the organization. Clarity of purpose gives leaders the capability to arrive at decisions that contribute towards realizing organizational meaning and value.

Practicing Decisiveness:

Practicing decisiveness is like practicing a muscle: it takes consistent effort and deliberate practice to strengthen. Leaders can cultivate this skill by actively seeking out opportunities to make decisions across a spectrum of situations—from minor daily choices to significant strategic moves. Each decision serves as a learning opportunity, allowing leaders to gain valuable insights into their decision-making process and refine their approach over time.

By embracing decisiveness, leaders build confidence in their abilities and a proactive mindset that propels them into action. Leaders make decisions, even in the face of uncertainty and ambiguity, and that shows the qualities of leadership and resilience. It makes these leaders become effective decision-makers for their organization. The very act of practicing decisiveness develops adaptability and agility as well, allowing leaders to navigate quickly changing environments.

As leaders acquire experience and refine their decision-making abilities, they earn a reputation for being decisive and action-oriented. This not only inspires trust and confidence in team members but also boosts the leader's credibility and influence within the organization. In the end, being decisive does have great value in today's dynamic business landscape and produces them as the leaders of successful organizations.

Learning from Mistakes:

One of the most important aspects of learning from mistakes as part of personal and professional growth in decision-making is realizing that not all decisions will deliver the intended outcome. Accepting failure as a part of the learning process allows leaders to embrace and learn from mistakes, seeing failure as a natural part of the decision-making process. When mistakes happen, it is important for leaders not to dwell on them negatively. They should instead take a growth mindset that considers failures as opportunities for reflection and improvement. Failures that occur are being analyzed by leaders; thus, the very act of analyzing them, helps one establish that the mistakes did not happen because they were not being followed by the action plan but to realize that there were mistakes and were made due to the serious operational shortcomings and misconceived attitudes among decision-makers. Knowledge of these weaknesses, mistakes, and patterns is a tremendous resource that leaders can use to act better in the decisions they have to make in the future. Furthermore, mistakes help leaders develop more tolerance, adaptability, and resilience to be able to accept and learn how to overcome challenges and setbacks in their professional organizations. In this regard, these failures turn out to be opportunities for growth and the cultivation of a culture of learning and continuous improvement. The conclusion is that a leadership is good by reflecting on mistakes is always able to evolve, become bigger, and succeed amid trials.

Adapting Hanuman's Quick Thinking to Modern Business Scenarios

Hanuman, the revered devotee of Lord Rama, is revered for his remarkable quick thinking and resourcefulness. His exploits in the epic Ramayana offer timeless lessons that are highly relevant to modern business scenarios.

Agility in Problem-Solving:

The agility in problem-solving, exemplified by Hanuman's legendary feats, brings home how adaptability and creativity are vital to today's complex business. What Hanuman did, swiftly adapting to changing circumstances and coming up with clever solutions, has stood the test of time in the face of dynamic market conditions.

In such an ever-changing business environment, agility is not just advantageous; it's needed. Rapid technological advancements, changing consumer preferences, and fluctuating global economic conditions are the triggers that demand a proactive method for problem-solving. Leaders must be able to pivot quickly to seize emerging opportunities and come up with solutions with agility and precision.

Agility sets organizations ahead of the game, making them adaptable to trends in the market, as well as flexible for market entry and exit. By cultivating a culture of flexibility and innovation, leaders empower their teams to embrace change, try out new ideas, and continuously enhance processes. In the end, agility in problem-solving is the hallmark of successful organizations that can find themselves in the strange world and drive sustainable growth.

Effective Communication:

Effective communication underlines pivotal roles in the attainment of organizational goals, as exemplified by Hanuman's ability to communicate effectively with beings of different races. This observation is reinforced by the fact that with Hanuman, there is clarity in communication which can makes a connection with all of the interfacing beings. Furthermore, in the business world, it is plain and clear communication that will foster understanding, alignment, and collaboration across teams and stakeholders. The management of ideas, visions, and expectations well-articulated means to inspire their actions and ensure results. Furthermore, effective communication is more important in providing tasks being assigned, allowing feedback, and resolving conflicts in a quick and constructive manner.

As leaders concentrate more of their energy on framing their ideas clearly, they can eliminate misunderstandings and errors and build an environment that cultivates transparency and trust among members within the firm. Besides, leaders who can articulate themselves well may go a long way in building long-lasting and meaningful relationships with their customers, partners, employees, and investors in an organization.

Finally, effective communication is the cornerstone of effective leadership and organizational success, allowing a team to work together towards common goals and overcome challenges with both clarity and confidence.

Strategic Planning:

Strategic planning, reflected in the meticulous approach to achieving Hanuman's objectives, is a cornerstone of success in both mythical quests and modern business endeavors. By following his meticulous planning method, Hanuman crossed all difficult points and managed to perform all his duties with precision and efficiency. In the business world, strategic planning plays an important role in guiding organizations towards their long-term goals. Strategic planning enables company executives to make sound decisions by setting clear priorities, managing their resource base, and aligning action to overarching objectives.

A strategic mindset can further empower leaders by enabling them to navigate through ambiguity with confidence. Strategic thinking-oriented leaders can inspire the organizations they lead to foster innovation, and resilience, and position them to live up to the future in the ever-changing dynamics of the marketplace.

Finally, strategic planning is not only an exercise of short-term tactics but of laying a foundation for sustainable growth and competitive advantage. Adopting the principles of strategic planning, leaders will map out a path to success for their organizations, in the way that Hanuman charted his path towards victory in the epic tale Ramayana.

Resilience in Adversity:

Adversity has always tested the character of Hanuman, challenging his courage, love, and love for his Queen. He displayed his steadfastness in the face of many obstacles, including daunting enemies and treacherous terrain, always resolute towards his work. This not only underlines what could have been an age-old lesson in mythological characters but also extends to modern-day leaders. Setbacks, failures, and unpredictable challenges are part and parcel of every business stage, but the resilience of a leader determines the success of such challenges. By inculcating a resilient mindset, a leader can confront uncertainties, rebound from adversity, and remain motivated in realizing goals. Furthermore, resilience enables leaders to inspire and elevate their teams during tough times, thus creating a culture of perseverance and determination within the organization. Witnessing their leader's resilience in the face of adversity, employees gain confidence and courage, empowered to surmount obstacles, emerging stronger. In the end, resilience is about embracing challenges as opportunities for growth and transformation. By cultivating resilience, leaders may move with grace and strength to navigate through turbulent times, ensuring that their organization does not only endure but thrives amidst adversity.

Team Collaboration:

One of the most critical skills that Hanuman exhibits in his legendary quest is how he teamed up with various allies. Hanuman's ability to work with diverse allies uncovers the power of collaboration and synergy to achieve shared goals. He worked in collaboration with different characters, including Sugriva, Jambavan, and the Vanara army, and this only fuels the power of cooperation in achieving the goal. In case of the business world, effective teamwork and collaboration are instrumental in the creation of new ideas, solutions, and goals. Leaders, by building collaboration cultures within their companies, can optimize the collective skills, knowledge, and perspectives of their team members to work in solving even the biggest challenges that occur and capitalizing on new opportunities.

Collaborative work strengthens people's sense of ownership and responsibility towards the achievement of a common goal. Hanuman had broken down silos, and he encouraged open communication and mutual respect. This helps in creation of an environment where collaboration can flourish, and teams that are not only working with each other but also collaborating can achieve extraordinary results that might be impossible for them to achieve individually. Ultimately, placing strong emphasis on teamwork and collaboration leads to the realization of the full potential of teams that work towards the success of any organization in today's dynamic business environment. The story of Hanuman's collaboration with his allies was crucial in achieving victory, just as teamwork and collaboration are vital determinants of success in the modern business world.

Overcoming Decision-Making Challenges Through Effective Strategies

Decision-making often faces challenges, most prominently in complex or high-pressure situations. Here are some ways to overcome common obstacles in decision-making:

Analyze the Situation:

Analyzing the situation is a critical step in effective decision-making, ensuring that leaders have a clear understanding of the context and implications of their choices. This step is for collecting all the relevant information, which could include trends in the market, financial data, and the opinions of stakeholders. Based on this data collection, one can easily identify patterns, trends, and potential opportunities or threats that might affect decisions. Seeking expert advice and the consideration of diverse points of view provide a valuable contribution to the decision-making process. In fact, seeking the help of experts who have valuable experience and knowledge, the leaders can gain more holistic knowledge of the situation to consider other parties' options. A risk assessment is also critical in determining the consequences of different alternatives of action that may be undertaken. By identifying potential risks and uncertainties, leaders can create strategies to mitigate negative outcomes and make better decisions. All in all, a comprehensive analysis of a situation helps leaders make decisions that have solid evidence, align with organizational goals, and take into account potential risks and opportunities.

Seek Input:

Seeking input from others is a core component of effective decision-making. It allows leaders to tap a wealth of knowledge and expertise that lies outside of their own. Leaders can obtain invaluable insights, identify blind spots, and consider different viewpoints by seeking out people with related experience or authority in the matter in hand. Moreover, involving others in the decision-making process fosters a sense of ownership and buy-in, as they'll know that their input is taken seriously. This collaborative approach not only enhances the quality of the decision but also establishes a culture of transparency, trust, and mutual respect in the organization. Moreover, seeking input from diverse perspectives allows leaders to identify innovative solutions and anticipate potential challenges or opportunities that may have been overlooked. By using the collective wisdom of their team or consulting with outside experts, leaders can make more comprehensive and aligned decisions with the goals and objectives of the organization.

Consider Alternatives:

Alternatives have become a very important aspect in the best manner of decision-making, so leaders are in a better position to decide between various options for evaluation. The process of various alternatives leads to a better understanding of all choices, and their respective advantages and disadvantages can be weighed. Analysis of different options aids leaders in measuring strengths and weaknesses as part of each of the alternatives, concerning the organizational goals, principles, and values. Further, in considering alternatives, creativity and innovation are facilitated because consideration encourages leaders to think outside the box and consider non-typical solutions to problems. Further, considering alternatives helps leaders anticipate potential risks and challenges associated with each option that might have resulted in the need to preclude contingency plans and mitigate potential negative outcomes. This proactive approach to decision-making thus makes the likelihood of success very high and significantly reduces any unforeseen obstacle that might have stopped progress.

Manage Risks:

Assessing risks—what those risks may be and the probable consequences from each decision—involves analyzing a variety of areas: it encompasses market conditions, regulatory requirements, and potential risks and impediments. This analysis enables leaders to think out the likely risks and devise compensatory mechanisms against them. Strategies to mitigate risks include putting measures in place for decreasing the likelihood of negative outcomes or for decreasing the severity of negative outcomes if they take place.

With careful management of risk, decisions can be taken with confidence, knowing that preventive measures have been instituted to avoid adverse impacts. This proactive way of approaching risk management may therefore enhance the effectiveness of the decision-making process and enhance the chances of obtaining the desired outcomes.

Trust Yourself:

Being confident in yourself is a foundational aspect of effective decision-making, empowering leaders to trust their instincts, experiences, and expertise to navigate complex situations. Although seeking input and considering alternatives are invaluable steps in the decision-making process, leaders must eventually find trust in their judgment and trust their abilities to make the right decision. Trusting oneself enables leaders to make decisions with conviction and clarity, even in the face of uncertainties or ambiguities. It allows them to tap into their experience and instinct in understanding the problem, weighing the options, and finally selecting the path that meets their goals and values. There is a lot of resilience and adaptability in trusting oneself, which gives leaders the power to learn from both successes and failures and from their failures, develop themselves. This trust in their abilities lead them to take up challenges with confidence and to lead with conviction, inspiring trust and confidence in themselves and in others.

Conclusion

The continually changing background of management, while advancing, has called for quick decision-making abilities and strategic thinking. In this chapter, we have explored not only how quick decision-making skills should be developed but also how leaders can make good decisions by thinking fast to enable them to grapple with the complexities of modern business. Besides, with inspiration derived from the legendary Hanuman, we sought to draw useful strategies and insights that can be used by leaders to make wise decisions and have them succeed in today's fast-paced world. We have outlined some methods of cultivating quick decision-making skills in leadership: gathering information and trusting instincts, setting clear goals, and practicing decisiveness. Additionally, we have delved into how the agility of Hanuman could be applied in modern business scenarios, from problem-solving and effective communication to strategic planning and toughness to face adversities as well as team collaboration. By bringing to life Hanuman's age-old principles to contemporary business problems, leaders may well bring forth new realms of creativity, flexibility, and achievement.

We have addressed some common obstacles faced during decision-making and provided ways for conquest, such as analyzing the situation, eliciting opinions, considering alternatives, risk management, and trusting oneself. By incorporating these strategies in their decision-making process, leaders will be more likely to make confident and effective decisions that increase organizational growth and innovation.

Finally, and to sum up, the journey of decision-making and quick thinking is not a smooth ride, but it can be done if the right strategies and mentality are in place. So, let us embark on this journey together, armed with the wisdom of Hanuman and the determination to succeed in the chaotic yet exhilarating world of management.

End of Chapter 15

Chapter 16

Coordination and Collaborative Efforts

In a complex environment, coordination and collaboration act as the basis through which teams can operate effectively while moving the project toward success. These two are the fundamental principles of teamwork, guiding individuals and groups towards their common goals and shared achievers. If one embarks on a journey back to ancient times and reaches the epic Indian mythological text, the Ramayana, the instances of coordination are given by the heroic duo Nal and Neel. These two were tasked with constructing a bridge that would serve as a connection between India on the mainland and the island kingdom of Lanka. Through unwavering coordination, notwithstanding the impossible barriers posed by treacherous terrains and hostile adversaries, they made it through and completed their mission. Their story stands as a timeless example of how alignment and cooperation drive one to achieve lofty objectives.

With the introduction of the modern business world to complexity in organizational structures and global operations, the principles of effective coordination are further required in the contemporary landscape. Effective coordination is one of the essential avenues for the working of diverse teams, departments, and stakeholders toward one goal. Whether one is dealing with a cross-functional project, managing a supply chain, or implementing strategic initiatives, it is through effective coordination. The core of coordination is the alignment of activities, resources, and efforts towards a desired outcome. It is the synchronization of timeframes, efficient allocation of resources, and providing free communication channels for smooth work and coordination. Fostering a culture of coordination helps streamline operations, eliminate redundancy, and boost productivity.

Among the major challenges faced in ensuring successful coordination within organizations is the necessity to provide coordination to complex projects and initiatives. Today, interconnected and at a fast pace, business involves different projects that include the participation of multiple stakeholders, diverse teams, and complex workflows. Coordinating these elements entails meticulous planning, transparent communication, and innovative problem-solving.

Lessons from project management frameworks, such as Agile and Scrum, indicate few of the practice-oriented ideas related to coordination. Through the breaking down of projects into smaller chunks and the identification of clear roles and responsibilities, as well as feedback loop mechanisms that support proper coordination, it can achieve adaptability and better alignment. Moreover, the use of technology tools, such as project management software and collaboration platforms, will ease real-time communication and information exchange, further coordination.

Consideration of effective communication helps to understand that success in coordination is highly bound to how people can share information and align priorities and aims. Clear and transparent communication channels foster trust, clarity, and accountability that lay the foundation for effective coordination. Better coordination can be achieved by leaders who have a better view of communication channels, thereby creating an environment for more communication and discussion.

Coordination with one's outside partners and allies is in addition to setting the achieved accomplishment and cannot be achieved by internal coordination. The so-called strategic alliances, joint ventures, and supplier relationships mean that effective coordination and alignment of goals and objectives will take place in organizations. By establishing equal partnerships where mutual benefits are taken and the lines of communication remain clear, the organizations can leverage outside resources and expertise in innovation and growth.

Nal and Neel's Coordination in Bridge Construction

Nal and Neel, the classical figures from the Indian epic Ramayana, representing the Indian epic Ramayana, testify to the huge potential of collaboration and coordination in monstrous realms. Their task was to build a bridge that would bridge the gap between the Indian mainland and the island of Lanka, and herein, the two display an unrivaled level of synergy.

Planning and Division of Tasks

This was especially evidenced in Nal and Neel's coordination, which greatly brought out the power of meticulous planning and a clear division of work as far as accomplishing their common objective is concerned. Nal's proficiency in design and strategic planning provided a blueprint for the bridge and materials needed with precision; his foresight strategically assured the smooth progression of the project without significant hurdles along the way. On the other hand, Neel's engineering and construction management expertise made him capable of executing the plan with minute attention to detail. He guaranteed smooth sails in the execution of every aspect of the construction project as per the known design parameters.

Their partnership was based on a collective understanding of the fundamentals of their respective skills and the role they were set to play. Their diverse competencies blended harmoniously and gave a great outcome. Nal's broader perspective and arrangement of plans for the team were evened with Neel's grounded touch to doing things and handling problems. Together, they formed a good team that was more than the sum of its parts; it underlined the importance of synergy in achieving complex goals.

Nal and Neel's coordination is a timeless illustration that has been provided as proof of the effectiveness of project management and collaboration. It reinforced priority awareness and task assignment to the team that reduced anguish in supervision and determination towards success and high-work efficiency. This approach brings accountability and mutual trust among members and is expected to lead to greater efficiency and success in the common goal.

Overcoming Challenges

The construction of the bridge posed huge challenges that tested Nal and Neel's resolution and ingenuity. With rough seas disrupting their activities, they stood resolute in accomplishing their assigned task. Instead of surrendering to the imperious forces of nature, they used creative approaches to overcome these hurdles. Their greatest challenge was brought about by wave power and to a larger extent by lack of resources. Strategic responses on their part ensured stability and strength for the bridge. They made sure that the massive boulders were strategically anchored to provide the structural integrity of the bridge against the adversely intense currents. They also reinforced it with strong support and had it meet the safety standards of the region.

Resource constraints were yet another major challenge. In such a condition, Nal and Neel had to apply the most efficient resources towards resource utilization. They laid down the most basic necessary elements of the construction process, keeping in mind efficiency and sustainability. Their zeal was to make the best use of available resources and prevent wastage. This frugality helped them to overcome this difficulty and not compromise the quality or safety of their work.

And to make matters worse, strict deadlines placed more pressure on this already daunting task. But Nal and Neel didn't lose heart. They meant to perform their jobs by meeting the deadlines. With proper planning and coordination, they optimized their work and managed their tasks cleverly. This proactive approach helped them stay on course and finish their project on schedule.

So, the success in overcoming these challenges shows how resilience, creativity, and effective collaboration in the face of adversity greatly helps in advancing and fulfilling one's goals. Nal and Neel were in a position to invent ways around obstacles and further develop their skills due to the recognition of the need for that. They succeeded in turning challenges into opportunities for learning and overcoming obstacles.

Complementary Skills

The collaboration of Nal and Neel was based on the recognition and use of complementary skills. Nal's strategic planning and innovative design provided the framework for the construction of the bridge. His strategic foresight enabled him to envision the layout of the bridge and anticipate potential challenges, laying the foundation for a successful project. In contrast, Neel's technical expertise and practical know-how played a pivotal role in putting Nal's designs into concrete structures. With an intricate understanding of engineering concepts and construction techniques, he ensured the bridge was technologically practical and long-lasting. With this hands-on approach to problem-solving, he overcame technical complexities and implemented Nal's vision with precision.

Moreover, Nal and Neel's collaboration went beyond individual skills to encompass a collaborative mindset. They addressed the challenges as a unified team, working together as partners for shared goals, where the sum of their strengths was the difference. They did it by coming together to manage their complementary roles and, at the same time, do things together that improve their effectiveness. This collaboration eventually led to their successful accomplishment.

Under this description, Nal and Neel's partnership is an example of how complementary skills can reach common targets. Their good understanding and rationalization of what needs to be done in forming strategic plans together with a technical partner and put into practice lead to broader chances and success. They not overcame the challenges but delivered quality of work. The impact of it established a long-term legacy of innovation and collaboration.

Coordinating Complex Projects Within An Organization

Coordination and collaboration are principles that not only apply to your cohorts, Nal and Neel, but even more so in modern organizational settings, especially when meeting complex projects and diverse stakeholders.

Establishing Clear Roles and Responsibilities

Defining roles and responsibilities is the way forward for coordination in complex projects. Once a team member has clearly identified their individual contribution, it will be much more efficiently pursued towards common goals. In complex projects, more often than not, there are multiple stakeholders who bring in different types of expertise and responsibilities. This clarity ensures that team members do not come to the crossroads or conflict over ambiguous or overlapping roles. With the specific tasks focused on, in such a manner that it does not require time or effort spent on what is beyond their purview.

Clear roles and responsibilities contribute further towards streamlined decision-making processes. When every individual understands what they are responsible for, decisions can be made rapidly and confidently. This agility is particularly prone in dynamic environments where fast responses to changing circumstances need to be given for success.

Moreover, the real-time clear roles and responsibilities optimization in resource allocation enable proper distribution of resources across the team. A clear definition of roles ensures that the resources provided to the team members are consistent with their specific duties.

In a nutshell, establishing clear roles and responsibilities lay down the very foundation for effective coordination in complex projects, with teams working harmoniously towards common objectives.

Effective Communication

In this modern world of communication, effective communication has become a crucial aspect in fostering coordination within teams and organizations. It serves as the lifeblood to ensure that the smooth flow of information, ideas, and feedback is rendered among team members. In today's fast-paced and interconnected world, organizations are adopting a host of communication channels to facilitate effective coordination. These may include traditional ways of communication like face-to-face meetings or phone calls, alongside digital tools like email, instant messaging platforms, and project management software. To make sure all stakeholders are kept in the loop and engaged, regardless of the location or time zone, organizations use these diverse communication channels.

Further, for open communication, setting up an organization-wide culture that values it, is imperative. Open communication of thoughts, feelings, concerns, and ideas makes a team member aware of an environment where all voices are heard and respected. This creates stronger discussions and better decision-making since the opinions, at their core, are fervently discussed, and hence they help foster a more united team dynamic.

Moreover, organizations that give high significance to effective communication and create open channels of communication can, in fact, improve coordination, foster collaboration, and lead to better outcomes.

Flexibility and Adaptability

Modern business is full of flexibility and adaptability as the major pillars for successful coordination. In many cases, complex projects tend to face unforeseen challenges, emanating from shifts in market conditions, evolving regulatory landscapes, or shifting stakeholder expectations. Leaders should have the ability to work swiftly to change strategies, reallocate resources, and adjust priorities quickly to keep the project moving forward. Agility to pivot in the face of such uncertainties is key to ensuring that the project would succeed in meeting objectives and delivering value to stakeholders. Moreover, embracing flexibility and adaptability enables organizations to view obstacles not as insurmountable barriers but as opportunities for innovation and growth. Building an environment that fosters experimentation and learning from failure empowers teams to capitalize on setbacks to foster creative problem-solving and continuous improvement. Flexibility and adaptability, blended into approaches to coordination, will enable a company to navigate the complexities of today's business environment with confidence and resilience. They will turn challenges into opportunities, channeling change to drive innovation and sustain success in a world ever-changing.

Lessons in Effective Communication for Better Coordination

Effective communication lies at the heart of successful coordination; it is the cornerstone upon which are built collaborative efforts. The organization can foster a culture of clear, open, and empathetic communication to enhance coordination, strengthen relationships, and drive collective success.

Clarity in Communication

Clarity in communication serves as a guiding beacon to ensure messages are communicated precisely and comprehensively in effective coordination. Therefore, a leader will have to articulate his thoughts and directives in a manner that is simple, direct, and devoid of unnecessary jargon or ambiguity. Clear language used to address all the stakeholders can make the leaders avoid confusion and minimizes the possibility of misinterpretation in the direction they have to work in. Similarly, understanding the broader objectives and strategic direction of the project, from which individual initiatives could be derived, makes the team apply it as a guide in their actions and contributions toward a common goal.

Additionally, creating a culture of openness and channels to clarify questions and issues further the initiative of clarity in communication. To encourage transparency, trust, and collaboration within the team, leaders should enable team members to seek clarification and express their thoughts openly. Such a culture not only strengthens the ties between team members but also breeds a spirit of curiosity and continuous learning, fostering innovation and growth within the organization.

In essence, clarity in communication forms an underlying aspect of effective coordination, facilitating teams in their challenges, aligning efforts, and accomplishments towards objectives. By emphasizing clear and transparent communication practices, leaders lay the groundwork for strong teamwork, collaboration, and the achievement of organizational objectives.

Active Listening

Active listening is a cornerstone skill in the field of effective communication and coordination, giving a pathway for individuals to truly understand the perspectives, concerns, and ideas of others. Active listening means understanding the emotional and motivational meaning behind the speaker. This involves more than just hearing words but a genuine effort to understand the underlying emotions and motivations behind the speaker's message. Leaders who foster active listening demonstrate profound commitment to their team members by offering their complete attention in conversations. By eye contact, nonverbal cues of engagement, and the lack of interruptions or premature judgment, leaders establish an atmosphere of safety and support for dialoging freely. Active listening, unlike mere acknowledgment of words, involves empathizing with the feelings of the speaker and validating his/her experience. When leaders are sensitive and respectful to each other's point of view, it fosters trust and mutual respect, in turn, strengthens team relationships. It is the active listening in which a leader has insights into various perspectives and viewpoints of the team members that has given valuable insights into the underlying dynamics of the organization, unveiling innovative solutions and opportunities for growth. Moreover, active listening builds a culture of collaboration and mutual support, where every voice is heard, and it contributes in making the team more inclusive and cohesive.

Feedback and Improvement

Feedback is a powerful instrument, by every definition, with which to actually foster effective communication and coordination within an organization, hence promoting progress, learning, and organizational improvement. It is like a mirror reflecting and mirroring back processes, strategies, and interpersonal dynamics within the team.

Leaders who put effective feedbacks in the first place build an open and free organizational culture, in which a team member is able to express their thought and contribute collectively. With such a setup, where an environment of safety and support is in existence for the discussion of feedback, these foster a trusting and respectful relationship among all team members as a prerequisite towards working towards realization of shared goals.

Feedback makes organizations identify blind spots and areas for improvement that may have otherwise gone unnoticed. Whether project performance, team dynamics, or leadership effectiveness is assessed, the insights gained are feedback points that leaders can use to refine strategies, streamline processes, and drive positive change.

Acting constructively on feedback is even more important than it may seem. Leaders should convey an attitude of listening to, learning from, and caring for the suggestions that are being fed into the organization. With improvements in areas that are seen to be ripe, organizations can foster a culture of continuous improvement and innovation.

In effect, it means that feedback is a growth catalyst for organizational growth and development, encouraging positive change and instilling the culture of excellence within an organization. If leaders accept and participate in this feedback as a vital source of knowledge for improvement, then it empowers the team to reach even higher levels of performance, collaboration, and success.

Conclusion

In the subtle dance of modern management, coordination and collaborative efforts are the bedrock upon which a successful team or organization is built. From the mythical realms of ancient epics to the dynamic landscapes of contemporary business, the principles of effective coordination remain steady, guiding people and groups towards their shared objectives. The story of Nal and Neel from the Ramayana is a classic example that stands as a timeless inspiration of how effective coordination can be, as the key to success even in the face of monumental challenges. Their unrelenting synergy, with their meticulous planning and complementary skills, could very well be what made them shine through obstacles and complete their mission before all others. Their story motivates and inspires leaders and teams alike to learn from the story of the previous two characters on the magnitude of alignment and collaboration that will see the dawning of real change.

Effective coordination has never been more relevant than today in this fast-paced and inter-connected world. Project management frameworks like Agile and Scrum offer practical insights in today's complex landscape on how to optimize coordination in executing complex projects, engaging diverse stakeholders, and maneuvering in dynamic market conditions. This helps in defining responsibilities for roles, a streamlined decision-making process, and an open communication environment that facilitates team collaboration in the effort to achieve common goals.

In addition, the requirements of coordination within an organization may include the recognition of the elements foundations of successful coordination. The definition of roles, decision-making processes, and communication are considered the key elements. By issuing roles to members, making decision-making processes easy, and making communication an open channel, leaders can create an environment in which teams can work together towards a common goal.

Moreover, feedback cannot be overstated when walking on the path to effective coordination. It is one of the most powerful levers in identifying blind spots, identifying the need to take action proactively, and spurring continuous improvement. In a regular manner, one must solicit feedback, and when ready to act on them, constructions can be attributed. With feedback, leaders can channel the collective intelligence of teams into positive change and innovation.

Finally, on the whole, coordination and collaborative efforts are part and parcel of success in this ever-changing and interconnecting world of ours. Through embracing principles of effective coordination, organizations can surmount challenges, grab opportunities, and end up achieving their objectives with confidence and resilience. And it is a memory of Nal and Neel that inspires us towards cooperation and coordination, based on their timeless tale of synergy and cooperation.

End of chapter 16

Chapter 17

Values and Upholding Principles

In the fast-paced world of management, with changing scenarios and ever-changing landscapes, the values and principles become indeed a fundamental cornerstone for success. These guiding stars provide direction and coherence amidst the chaos of organizational dynamics. While strategies change, technologies evolve, and markets fluctuate, the core values and principles remain steady, anchoring individuals and organizations alike in their pursuit of excellence. In every successful organization, a strong set of values define its identity and guides its actions. These values form the foundation of corporate culture and are a common language used to meld attitude, behavior, and choice within every individual of an organization. It could be integrity, accountability, or innovation; these values provide a shared vision and common language that unite employees in their efforts towards a common purpose.

Moreover, values help foster positive work environment and drive employee engagement. When employees align with the values of the organization, they become more motivated, dedicated, and passionate in their work. This sense of alignment with the values not only improves job satisfaction but also leads to higher levels of productivity and performance. Encouraging the adoption of organizational values go beyond merely stating them; it requires active leadership,and committment to practical implementation and communication.

Leaders must embody the values themselves, leading by example and demonstrating their commitment to ethical behavior and integrity. Additionally, organizations can create opportunities for employees to contribute in value-based efforts, reward behavior that aligns with the values, and organize frequent training and development sessions to keep the importance of values alive.

When organizations find themselves in the throes of organizational challenges, they turn to values and principles as beacons to steer through the uncertainties and difficulties with integrity and resilience. Enabling the upholding of principles in difficult times requires courage, conviction, and a steadfast commitment to doing what is right, even when it is not easy. By staying true to the values, organizations can maintain trust and credibility with stakeholders, develop resilience in the face of challenges, and emerge from adversity stronger and more united.

The Role of Values in Shaping Corporate Culture

Defining Organizational Values

Defining the organizational values is a crucial step in laying a foundation and shaping the culture and identity of a company. These core beliefs and principles drive the organization's ethos. This process starts with an introspection whereby the leaders and stakeholders first reflect on what is most important to the company and, thus, what values it should want to maintain. The values should be aligned with the company's mission, vision, and goals so that it acts as a guiding principle for all decisions and actions of the employees and stakeholders. It may be fostering a culture of honesty, creativity, and teamwork, among others. By making clear how these values translate into action in day-to-day operations of the organization, the company needs to communicate these effectively. Through communicating the values themselves, supported by demonstrations of such by the management, not just through letters but actions, communication channels, and organizational policies, companies can build a culture where those values are not mere words on a page but an experience that lives through a person who does things as they normally do. Finally, the definition of the values should lead to more than just writing down the virtues; it should set in a shared sense of purpose and identity that binds employees together and drives collective success. Clear, understood, and embraced by every individual in the organization, the values are a powerful driving force for the culture, fostering engagement, and driving performance.

Cultivating a Values-Based Culture

Creating a values-based culture is much more than defining values for organizations; it involves ingraining the values within the fabric of the operations and interactions of the organization. This effort requires the commitment of leadership to ensure that the values are more than mere words on a page but are lived experiences and are all about guiding behavior and shaping outcomes. Leadership sets the tone for the organization by modeling and reinforcing the values through its action, decision-making, and behavior. When leaders consistently display a commitment to the values, it sends a powerful message to employees that this is the expectation and the value they hold for the organization. That, in turn, promotes employees into emulating these values, and it promotes accountability, ownership, and improvement.

Apart from leadership, there is active involvement from employees at all levels of the organization in creating a value based culture. Employees should be encouraged to embody the values through their daily work, recognizing and celebrating those times when the values are demonstrated. This can be done in recognition programs, storytelling, and other initiatives that build on and highlight the importance of values in driving organizational success. By creating an environment where values are embraced, celebrated, and integrated into everyday practices, organizations can foster a culture that is conducive to trust, loyalty, and engagement among the employees. This, in turn, yields higher levels of performance, higher employee satisfaction, and a deeper sense of purpose and identity within the organization.

Impact on Employee Engagement

The impact of organizational values on employee engagement is unmatched. When employees find a strong match between their values and those of the organization, it creates a feeling of connection and belonging that fosters engagement and commitment to work. Resonation with an organization's values leads to higher motivation, a sense of purpose, and above-average job satisfaction. They feel proud to contribute to an organization that shares their beliefs and principles, which ultimately motivates them to work with excellence and devote extra effort to meet organization's needs. Furthermore, values offer a guiding light to the employees during times of crisis or turmoil, making them feel directed stablity. When faced with decision-making, potential conflict resolution, and complex situations, employees can fall back on the guiding lines of the organization's values to support and define their choice of direction and actions, thus upholding the values laid out. Organizations that create a culture premised on values have an advantage in attracting and retaining top talent. They attract and retain the talents since working in a cultural fit where personal values fit is ascertained within an organization. By fostering a value-driven environment, organizations can create a competitive advantage in the talent market, positioning themselves as of choice for top performers who share the values and vision of the organization.

Encouraging Employees to Align with Organizational Values

Communicating Organizational Values

Effective communication is essential in the relay of organizational values from being only the words in the paper to being deeply integrated into the fabric of the company culture. In leadership, clear and consistent communication of values should be given high priority for delivering across all levels in the organization, using various means that would take the leadership's message across to the staff. Discussions, both in physical meetings and via virtual channels, are also opportunities through which leaders will be able to articulate the importance of values and tell success stories such that their impact is felt. The leader must weave messages on values into conversations and discussions, illustrating their relevance and effect on organizational success. For instance, e-mails, newsletters, and intranet platforms are other means that the values can be communicated to employees regularly. In such platforms, leaders have the opportunity to share stories, case studies, and testimonials that are towards the living of the values in everyday business operations and bringing in the positive impact they bring to the organization and its stakeholders.

Social media can also be used as a tool for displaying organizational values and culture to the broader public—i.e., candidate pool, customers, and partners. Leaders can leverage this platform to share photos and videos of the company's values lived out and develop a great reputation as a values-based organization.

It is also essential that values are woven into onboarding, training programs, and performance evaluations for one to reinforce their weight and put it among staff as a priority they should heed. Integrating values into every single aspect of the employee experience, from recruitment to retention, will keep them alive and, therefore, relevant in the hearts and minds of employees as they seek to understand their part within the organization.

Leading by Example

Leading by example is much more than just a leadership principle; it is a powerful tool that provides a powerful opportunity to shape organizational culture and reinforce core values. Leaders, being role models to their employees, show other employees what this organization stands for through their actions, decisions, and how they interact with other people. The actions of the leader should exude his or her commitment to organizational values every step of the way. Whether it's acting ethically, being accountable for their actions, or being respectful towards everyone around, leaders will institute an authentic and transparent work culture that makes employees feel appreciated and valued.

For instance, when workplace leaders demonstrate by action— through their daily activities, decisions, and interactions with others—they create a culture of authenticity and transparency that are good representation of the values held within the organization. When employees get to see their leaders living up to organizational values, they are likely to internalize those values themselves and apply them in their work and interactions.

Additionally, leaders should be able to publicly recognize and reward employees who practice organizational values in their day-to-day lives. Public recognition and reward reinforce the importance and commitment of the leaders towards those values. This not only encourages employees to carry on those values but also indicates to all the people working in the organization what is worthwhile and commendable behavior.

Essentially, leading by example is not just in words; it is in deeds. When leaders consistently demonstrate their commitment to organizational values, they create a culture that gets people aligned and working towards a common goal with trust, credibility, and loyalty.

Employee Empowerment

Employee empowerment is a way to help develop an organization. It means the creation of an environment in which there is an attitude that people feel guided by and work together according to organizational values. One way of achieving this is through inclusivity and respect. When employees feel that the organization regards them positively and respects them, they will feel more engaged and committed. It could be achieved in a way that unbiased and friendly dialogues exist among employees, open and free to express ideas or opinions without fear of rejection. Getting the organization to be reliant on the opinions and ideas of the employees will also help to empower them; in this case, they also get to share their involvement in molding organizational culture and values.

For instance, it also includes opportunities for personal development, growth, and recognition. When employees feel the organization recognizes and rewards their contributions, motivation, and engagement are increased. Organizations can show that they recognize and appreciate the people's growth and success by investing in professional development and the opportunity to advance. This not only reinforces organizational values but also breeds a sense of organizational loyalty and the feeling of being part of something bigger.

In summary, the empowerment of employees to align with organizational values requires the creation of a conducive environment, wherein employees feel valued, respected, and heard. With open dialogue, collaboration, and feedback channels, companies can encourage active contributions from employees to grow their skills, experience upward mobility, and be recognized.

Upholding Principles During Organizational Challenges

Transparency and Integrity

Transparency and integrity are foundational principles that underpin the trustworthiness and credibility of an organization, especially in times of difficulty and ambiguity. Transparency is a matter of being transparent, open, and honest in communication, assuring that the stakeholders are informed of critical issues such as problems, risks, and decisions. It consists of giving timely and factual information to avoid hiding or misrepresentation of facts. By practicing transparency, organizations create a culture of honesty and accountability, to be successful in communicating effectively with employees, customers, investors, and other stakeholders. Integrity, which hand in hand with transparency, is a matter of standing up and acting ethically across all aspects of operations. In upholding integrity, it is about always acting in an honest, fair, and ethical manner, even when under temptation or pressure to deviate from the path. Organizations with a commitment to integrity exhibit the spirit of doing the right thing, regardless of circumstances, and thus build trust and respect among stakeholders. Besides, it helps in protecting reputation and credibility from damage caused by any unethical behavior or misconduct. Therefore, in essence, transparency and integrity are guiding beacons through which organizations can move through challenges and uncertainties. By embracing these principles, an organization can develop trust, credibility, and resilience that are essential in sustaining long-term success and effective management of crises as and when they arise.

Decision-Making Frameworks

In times of crises or organizational challenges, effective decision-making thus becomes more critical in times of uncertainties and risk management. Decision-making frameworks apply structured approaches that guide organizations in the sound and ethical directions to come, in keeping with their values and principles. The processes generally comprise input from key stakeholders, the consideration of different options, the evaluation of the possible risks and benefits, and eventually, choosing the way to go that is most consistent with the mission and purpose of the organization. Underpinning these frameworks are core values, like honesty, taking responsibility, and being socially responsible, among others. These decisions are thus strengthened by values, in a way that makes them ethical and towards the betterment of the society at large. For example, decisions taken with integrity will value transparency and honesty, and this will make sure one maintains a high ethical standard for their courses of action.

Moreover, the stakeholder's involvement in the decision-making process makes it possible to get a range of perspectives and vistas. By hearing from employees, consumers, investors, and other interested parties, an organization can better gauge the possible reverberations of their decisions and identify unforeseen consequences. This approach is both transitive in scope and vision, hence raising the quality of decision-making while simultaneously supporting a broader constituency's sense of ownership.

Through the establishment of clear decision-making frameworks guided by values and principles, organizations will navigate challenges confidently and ethically. These frameworks provide a path for making appropriate, well-informed decisions that take in the long-term interests of all stakeholders, hence making the organization resilient and sustainable.

Building Resilience

Building resilience is paramount in sustaining or thriving through instability and hardship. Resilience empowers a firm to be able to adapt to changing circumstances, recover from setbacks, and emerge more powerful than what they were before. The way of investing in robust systems, processes, and capabilities that can withstand various challenges is one of the ways through which resilience may be nurtured. These may include such varied measures as upgrading their technology infrastructure for optimization of efficiency and flexibility, developing flexible workflows that are easily adaptable to new events, and creating talent development programs to ensure that employees have the skills and knowledge to overcome challenges adequately.

Moreover, creating a culture of learning and collaboration is important in building resilience. When employees are encouraged to share their knowledge, work collaboratively on problem-solving, and learn from failures, they will be better able to face future challenges. By embracing a growth mindset and treating failure as opportunities for learning and growth, organizations can convert adversity into innovation and growth.

Courage and resilience are needed to thrive in a dynamic business environment. If an organization can build resilience, it can not only survive the challenges but also emerge stronger and more adaptable, positioning itself for long-term success. By committing strategic investments in technology, talent, and culture, organizations can create the resilience needed to handle uncertainties and seize opportunities in a world that is always changing.

Conclusion

In the dynamic and ever-changing business environment, where cultural changes are as inevitable as profits, the role of values and principles comes to the fore. Moving into the concluding chapter on the role played by values and practices in organizational management, it can be seen that those guiding lights are none other than indispensable in helping us manage the complexities of the business world with integrity and resilience. In the scope of this chapter, we considered the underlying impact of values on corporate culture formation and how they translate into driving employee engagement and decision-making at times of organizational challenges. We understand that how organizational values are interpreted helps define the cultural direction of an organization and provides identity and purpose among employees. One needs active leadership, employee participation, and a commitment to embedding values within day-to-day activities.

In addition, values are very critical in the sense of driving employee engagement and performance. When employees are in sync with organizational values, they get a greater sense of being connected and committed to the organization, thus increasing motivation, satisfaction, and loyalty. To allow employees to reflect their organizational values, prepares them to make decisions with regard to issues affecting the mission and the vision of the organization.

It is during crisis or uncertainty times that upholding principles becomes most important in creating trust and credibility among all stakeholders. Transparency and honesty are guiding principles that enable the organization to move through difficult times with integrity, accountability, and resilience. Organizational value-based decision-making frameworks ensure that decisions are made in the interest of all the stakeholders while considering long-term objectives, thus promoting trust and perpetuity.

Building resilience is important for organizations to become stronger and more adaptable to conditions of ambiguity and adversity. The strong systems in place, the learning and collaboration culture, and the acceptance of changes with courage and resilience help organizations to come out stronger and more adaptable to be able to tackle long-term success.

In closing, the real values and principles are not just mere words but solid aspects of organizational management. In this regard, some concerns include how these values are incorporated within a culture of integrity and resilience and how they help keep employees valued, motivated, and ready to bring their best. In order to help manage the dynamic landscape of management, let us recognize that values and principles serve as the guiding stars which illuminate the path towards excellence and enduring success.

End of Chapter 17

Chapter 18

Effective Communication and Leadership

Effective leadership is not all about dictating orders or stating decisions; it is about forging relations, initiating activities, and guiding teams towards shared goals. At the core of this transformative process lies effective communication, the cornerstone upon which successful leadership is built. In this chapter, we delve into the reciprocal relationship between communication and leadership, thus relating communication as the vital conduit through which leaders articulate their vision, mobilize their teams, and work through obstacles. Imagine the leader standing before his team, communicating a compelling vision that ignites the passion and purpose within each member. It's not just the words he speaks but the way he conveys them—tone of voice, sincerity in gestures, and clarity in the message. Effective communication is more than mere communication of information; it enhances understanding, trust, and also helps in framing a collective purpose.

As we embark on this journey, we unravel the complexity of effective communication skills and its profound impact on leadership effectiveness. We explore how leaders, like skilled conductors, can orchestrate the communication strategy in such a way that they are inspired, motivated, and empowered by the respective teams. From active listening to visionary storytelling, we trace down the many techniques of communication which effective communicators as leaders use to build a closer connection with their teams.

The way we navigate this terrain unfolds the intricacies of communication in leadership, understanding its power to change organizational culture, drive performance, and facilitate resilience. We navigate into the gray areas of nonverbal communication, articulation of visionary stories, and the quality of an inclusive communication environment where all voices can be heard and invaluable.

By traversing this terrain, we gain a deeper appreciation of the transformative potential of effective communication in leadership. We witness how leaders who master the art of communication not only inspire greatness in others but also cultivate a culture of collaboration, innovation, and excellence. Join us in this exploration as we unlock the secrets to becoming a more effective communicator and a more impactful leader.

Rama's Communication Style and Its Impact on Leadership

Let us first venture into the realm of Rama, a fictional manager renowned for his exceptional communication skills and its profound influence on his leadership effectiveness. Rama exemplifies the concept of effective communication in leadership, reflecting pivotal elements resonating with his team and sustaining them towards shared objectives.

Active Listening:

Active listening were the principles that followed the clarity exhibited by Rama in his communication style, a crucial skill in effective leadership. In contrast to passive listening, where one merely hears the words of a speaker, active listening entails real engagement and the comprehension of the message. Rama absolutely stood out in this area, proving an unusual knack for tuning into the perspectives, concerns, and aspirations of the team members under his leadership.

In the context of active listening, Rama sets up an environment where every person in the team feels recognized and respected. He gives much attention not just to the words spoken but also to the emotions that go with them, implying that his approach is very empathetic. This builds trust and rapport between the team members.

Furthermore, Rama's skill at active listening aids him in unearthing golden nuggets of valuable insights and ideas that might otherwise be overlooked. In that way, this empires an opportunity for Rama to foster collective wisdom in the team to contribute towards the decision-making process and the problem-solving process.

Transparency and Openness:

Transparency and openness are key tenets of Rama's approach toward leadership, guiding his interactions with his team and shaping the organizational culture. Rama believes transparency is very necessary for developing a relationship with another where one can feel there is trust as well as building a shared purpose. He ensures that information regarding the organization's goals, strategies, and decisions is readily accessible to all team members, promoting clarity and alignment.

In heralding transparency, Rama does more than disclose information; he promotes an open environment of honesty and integrity. He encourages open communication channels where team members can express their thoughts, fears, and suggestions without fear of judgment or reprisal. It is an environment that rewards trust and collaboration, one where people feel appreciated and respected for the contribution they make.

Secondly, Rama's openness stands to disclose not only successes but also failures to his team. He believes transparency is not only celebrating achievements but it also provides us with a valuable learning opportunity from failures. Through this, he openly discusses challenges and learning opportunities with challenges in order to cultivate a culture that looks for continuous improvement and innovation within his team.

Overall, Rama's insistence on transparency and openness creates a positive workplace where team members feel supported and motivated to deliver at their best. By fostering a culture of trust and credibility, Rama empowers his team to withstand any challenge coming in its way with strength and confidence, focusing on collective success towards the aim of realizing the organizational goals.

Clear and Concise Communication:

Effective communication is evident in Rama's leadership style, putting forward his ideas and information in a way that is easily understood and comprehended by the team. Rama understands that it's the most important factor to ensure that his information is indeed understood correctly and wholly by everyone involved. He then observes great care in using words that are easy to understand in a simple and straightforward manner.

Through clear and concise communication, Rama minimizes ambiguity and confusion, bringing complete and proper understanding of objectives, expectations, and strategies within his team. He shies away from technical language or jargon, instead opts for a plain and simple way of expressing himself that his audience will be able to comprehend.

Further, Rama appreciates brevity in communication, knowing that lengthy talks can be confusing and uninteresting. Therefore, he only intends to explain in a concise and brief manner to be able to communicate what he wishes to.

The kind of clear and concise communication done by Rama fosters a culture of understanding and alignment within his team. With clear information on the roles and responsibilities of each member, Rama ensures that every member is on the same page, thus paving the way for effective collaboration and task execution.

In summary, Rama's focus on clear and concise communication translates into effective leadership of his team towards the achievement of goals. The clarity and certainty he offers in his messages is crucial in encouraging his team members to do their best and add real value to the organization.

Enhancing Communication Skills for Effective Leadership

In this part, we explore practical methods and tactics for the improvement of communication skills to lead efficiently. From active listening to assertive communication, these skills would enable leaders to communicate more effectively with their teams and cultivate engagement across the organization to ensure success.

Active Listening Techniques:

Active listening techniques are valuable tools for leaders, enabling them to nurture strong relationships with their team members and develop an open communication and collaboration culture. One such technique is paraphrasing; leaders restate what they've heard in their own words to ensure understanding and demonstrate empathy. This not only confirms that the leader has grasped the essence of the message but also shows respect and validation for the speaker's view.

Another valuable active listening technique that leaders may use is summarizing, which helps them to synthesize the key points and themes from the conversation, helping to distill complex information into manageable insights. The summarizing of information helps them to ensure that they are able to provide clarity regarding the main takeaways from the discussion.

Moreover, asking clarifying questions is important in the best practice of active listening. Through questions, leaders may seek clarification about any confusion, probing deeper meanings, and understanding underlying issues. It shows genuine interest to understand the other person's view and encourages further dialogue and engagement.

In sum, using techniques such as paraphrasing, summarizing, and asking clarifying questions enables leaders to create an environment within which team members feel valued, respected, and understood. This not only fosters good relationships and trust but also improves communication effectiveness and contributes to overall team cohesion and success.

Clarity and Brevity:

Clarity and brevity must be integral elements of effective communication for leaders, especially in environments where rapid communication is a prerequisite, where messages must be concise. Clear communication provides directional and expectation clarity, thereby reducing the likelihood of ambiguity or misinterpretation by members of the team. Thereby, the clear language used helps ensure the meaning behind any given communication is easily understood and put into practice. Further, brevity in communication is relevant since it captures the attention of busy team members and conveys the information effectively. Long-winded or convoluted messages may result in confusion and disengagement, which reduces productivity and decision-making. Leader communication, therefore, that is succinct in content delivery, respects the time and attention span of its team members. Clear and concise communication helps in fostering alignment and cohesion within teams since everyone understands the goals, priorities, and expectations. When messages are communicated with precision and brevity, team members can focus on executing tasks and achieving objectives without being burdened by unnecessary details or ambiguity. Moreover, clear and concise communication enhances trust and credibility in the team members, for it exhibits transparency and sincerity in leaders' interactions. Therefore, simplicity and clear communication enable the leaders to convey their messages with a high level of precision, impact, and authenticity. By focusing on clear and concise communication, the leaders build the spirit of understanding, alignment, and trust among the team members, and this goes a long way in ensuring success and the desired outcomes.

Nonverbal Communication:

Nonverbal communication is another critical element in effective leadership that often transmits more information than what is being articulated through verbal communication alone. An experienced leader who skillfully uses nonverbal cues can bolster his ability to relate to and get through to his members. For instance, a leader who smiles warmly during a team meeting communicates approachability and positivity, while a frown suggests deep concentration or concern, encouraging other team members to focus on intricate details.

Gestures form part of nonverbal communication, assisting leaders in emphasizing critical points, illustrating concepts, and connecting with the audience. A leader who uses open, expansive gestures shows confidence and enthusiasm; meanwhile, small gestures like nodding or tilting forward can translate to attentiveness and nodding of approval.

Posture and stand are other key aspects in using nonverbal cues. Standing tall with shoulders back can communicate confidence and leadership, while an open and relaxed body language can make members feel free to approach the leader with questions or issues at ease.

Leaders can use nonverbal cues and the signal of others' nonverbal cues to enhance the effectiveness of their communication. This heightened awareness ensures that leaders change their communication style to form closer connections with their team members and better build relationships that are based on trust and rapport.

Adaptability and Flexibility:

In today's diversified and changing environment, what matters the most in effective leadership is flexibility and adaptability in communication. Leaders with these qualities are able to deal with challenges in communication with one ease, ensuring that the message they are trying to relay is correctly interpreted by different audiences. One part of adaptability in communication includes fitting the content of the message to the preferences and needs of the audience. Different communication is carried out according to diverse style and preference, cultural backgrounds of the people; hence, leaders must learn how to adjust their tone, language, and delivery in order to be able to make good use of them, considering these differences. For example, it is possible that the response is more suitable with direct and brief communication than a conversational, inclusive one, for example. Realizing these differences and respecting them, leaders ensure that their messages are received and interpreted by all the team members adequately.

In addition, flexible communication involves welcoming feedback and changing its strategies whenever necessary. That is, successful leaders remain flexible and promptly respond to changing communication needs and staff demands. This might also mean the willingness to use different communication channels, ranging from face-to-face meetings to email or video conferencing, depending on circumstances and the preferences of the team.

Moreover, with adaptive communication, team members are inspired to make a productive team by fostering a culture of inclusivity. Leaders that display flexibility in their communication style give an atmosphere in which every person's voice is heard and respected. This creates an opportunity for greater conversation, ideation, and innovation as one feels comfortable sharing their ideas and thoughts without worry of judgment or misinterpretation.

Communicating a Vision to Inspire and Motivate Teams

A powerful vision is a guiding light that helps organizations succeed by inspiring teams to surmount challenges, draw on innovations, and strive for excellence. Leaders who are effective at vision communication help imbue it with fervor, purpose, and feasibility, thereby lighting up the passions and minds of their teams.

Vision Articulation:

Vision articulation is a solid cornerstone of good leadership since it offers direction and purpose for team members to unite for. Effective leaders will be able to articulate a compelling vision that not only outlines the future state but also resonates deeply with the values, aspirations, and aspirations of their team members. One of the elements of vision articulation is painting a vivid picture of the future that team members can visualize and aspire to. The leader can describe what success looks like in more tangible terms that make the vision more related and interesting for their teams. This clarity leaves team members knowing what the outcomes are and the part they play toward accomplishing these goals. In addition, vision articulation involves meaningful communication about the "why" behind the vision and why it deserves consideration. When leaders are able to tie the vision to the general mission and values of the organization, they inspire a sense of commitment and alignment among team members. When team members realize the value of the vision and how it follows their own values and aspirations, they will tend to become more motivated and enthusiastic towards contributing to the realization of the vision. Lastly, vision articulation involves listening to the perspectives and ideas of team members and inviting their input and feedback. The leaders who listen to the perspectives and ideas of their team members show respect and inclusivity, but also ensure that the vision reflects the collective aspirations of the team. This collaborative approach fosters a sense of ownership and buy-in, empowering team members to actively contribute towards the vision.

Inclusive Visioning:

Incorporative visioning is a very powerful form of leading teams to shape the vision for the future of the organization. Instead of imposing a single top-down definition for the vision, inclusive visioning calls for active requests for input, feedback, and collaboration from all the teams in an organization.

Leaders stimulate their ownership and belongingness to the organization and team by having open dialogue with them, and hence, the leadership is made responsible for reducing the barriers that may be creating misunderstandings, differences, and conflicts in the work process. It becomes significant to encourage communication that helps boost the commitment of team members towards the vision. This inspiration helps to create a sense of empowerment that motivates individuals towards the development and fulfillment of the vision.

Moreover, inclusive visioning makes sure that the vision will bear representation to the whole team's diverse perspectives, experiences, and aspirations. By taking into account the views of the whole team, leaders can ensure that the vision resonates with the values and priorities of all stakeholders and hence creates more buy-in and commitment to its implementation.

It also boosts collaboration and teamwork within the organization. When team members share their common roles, responsibilities, and how they contribute to the vision, it helps them understand each other. This common understanding breeds trust, cooperation, and synergy between teams and develops collaboration in order to fulfill the common goal.

Overall, inclusive visioning transforms leaders from mere captains to architects of shared visions that inspire, motivate, and unite. Leaders, therefore, need to embrace inclusive visioning in the processes and engage the whole team so that a common, unified goal is to bring out the best in people and the organization.

Consistent Communication:

Communication of the vision is an important feature that ensures the organizational vision remains alive and resonant within the team. The vision should, therefore, be periodically reinforced by effective leaders through different communication channels to remain fresh, relevant, and inspired. Leaders can ensure that they maintain consistency in propagating the vision by including vision messages in all forums, such as team meetings, town halls, or presentations, among others. Regular weaving of vision into these interactions by the leaders helps remind the team about the purpose of the organization and what should be done collectively. The repetition helps reinforce the importance of the vision and its compatibility with the activities of the team in everyday activities and long-term objectives.

On the other hand, consistent communication of the vision through organizational channels such as emails, newsletters, and internal platforms helps reach a broader audience and reinforces the message across different departments and levels of the organization. By employing these channels, leaders can ensure that every team member is updated and reminded on a recurring basis about the vision to make sure that they have an active understanding of its meaning and importance in their work.

Additionally, leaders should conduct themselves in such a way that they demonstrate a consistent embodiment of the values and principles outlined in the vision. This helps to reaffirm the sincerity and relevance of the vision in the minds of the team because when they witness leaders actually living their beliefs and principles expressed in the vision, it causes them to believe that the vision is authentic and relevant. This consistency builds trust and credibility, further strengthening the team's commitment to realizing the shared goals.

Conclusion

In conclusion, effective communication is the cornerstone that connects leaders with their teams, aligns efforts, and propels the organization towards their goals. This chapter has explored the relationship between communication and leadership as it allows for excellent leadership effectiveness. We first had an exemplary communication style of Rama, a fictitious manager, who nailed active listening, transparency, and clarity in communication. Rama's approach highlights the importance of nurturing trust, empathy, and collaboration through active listening, openness, and clarity in communication.

We then went into the instrumental communication skills for effective leadership and involving active listening techniques, clarity, and brevity of nonverbal communication, adaptability. These abilities enable the leader to form a link to the employees in terms of the important understanding between them, make them understand the nuances of difference in the communication preferences and contexts of the employees, and all the rest.

We also discussed the importance of a visionary communication to energize and motivate the team. A leader like Rama cannot be described but could be seen as one of his visions that have captured the values and aspirations of his followers in their role of guiding their life together toward a common purpose, direction, and in fact, reality. Visioning with inclusivity ensures that the vision will include all the members and shall collectively result in ownership, collaboration, and unity.

Consistent communication of the vision boosts its significance and relevance, knowing that everything continues being relevant, and nothing gets worn out. For leaders to instill trust, credibility, and alignment in teams and make the teams find motivation and incentives to work in an effective manner, vision messaging should be propagated through every communication channel. Leaders who demonstrate the vision through example, create an environment that builds trust, credibility, and alignment with the other teams and individuals in the organization.

In light of the said, it is pretty evident how effective communication skills can make a very massive difference within an organization's leadership. Therefore, in this context, mastering communication skills becomes not just a necessity but a catalyst in driving organizational success. Through effective communication, leaders could change greatness within others, conduct collaboration, and develop a culture of innovation and excellence.

To put it another way, effective communication in that case is not merely a tool but a fundamental pillar of effective leadership. It is by implementing the principles of effective communication, as well as learning, will certainly release the full potential of our teams and address challenges with strength, based on the course towards the proper pathway for the organizations towards the future. Together, let us embark on this journey of growth, learning, and transformation, as we strive to be more effective communicators and impactful leaders.

End of Chapter 18

Chapter 19

Conflict Resolution and Team Collaboration

Conflict is one of the most inevitable subject in any workplace. When diverse individuals gather, each having its unique perspective and approach, conflicts will occur. But the key does not lie in avoiding conflict altogether but rather how we work out and manage it. This chapter delves into the realities of conflict resolution and team collaboration, presenting straightforward strategies accessible to anyone.

In any professional setting, be it an office, factory floor, or virtual workspace, conflicts will rise for various reasons. There could be disagreements over project priorities, clashes of personalities, or a miscommunication that escalates into tension. Whatever the trigger, conflicts are naturally part and parcel of human interaction. Rather than viewing conflicts as obstacles, it is crucial to recognize them as opportunities for growth and improvement.

The heart of effective conflict resolution lies in communication. When faced with a conflict, the first step is to engage in open dialogue. This means actively listening to all parties involved, understanding their perspectives, and empathizing with their concerns. By creating a safe space for honest communication, teams can lay the foundation for finding common ground and working towards a resolution that satisfies everyone involved.

Collaboration is another cornerstone of conflict resolution. When team members collaborate well, they can optimize their diverse skill sets and experience pools to handle situations and achieve common goals. But fostering a collaborative environment requires much more than just assigning work and setting deadlines. It involves creating a culture of trust, respect, and mutual support where each team member feels valued and is given the freedom to contribute.

As leaders, it's about cultivating the ability to manage conflicts and setting the example within a team. This involves providing active listening, a show of empathy, and impartiality while mediating conflicts within a team. By showing a commitment to fairness and inclusivity, leaders can inspire their teams to have a constructive mindset and develop a collaborative approach towards more mutually beneficial solutions.

What is explored throughout this chapter is how conflicts are resolved, and how collaboration is fostered within teams. We try to break down complex concepts into easily understood language, so we are able to give readers the tools that they need to navigate conflicts effectively and foster a culture of teamwork and cooperation within their workplaces.

Resolving Conflicts Through Open Dialogue and Equitable Solutions

Communication is where conflict resolution starts. In fact, any disagreement or conflict has to be put in simple language. Here's how to do it step by step:

Step 1: Listen Carefully

Listening attentively is indeed one cornerstone of conflict resolution. When people bring grievances or disagreements to the table, lend your undivided attention—that shows respect and willingness to understand their point of view. Don't interrupt, rather, affirm their right to be heard; this helps create an environment of mutual understanding. Even if their perspective differs from your own, giving them the space to express it shows empathy and a willingness to find a fair resolution. In other words, attentive listening creates a foundation for constructive dialogue that sets the stage for finding common ground amidst divergent viewpoints.

Step 2: Find Common Ground

The next step is to seek out commonalities among the speakers, which are shared principles, objectives, or aspirations that unite the individuals that are in conflict. This entails finding common ground in goals, values, or interests transcending the conflict's own. One can get unify and undertake collaborative efforts with regard to differences in approaches on the basis of recognition of commonalities. This common ground forms a base for effective dialogue, such as looking for ways to realize reciprocal gains.

Step 3: Brainstorm Solutions

With a common-ground basis, the next phase is the part of collaborative brainstorming to come up with possible solutions. This phase is characterized by openness and inclusivity, inviting input from all parties involved. Encouraging diversity and out-of-the-box thinking can result in an atmosphere of exploration and experimentation, with each participant contributing ideas worth considering. When anybody has an idea for a solution, in encouraging the notion that solutions may come from unexpected corners, everybody gets encouraged to contribute a probable suggestion. The collective effort of the team to resolve the conflict becomes all the more successful, and every suggestion is valued for the particular contribution that it makes. From the above approach, possible innovative and unique solutions may be generated that can directly tackle the issues.

Step 4: Agree on a Solution

Once there is a full, in-depth discussion and evaluation of each of the possible solutions, the focus changes to determine the best possible solution. Often, it involves a readiness to compromise and adapt from all the stakeholders. The intention is that a resolution should be found, which not only resolves the current conflict but also addresses its underlying causes. Achieving unanimity is achieved with the realization of mutual understanding and agreement that, for some time, collective well-being is of paramount importance as opposed to individual preference. It is of great importance to make sure that once a solution has been agreed on, all those concerned should bind themselves to implement and follow the actions that they had agreed upon.

Step 5: Follow Through

Although reaching a resolution represents a significant milestone, it is important to recognize that it doesn't mean the journey ends. Follow-through is essential to ensure that the agreed solution is properly implemented. Regular check-ins enable ongoing assessment of progress and identification of emerging issues or concerns. The active involvement and monitoring of the implementation process help address potential obstacles in a timely manner, helping prevent future conflicts. Consistent follow-through exhibit a commitment to the resolution process and creates a culture of accountability and transparency in the team or organization.

Strategies for Promoting Healthy Collaboration Within Teams

Collaboration is an important skill in reaching success in any organization. When teams work effectively, they are capable of getting more done than if each were alone. Here are some strategies for encouraging healthy collaboration within teams:

Clear Communication

Effective communication builds the bedrock for successful collaboration. It includes ensuring that each team member is aware of their duties, the meaning behind their contribution, and the relevance of these contributions toward the team objectives. This lets create an open and trust-based, where each member feels more secure to share his or her viewpoints, thoughts, concerns, and ideas without fear of being judged by other team members. People need to be updated periodically on the progress of the project and about the state of affairs that might involve changes as well.

Respect and Trust

The essence of productive teamwork lies in respect and trust. Being treated decently, valuing expertise and opinions, and actively listening to their input provides a sense of belonging and team spirit within the group. Trust is built by giving space for independent ownership of responsibility to the team members and accepting its members' competency to perform the role at the required level. The diversity that enriches collaboration by providing an opportunity for innovation and inclusivity in problem-solving and decision-making is brought to bear in appreciating the unique strengths and talents that each individual brings.

Encourage Participation

A culture of inclusivity and empowerment is nurtured through active participation from each team member. Everyone, with the active encouragement of their contribution of their ideas and perspectives, explores a wide range of ideas and viewpoints. Creating a supportive atmosphere where people are valued and respected for their contributions cultivates a sense of psychological safety, thus giving way to even those holding opposing opinions to freely express themselves. Embracing the diverse perspectives enriches the discussions and enhances quality decisions—tapping the collective wisdom and creativity of the team to formulate innovative solutions and lead to project growth in unison with set objectives.

Celebrate Successes

One of the critical ways to encourage a positive and goal-motivating work environment is by honoring successes, whatever their size. Celebrating the achievements of the team cultivates appreciation for the difficult and specific efforts they have made in pursuing the objectives. Allowing the team time to celebrate milestones and accomplishments not only raises the morale but also reinforces the value of teamwork and collaboration. Recognizing individual and collective efforts will foster pride and satisfaction among the team members, encouraging sustained dedication and commitment towards the shared objectives. In the end, celebrating the successes has thus developed a culture of appreciation and camaraderie that drives sustained motivation and engagement for the team.

Address Issues Promptly

It communicates your commitment towards making the working environment harmonious and efficient, and dealing with disputes or challenges immediately prevents them from becoming serious and rising to a greater level. Actively listening to all parties and collaborating on finding the best possible solutions create the impression of equity and a deep-seated inclusiveness within the team. Rapid problem-solving not only preserves the productivity of the team but also improves the atmosphere of the team and employees feel positively about being heard and appreciated. All this nurtures mutual trust and provides a fertile ground for successful collaboration in fulfilling its objectives.

Building Conflict Resolution Skills for Effective Leadership

Being a leader, it is important to develop good conflict resolution skills for managing your team effectively and making the work environment lively. Below are some of the tips that would aid:

Active Listening

Active listening is not just listening; it's about fully engulfing what is being communicated. That way, you demonstrate respect and empathy towards your team members, that is paramount for you to develop a supportive and understanding working environment with all the different people under your direction. Avoiding interruptions and not being judgmental fosters an open space for them to express their thoughts and feelings. Active listening helps to gain insight into their point of view. Through this mechanism, shared experinces and concerns enable finding a common ground that can lead to some meaningful collaboration. In the end, active listening creates opportunities for building relationships, building trust, and effective communication in the team.

Empathy

Empathy means being able to put oneself in another person's place and understanding how they might think, feel, and experience things. This kind of empathy for your team members is a sign of compassion and an interest in their well-being. Getting into other people's shoes creates a sense of understanding and earns mutual respect that lays the groundwork for smooth collaboration and conflict resolution. The ability to understand their feelings and motivations creates a platform upon which team members feel worthy and appreciated. Empathy brings more intimacy and meaningful interactions among team members. It helps to engender a climate of understanding and inclusiveness within the team, leading to more meaningful and productive interactions.

Mediation Skills

Leaders acting as impartial facilitators in such disputes bring immeasurable value to their teams in developing skills in mediation. The leader here facilitates open communication, wherein differing perspectives are presented openly, and solutions can then be found that are in line with each other. The leader should focus on bringing understanding and empathy between the conflicting parties, encouraging active listening and respectful dialogue. The leader's ultimate goal is that through skilled mediation, members of the team share their concerns and perspectives, and they work collaboratively to address problems in the process of resolution. In sum, effective mediation of conflicts fosters understanding and promotes mutual regard. It strengthens relationships, builds trust, and instills in the team members a spirit of cooperation and unity.

Emotional Intelligence

Emotional intelligence is one of the most important leadership skills that cannot be neglected by any leader. It comprises self-awareness, self-regulation, empathy, and social awareness. By improving emotional intelligence, leaders could be able to understand their own feelings better and how they form the basis for what they do and say. With this awareness, they may understand other people's emotions better, encourage a deep sense of connection with others, and increase trust. By overcoming both anger and intrigue in handling conflict, leaders remain composed and don't let emotions affect them since they're ready to resolve problems thoughtfully and sensitively.

They then use this heightened awareness to assess every situation more empathically and respond in a way that is definitely better than their opponents.

Lead by Example

Leading by example is the behavior of setting an example of the principles and behaviors that you desire your team to emulate. As a leader, your actions actually speak far louder than words. The way you handle conflicts will set a standard that others will follow. Your team will follow you in using strategies like active listening, empathy, and compromise to deal with conflicts that you show them. Open to feedback and committed to finding solutions that prioritize teamwork, account for yourself and others. Ultimately, leading by example makes it possible to create an environment where conflicts represent opportunities for growth and learning, and it is in that context that teamwork really flourishes.

Conclusion

Effective conflict resolution and team collaboration, on the other hand, are sine qua non for a healthy workplace environment. In this chapter, we examined how conflicts are managed and how teams should collaborate, providing real-life tactics that are practical and applicable to all. Conflict is one of those intrinsic issue that comes with human interaction; hence, it's an inevitable part of being human. Conflict will rather serve as a path to growth and improvement, because if it is presented to a team as a path of self-improvement, the team could turn conflict into a means of realizing positive change.

Central to conflict resolution is, therefore, effective communication. By letting the parties involved in the conflict express themselves and listening actively to them, the teams lay a foundation on which to build mutual understanding and respect. Through active listening, with transparency in communication, they can provide a platform to settle conflicts collectively.

Collaboration is also important in conflict resolution. When team members collaborate well, they use a combination of their abilities and experiences to handle the challenges and work towards the common goal. A culture that engulfs trust, respect, and support among team members creates an environment that can facilitate a seamless collaborative effort and achieve great results for leaders.

As leaders, it is our responsibility to nurture the skills that are necessary in the process of handling conflicts and set an example in our teams. By expressing active listening, empathy, and impartiality, leaders can influence their teams to take a constructive stance and tackle conflicts collaboratively.

Throughout this chapter, we aimed to simplify complex concepts into understandable language to help readers develop skills in handling conflicts without losing sight of their workplaces. In essence, conflict resolution and team collaboration are not skills that need to be mastered, but rather continuous processes which require commitment, empathy, and readiness to change their attitudes. By embracing conflicts as a means of self-improvement, a collaborative culture can unleash team potential towards ultimate success.

End of Chapter 19

Chapter 20

Trust and Empowerment in Leadership

In every workforce, there is a bedrock for constructing successful relationships and collaboration: Much like the sturdy foundation of a house, trust should provide stability and confidence, enabling individuals to work harmoniously in order to come out with a joint goal. When employees trust their leaders, it breeds confidence and loyalty, making them feel safe to invest time, energy, and talents into their work. In this chapter, we shall enlighten how these qualities—trust and empowerment—are catalysts towards a vibrant, cohesive work environment, and how their existence nurtures such a situation.

Trust is the cornerstone of effective leadership, being the linchpin that binds leaders and employees together, united in one purpose for the common achievement of organizational objectives. In the way a captain relies on the trust of his crew to navigate a ship through rough waters, a leader depends on the trust of their team members to chart a course toward success. When leaders inspire trust through their actions, communication, and decisions, it builds a ripple effect throughout the workspace, instilling confidence and motivation in employees to get it right.

Furthermore, trust is not a one-way street: it is a reciprocal relationship that calls for active contribution from leaders and employees alike in building it. Leaders need to demonstrate honesty, openness, and reliability in their dealings with employees, fostering a trusting relationship with them by offering consistent and ethical behavior. Meanwhile, employees need to play their part, too—by maintaining professionalism, honesty, and accountability in their work—to make this work. With this flow of trust, an atmosphere of mutual respect and collaboration is built that leads to innovation, productivity, and organizational success.

Empowerment is another critical aspect of effective leadership to empower employees to take ownership of their work, provide resources, and extend support in order for them to rise to the occasion. Empowerment is how a gardener nurtures a garden by giving the proper environment for employees to be able to take ownership of their work, to come up with their own ideas, and to contribute according to the collective vision. By empowering employees to think creatively, take initiative, and solve their own problems, leaders unleash the full potential of their teams to drive innovation and organizational growth.

Trust and empowerment are indispensable elements of effective leadership, serving as the bedrock for a positive and productive work environment. By focusing on trust-building behaviors, open communication, and empowering employees to take charge of their work, leaders can create a culture where collaboration thrives, morale soars, and organizational goals are achieved with excellence. Throughout this chapter, we shall explore the strategies and tools to how trust and empowerment should be cultivated within leadership, where it delivers useful insights with insights and practical advice to cultivate an atmosphere of trust and empowerment in any type of workplace.

Building Trust Through Consistent and Transparent Leadership

Trust is the bedrock of any healthy relationship, including the one between leaders and employees. It's like the firm footing that gives you stability and confidence as you step through your workday. Trust is not something that magically develops; it needs to be built consciously through consistent and transparent leadership.

Consistency:

Leadership consistency equates to a steady drumbeat rhythm, and rhythm is the soothing law of musical performance. In this sense, consistency provides employees with a sense of stability and predictability for their work environment. In such a case, if a leader is consistent with his words and actions, employees would be confident on how to handle certain situations, hence the assurance that the same level of expectations is maintained from the leadership level. A leader who demonstrates consistency in leadership results in trustworthiness among employees with the assurance that their leader would be good and keep up to all the elements they share with them. Employees should trust in their leader because he will meet the promises they have made, maintain consistency in execution of projects, and maintain a consistent approach to management of tasks and challenges. Trust creates an environment with a collaborative and friendly atmosphere, where every individual is harmoniously working towards common objectives. In this way, leading the team with certainty and direction would bring about mutual success and creativeness in achievement.

Clearly, consistency is an effective approach in the leadership process that brings success within the workplace. When a leader exercises consistency within its team through actions and decisions, employees will be able to work under one easy framework of operating successfully. This builds trust and stability in unity within the team, with the leader devising a pattern that supports success in the workplace.

Transparency:

The illuminating work of transparency, as it radiates the light in a dark room, shows that there are areas with clarity and visibility to the road ahead. In transparency, leaders only make decisions under illumination—sharing information openly and honestly, letting people understand the purposes of decisions with nothing vague. This transparency builds confidence and legitimacy throughout the team, having said that the employees feel that they have taken part in deciding. The open revealing about decisions affecting team interests brings them greater respect as to intelligence and sound judgment, while the transparency adds value to the employee base. The transparent leaders also provide some context and rationale, along with further listening, so as to be able to think and contribute within the reasonable framework that they lay out. This transparency provokes a culture of trust and interdependence, where the employees feel appreciated for their contribution. Besides, open-door policy and feedback, within the team, enables employees to give their opinions and ideas without much fear. Once the leaders listen to the feedback put forward by employees and use them to finalize the decision-making process, it is a way of convincing employees that they are part of this organization and need to feel committed to making this work. In this manner, the constructive nature of the collaborative effort leads to fresh ideas, problem-solving, and constant self-improvement.

Summing up, transparency is a legacy in effective leadership; it introduces the culture of openness, honesty, and trust in a team. It provides a transparent platform through which the leader can reveal its decisions while conversing openly with the employees. It may foster some incorporation and engagement from its employees, ensuring that it sets ownership and investment.

Empowering Employees with Autonomy for Increased Engagement

For a person, empowerment is like giving them the keys to their own car: it lets them chart their own course, take control, and own their destiny. When employees are empowered, they get a chance to decide, take initiative, and solve problems on their own. They feel the trust and value their leaders lay in them, boosts their confidence and engagement.

Autonomy:

Autonomy in the workplace is akin to handing someone the keys to explore a new city by themselves: an opportunity for individuals to navigate their own path, make decisions, and take responsibility for their actions. Just like traveling to a new city empowers the individuals to discover hidden gems and create unique experiences for themselves, giving autonomy to the employees empowers them to unleash their creativity, expertise, and potential within their roles.

Leadership that embrace autonomy empowers employees to make informed decisions within their areas of expertise, giving them ownership of their work and contributing meaningfully to the team's objectives. Autonomy from leadership encourages employees to explore new ideas, solve challenges, and innovate solutions. This empowerment and accountability leads to higher team engagement.

Moreover, autonomy fosters intrinsic motivation, as employees derive satisfaction and purpose from making decisions that impact their work. That is to say, autonomy in the workplace fuels a spirit of adventure and curiosity in employees.

Thus, autonomy is one of the most potent tools in fostering engagement, creativity, and productivity amongst employees. By giving employees the freedom to explore, experiment, and take risks, leaders create a culture of innovation and excellence within their teams, driving success and growth for the organization.

Support:

Empowerment is the energy that acts as a platform for employees to take hold of their work and, in turn, translates into the tremendous innovation capacity they have. While autonomy gives a person freedom of choice and decision-making, support bears this out by providing the infrastructure to buttress and execute these efforts, ensuring success. Leadership of support takes into account the need for individual employees to be provided with the tools, resources, and knowledge necessary to succeed. This may include everything from setting clear expectations and objectives to providing comprehensive training and development opportunities and continued guidance and mentorship. When the leaders involve themselves in the employees' growth and development, it shows employees that leaders and the organization are committed to them.

Second, support fashions a sense of trust and courage within the employees, who know that, with challenges or endeavors, they are supported by their leaders and colleagues. Similarly, just as a sturdy support system will support and ground the person, leadership support gives the staff the confidence to take calculated risks, to come up with innovative solutions to problems, and to advance the frontiers of their potential.

Furthermore, support builds a culture of collaboration and teamwork, where individuals feel recognized and respected for their contribution. When leaders deal with support, they create an environment that is safe for people to seek support, share ideas, and participate in projects. The innovational spirit will remain, though, as this collaborative environment pushes forward a workplace of creativity and accountability.

Creating a Culture of Trust Within an Organization

Trust is the soil in a garden, giving nourishment and support to the growth of plants. In the same way, trust is the bedrock of a healthy organizational culture: a platform where employees can feel safe, supported, and valued.

Leadership Example:

Trust acts as the central guiding beacon within an organization that sets the benchmark for trust, providing a guiding principle for employees to emulate. When leaders demonstrate trustworthiness through their words and actions, a strong foundation of integrity, honesty, and respect is established across the entire organization. By consistently exhibiting integrity and honesty in their dealings, leaders build credibility and earn the trust of their team members. Leaders provide leading by example to their employees as they closely watch how leaders solve problems, openly communicate, and maintain the proper ethics. In a culture of trust, where people feel safe and supported, leaders prioritize transparency and authenticity in their interactions.

Leaders moreover hold themselves and others accountable to upholding trust in their organization. They lead by example, sticking to ethical principles and showing good faith in every action they take. Leaders make their decisions and keep account of their actions and the decisions they made. This acts as a guiding factor for employees, where they trust that anything said and done by their bosses is going to be truthful.

Apart from that, leaders actively listen to the concerns and opinions of their employees, putting importance to their ideas and conveying respect for their perspective. In this case, through promoting open communication and giving feedback, leaders create an environment that cultivates trust and cooperation, giving employees freedom of expression over ideas and concerns.

Essentially, the example set forth by leadership acts as a pivotal role in the organization's culture of trust. With embodiment of trustworthiness in word and deed, they inspire confidence, promote transparency, and formulate an enabling environment where an individual can develop full capacity to the extent and strive for success.

Employee Contribution:

Creating a culture of trust and accountability in the organization needs the contribution of employees since trust is an effort from all: from the top leadership to the bottom-line workers. When it comes to the generation of trust, the employees are important because their work puts them into positions where they reflect the responsibility, honesty, and consideration that they practice in their interactions with colleagues, customers, and others in the working environment.

Where reliability is concerned, employees establish trust by discharging their duties and keeping deadlines. When colleagues have confidence in the commitments made to them and the deliverables given, they instill trust where there is a more collaborative work environment.

Another criterion that builds trust is the honesty with which people interact. Straightforwardness in dealing with each other, with managers, and even with clients instills confidence within employees, making them feel reliable and credible at workplaces.

Behavioral aspects such as respectful behavior should also be part of building trust within an organization. When employees treat their fellow workers, partners, and customers with respect, they are fostering an environment that is inclusive, supportive, and welcoming, where trust can flourish.

Moreover, trusting relations have much more possibilities when it gets embedded in the organization's fabric. Then, employees feel safe and supported, and they feel free to take the initiative, contributing their idea for optimizing the working regime and associating with others, where their contribution is appreciated and valued.

Conclusion

In the present-day workplaces, with the ever-changing landscape, trust and empowerment emerge as the pillars on which successful leadership is built. For effective leadership, trust and empowerment create an environment in which the employees are valued, involved, and motivated towards the organizational targets. Trust, like a sturdy framework or bedrock of a building, provides safety and security to an individual. Effective leadership is built on trust, which fosters trust, loyalty, and collaboration in team members. Through transparent and honest action and decision-making, trust is built by leaders, and a culture of open communication and mutual respect prevails. Through all these factors, empowerment provides an environment in which the employees are free to think without restrictions and innovate or grow with the organization. In empowering employees, leaders build a culture of creativity, autonomy, and accountability that values employees and helps them achieve exceptional results.

In this section, we have explored the various ways to instill trust and empowerment within leadership. These include consistency and transparency in action and decisions by the leader, and provision of autonomy and support to the employees. All the above elements assist to create a culture where trust and empowerment could be fostered. A leadership driven by example, employee involvement in the decision-making process, and open communication create a trusting and empowering environment.

In sum, trust and empowerment are not mere buzzwords but are fundamental elements in leadership that deliver organizational success. By focusing on behaviors that create a culture that is built on trust and support for employees, leaders can create a culture where teamwork thrives, innovation takes off, and everyone feels appreciated and energized. Let us remember that, in this modern-day landscape, trust and empowerment are the catalysts that transform workplace culture for the better.

End of chapter 20

Chapter 21

Managing Change and Adaptability

Change is just the wind that never stops blowing; it can be gentle, like a breeze blowing through the trees, or it can be a whirlwind that throws us off balance and leaves us feeling disoriented. However, just as the wind brings with it new scents, sounds, and sensations, change also presents us with fresh opportunities and adventures if we approach it with an open mind and a willingness to adapt. In this chapter, let's journey through real-life examples and simple language to help unravel the complexities of change management, equipping you with the tools and insights required to navigate transitions effectively.

Change is not an abstract concept, but rather a given aspect of our professional life. If it is a company's change of direction, new technologies that are coming in, or just the way that work has got to be done differently, change will shake up routines and push into uncomfortable zones. Since adapting to change and nurturing an adaptable mindset is a necessity, it comes to our rescue. With the help of the chapter, we'll bring out practical strategies and actionable tips towards being comfortable and resilient with change. By knowing from real-life experiences and applying proven principles of change management, we will get a deeper sense of moving through the transitions effectively, both as individuals and leaders within our organizations.

Join us on a journey of exploration and discovery as we unravel the mysteries of change and open the secrets to mastering adaptability in the ever-evolving landscape of the workplace. Each of us can learn how to harness the power of change to propel ourselves and our organizations towards greater success and fulfillment.

Adapting to Change Through Rama's Experiences

Meet Rama, a manager at a small tech company. Rama's company is constantly changing—new technologies and trends shaping the industry. Rama first found it hard to keep up with the new changes. With time, Rama managed to adapt and grow, even taking change as an opportunity.

Rama's journey taught him some valuable lessons about managing change:

Stay Flexible:

Rama's journey taught him invaluable lessons to be adaptable in a changing environment. He did not rigidly cling to the comfortable; he had a mind open to the unknown and an ability to be adaptable in such situations. Cultivating such an attitude, he found that resilience and adaptability, in concert with flexibility, gave him the power to face turbulence in a calm and comforting manner. He realized how to change his approach, take on opportunities, and solve unexpected problems. Due to this, he not only survived change but emerged stronger and more capable than ever before.

Keep Learning:

Rama realized that with most changes come new opportunities for growth and development. He understood the value of staying curious and open-minded, especially in times of uncertainty. He knew to stay ahead and not be one who reacts but rather one who is ready for the unexpected change. Whether it be attending workshops, seeking mentorship, or pursuing online courses, he always ensured he sought out ways to expand his knowledge base and acquire new skills. This commitment to lifelong learning not only bolstered Rama's confidence but also equipped him with the tools needed to thrive in a rapidly evolving environment.

Stay Positive:

Amidst the turmoil of change, Rama felt the power of maintaining a positive outlook. However, Rama took up change with optimism and resilience. Rather than dwelling on the uncertainties or setbacks, he chose to tackle change in such a way that he made constructive progress within the organization. This mindset has motivated Rama to always view obstacles as opportunities for growth, learning, and innovation. By perceiving change not as an obstacle but as an opportunity, Rama empowered everyone around him to do the same and excel. Instead of being weighed down by negativity, Rama used change as a chance to learn, evolve, and ultimately, gain bigger successes.

Rama's experiences reveal how change will always occur, but with a good attitude and approach, we can adapt and cope in any situation.

Guiding Teams Through Organizational Change

Managing change isn't just about individual adaptability—it's also about guiding teams through transitions. Here are some tips for leaders to help their teams navigate organizational change:

Communicate Effectively:

It is during times of change that communication becomes very important. In this respect, transparency is paramount since the teams have to be updated at each stage of the process. Open communication builds trust and lowers uncertainty, as team members feel more secure and involved. Regular communication, answering questions, and addressing concerns to improve understanding are all things leaders need to do in order to create an environment of making changes. Effective communication also encourages collaboration and alignment so that the team can navigate through change collectively. Overall, good communication helps the individuals understand why change is taking place and how they can adapt to it and assist in its success.

Provide Support:

The employees during periods of change might find themselves wondering and fearful of what might happen, so that support needs to be given by their leaders. The support may take the form of offering training sessions in developing new skills; providing access to resources or tools that may be required to adjust to change; or simply being available to listen to their fears and reaffirm a reassuring feeling. By feeling heard, and with leadership showing empathy and standing in solidarity, employees can feel less anxious and more certain in how they approach a change. In the end, support during a period of change develops a sense of trust and reliability among employees that can steer them through hard transitions more easily.

Foster Collaboration:

Teams must collaborate and work together more effectively for smooth sailing through transitions. Leaders could encourage collaboration by availing team members of opportunities for them to come together, brainstorming, and sharing insights. Leaders empower their staff to innovate within change-bred challenges by promoting an environment of teamwork and cooperation, sharing talents, and resources to solve problems. Moreover, team collaboration should foster trust and camaraderie among team members, creating an atmosphere of support where each person feels valued and motivated to participate for the success of the team's goals.

Lead by Example:

In this regard, the most natural way to realize the vision of change is through setting an example in action. When the lead is demonstrating flexibility and resilience in their actions, it does not only automatically set the pace for all other teams in place but also becomes a crucial piece to the puzzle of creating a strong team spirit. The more proactive, adaptable, and open-minded a leader is, the more likely they are to succeed in the face of uncertainty and emerge stronger and better. And seeing their leaders displaying these characteristics can trigger confidence and trust in their employees, assuring them dependency on the support and guidance needed to adapt and thrive in trying conditions. In the end, leading by example helps cultivate a culture of resilience and adaptability within the organization.

Through empathetic support in guiding their teams through change, leaders can help minimize resistance and facilitate a smoother transition.

Proactive Approaches to Managing Change Effectively

Rather than waiting for change to occur, proactive leaders provide solutions to anticipate and allow opportunities to develop. Here are some proactive ways to manage change effectively:

Stay Ahead of the Curve:

The rapid business environment of today calls for staying ahead in order not to get left behind. Keeping an eye on all the developments and trends in the industry prepares the team for the changes that come in the course of time. Being proactive while adapting to new technologies and market shifts is a way of ensuring that the organization remains competitive and resilient in face of evolving challenges. This proactive approach also helps in mitigating any potential risks, but more than anything, it opens up opportunities for growth and innovation. Staying ahead of the curve means positioning teams to succeed and being capable of adapting through change with confidence and agility.

Foster a Culture of Innovation:

Building a culture of innovation is like planting seeds of creativity throughout your organization. This would mean that when team members are thinking outside the box and experimenting with novel ideas, this creates an environment that fosters innovation. Such a culture does not merely facilitate quicker adaptation to changes and turning your organization into an industry leader; it also supports collaboration. Facilitation of creativity and experimentation fosters a mindset of continuous improvement and adaptation, empowering your team to stay ahead of the competition. By nurturing a culture of innovation, you unleash the full potential of your team and drive sustainable growth and success.

Develop Change Management Plans:

Building change management plans may be preferred to develop a roadmap to navigate through the ever-changing terrain of change. Such plans describe specific strategies and actions to be taken in response to various types of change. They provide clear communication strategies, comprehensive training programs, and effective implementation tactics for proactively addressing potential challenges and capitalizing on opportunities presented by change. These plans offer a structured framework for managing transitions, ensuring that everyone in the organization is aligned and equipped to adapt smoothly to new circumstances. In essence, change management plans form the foundation to successful change initiatives, which nurture resilience and agility within the organization.

Seek Feedback:

Seeking feedback is akin to opening a window to fresh perspectives and insights. That is, there exists the active invitation of input from employees and stakeholders regarding their experiences, concerns, and suggestions regarding proposed changes in processes and operations. An organization can therefore harness the collective wisdom of its teams to identify blind spots, uncover innovative solutions, and ensure that proposed changes resonate with those directly affected. Involving others in the change process fosters ownership and buy-in, which in turn increases the likelihood of successful implementation and sustained success. Finally, seeking feedback empowers people to contribute meaningfully to the change journey, leading to positive outcomes for an organization in general.

Embrace Continuous Improvement:

Continuous improvement is equivalent to nurturing a garden: it needs a lot of attention and care for development and life. Sowing the seeds of continuous improvement within your team or organization is a way to create an environment where innovation, flexibility, and adaptability are promoted. Be it through the review and retooling of processes, products, and strategies in alignment with ever-evolving market trends and customer requirements. Converting change from disruption to a means for growth and refinement opens up a path towards long-term success and robustness in a dynamic setting.

Leaders who have the capability of being proactive with change management will hence position their organizations to be the best in this ever-changing world.

Conclusion

In a nutshell, coping with change and flexibility are mindset things, not skills that merely imply knowing when to do things. For this section, we have offered a critical endeavor to demystify the transitions in real-life examples, generally using simple language, for easy understanding. We have delved into valuable insights and actionable strategies for what to do in guiding teams through organizational changes and adopting proactive approaches. Change is something that happens; it's how we respond to it that makes all the difference. For adapting well to change, keeping our mindset open, continuously learning, and remaining optimistic are key factors. It involves quality communication, support, collaboration, and following an example with the help of this for leading teams in change, to develop a culture of resilience and adaptability.

Further, proactive leaders who prop up in advance of challenges, creating a culture of innovation, developing change management plans, learning to communicate by example, and working to be continuously improved lead the team effectively and with flexibility in coping with change. With this kind of approach, the organization can position itself in a position to lead long-term success and sustainability against an ever-changing scenario. In this concluding chapter, we should bear in mind that change is not something to run from but rather a catalyst for progress. By instilling an adaptable mindset and proactive approaches, we can transform challenges into opportunities, and by doing this, be better off than living under the cloud of uncertainty. Let us get together and unlock the power of change to help us achieve greater success and fulfillment in ourselves and in our organizations.

End of chapter 21

Chapter 22

Resilience and Perseverance in Leadership

In the voyage of leadership, turbulent waters are an evitable manifestation: times where impediments and hindrances loom large, threatening to derail progress and blur the path towards achievement. However, in such moments, it is precisely the turbulent waves that illuminate the road ahead with glimmers of resilience and perseverance in leadership. This chapter illuminates nurturing these virtues in practice and provides a practical approach that helps leaders navigate through the adversity and attain lasting ends.

In essence, leadership is preferred to the leadership of a ship that might steer its way along turbulent waters and uncertain weather conditions. Sometimes, the storms might arise suddenly, testing even the mettle of the most seasoned captains. However, it is the resilience and perseverance of the leaders that decide whether the ship would be hurled by the tempest's fury or emerge unscathed. This chapter embarks on a journey that enables us to understand how cultivating these essential qualities can empower leaders to weather any storm and steer their teams towards success.

Considering the practical example of real-life experiences and easily-understandable anecdotes, we shall find easy-to-follow advice on what steps to take to develop resilience and perseverance in leadership. Whether you are charting a course through choppy seas or navigating uncharted waters, the principles outlined in this chapter will arm you with the tools and techniques that will allow you to cross the line of adversity and emerge on the other side, stronger.

Join us on a journey into the heart of leadership, where resilience and perseverance are the guiding stars that illuminate the path to enduring success. By providing practical examples and easy-to-understand guidance, this chapter hopes to simplify the art of leadership, empowering you to navigate the stormy seas of uncertainty with confidence and determination.

Cultivating Resilience in Leaders During Challenging Times

Resilience is like a sturdy ship that sails through rough seas, weathering the storms and emerging stronger on the other side. As a leader, the cultivation of resilience is crucial in handling the harsh environments and difficulties that come along the way. Here's how you can develop resilience in yourself:

Embrace Change:

Change is like steering the sails of a ship to catch the next wind. Resilient leaders understand that change is not a disruption but rather an opportunity for evolution. They approach change with curiosity and adaptability mindset, whereby challenges represent gateways to innovation and growth. Instead of resisting the currents of change, they harness its momentum to propel their teams forward. By instilling in their teams a culture that is open to change, resilient leaders embold their members to embrace uncertainty with confidence and creativity in navigating towards an adversity-evading outcome.

Stay Positive:

Optimistic leadership, in other words, is like being a beacon of light amidst darkness. Resilient leaders understand the strength of positivity to uplift people's spirits and drive motivation. They cultivate a mindset of positivity by choosing to focus on solutions rather than dwelling on problems. For instance, leading by example and ensuring that all have a positive outlook, they inspire teams through the challenges to persist with renewed determination. Positivity radiates like sunshine, infusing energy and hope into the collective spirit of the team. In times of uncertainty, a leader's unwavering positivity becomes a guiding force, illuminating the path forward and instilling resilience in every team member.

Build a Support Network:

Building a support network is like erecting a safety net below the tightrope of leadership. Resilient leaders appreciate and cultivate beneficial alliances as their support system, which helps them seek advice, disclose problems, and always get a timely second opinion or support from trusted allies. In times of hardship, their network of friends, colleagues, and mentors will offer the leader a listening ear, invaluable advice, and resolute encouragement. Leaders, with this, gain fresh perspectives and fresh ideas that will help them meet obstacles with greater clarity and resilience. Similarly, resilient leaders offer support to other people, instilling a culture of mutual aid and solidarity. Together, they make a resilient community that can stand firm against challenges.

Practice Self-Care:

Practicing self-care is like tending to the garden of your own well-being, nurturing and attention that will flourish. This is made evident by resilient leaders who resort to activities promoting physical and mental health in actualizing that self-care is paramount to remain resilient in the face of adversity. They carve out time for exercise, meditation, hobbies, and quality time with loved ones, knowing that these activities help restore their energy and improve their emotional resilience. With a balance in self-care, leaders guarantee that they have the necessary strength and stamina to endure any hardships and lead with clarity and confidence even during the most times.

Learn from Setbacks:

Learning from setbacks is like panning for gold in adversity: patience, resilience, and a sharp eye for opportunity. Resilient leaders understand that failure is not the end, but rather an invaluable source of insight and growth. They view setbacks as stepping stones toward success, extracting lessons from every experience in order to fine-tune their strategies and approaches. By embracing failure as an inevitable part of the journey and adopting a growth mindset, leaders cultivate perseverance and resilience, transforming setbacks into catalysts for continuous improvement and future achievements.

Motivating and Supporting Teams through Adversity

For being a leader, your role is not just about getting through adversity by yourself but also keeping on the runaway line the people under you as well. Here is how:

Lead by Example:

Leading by example, that's being the guiding force like a lighthouse on a stormy sea—guiding others with resolute power. Resilient leaders can appreciate how every action they undertake has a bearing on their teams. By delivering a profound sense of optimism, adaptability, and determination in every instance of decision and interaction, the leaders set the standard for resilience within their organization. Their unrelenting commitment towards the face of every problem that comes along in their way and accomplishing their goals forges the attitude of indomitable spirit among every individual in the group.

Communicate Effectively:

Effective communication is the beacon that guides teams through the storm of adversity. Resilient leaders know the value of communicating their team with details regarding challenges and ways of dealing with them. They provide transparency and openness about the situation, which forms a trust environment for collaboration where people feel valued and supported. By listening and encouraging openness, the leader instills a sense of unity and purpose amongst them in uncertain situations. Through clear and honest communication, resilient leaders empower their teams to navigate through adversity together, emerging stronger and more cohesive than ever before.

Provide Encouragement:

Resilient leaders are one of the shining lights that can be seen amid the darkness by their teams of employees during difficult times. They understand that in tough times, the journey can take a toll on morale, hence making it a priority to offer encouragement and lift up the spirits of their teams. In this sense, through the recognition of their strengths, the tiniest of victories, and the appreciation of the team's efforts, resilient leaders ensure a grounded sense of optimism and determination amongst their teammates. With consistent encouragement and positive reinforcement, they stay motivated and continue to endure, certain that their efforts are counted and valued.

Offer Support:

You cannot offer a listening ear for life; hence you need to offer help whenever possible. As a leader, being there for your team implies offering them the needed resources, advice, and emotional support to help in overcoming hurdles. It might mean providing access to training, tools, or merely being available when needed. Your support can make a real difference when it comes to perseverance, where your team is faced with problems together. You demonstrate empathy and understanding to create a safe and supportive atmosphere where team members feel that they are valued and empowered.

Foster Resilience:

Fostering resilience within your team is not merely a matter of weathering the storm; it is about thriving in spite of the challenges. As a leader, you can encourage resilience by creating a milieu where team members feel enabled to develop, learn, and adjust. Do you know? Acknowledge and identify their wins, and provide occasions for sharing experiences and building each other up. This helps to create a culture where your team members are effective at getting through a tough time with confidence and determination, ensuring that your organization can survive even the toughest trials with flying colors.

The Role of Perseverance in Achieving Long-Term Goals

Perseverance is just like a marathon runner who keeps pushing forward, step by step, until he reaches the finish line. In leadership, perseverance is the heartbeat of every person that leads to the development of dreams into reality with the help of innovation and the journey toward success. Here are some of the steps one can harness perseverance to its full potential:

Set Clear Goals:

Setting well-defined goals is like charting your course to success, with a clear direction and purpose. When your goals are defined and SMART, you know exactly what you are aiming at and how to attain them. Cutting down big goals into smaller milestones makes them more manageable and keeps you motivated, and always maintains a sense of progress as you move forward towards your goal. By that, you have a clear roadmap that will guide you to overcome challenges with confidence, knowing that every step of yours gets you closer to your final destination. Clarity of purpose is how you set yourself up for unquestionable success and guarantee yourself a process to get to it, no matter how difficult the challenges might be.

Stay Committed:

Having commitment to the goals one is seeking is like traveling with the North Star; you will find a path to get you through the toughest nights and roughest seas. The road to perseverance demands an unwavering dedication and a steadfast resolve to face and overcome any challenge that come your way. Recall the passion and purpose behind your goals, as they fuel your inner drive and resolve. While the challenges do test your resolve, your commitment to your vision will see you through the hardest of times. Keep it together, keep on grinding, and never lose sight of where you're heading—knowing that each step brings you closer to your dreams.

Be Flexible:

Flexibility has to be the dance partner to commitment in the waltz of perseverance. While the goals give the destination, flexibility allows one to tread on the winding roads and unexpected detours towards the same. Treat every change as a chance to grow and innovate, rather than viewing it as a sign of failure. Do not become rigid to new ideas and approaches but keep being agile to reach your successes. Like a tree bending in the wind, the flexibility gives you a shot at surviving adversity without breaking. Embrace change, and the flexibility to survive the journey for a stronger you. Your dreams are sure to become reality one step at a time when you keep this strategy in mind.

Stay Positive:

The fuel of perseverance is the force of positivity, pushing one ahead to face the rough road ahead. It's how you keep positivity in your life, being optimistic about the odds, finding a silver lining in each cloud, and having belief in the world of possibility. Unlike focusing on setbacks, place your emphasis on lessons learned and the strides you've made. Maintain a mode of gratitude, embracing every small victory along the way. Positivity can keep your motivation running at full speed and your spirits up in any fight against odds. Positivity isn't simply a mindset; it's a superpower.

Seek Support:

Seeking support is not a display of weakness but rather a true sign of your strength and resilience. Take support from friends, family, mentors, and colleagues, drawing strength from their encouragement and guidance. Share your challenge openly, and seek advice whenever necessary. Friends or colleagues may offer new perspectives, fresh ideas, and even some emotional backing that may motivate and help you stay strong. Together, weather any storm that comes your way.

Conclusion

In the journey of leadership, the compass is resilience and perseverance. If you think of the journey of leadership as a ship sailing, then it is these qualities that will help the ship withstand all kinds of winds, tides, and waves. On the other hand, looking at what the chapter has covered, it becomes clear that these qualities are not just desirable but must have skills for navigating effectively through the challenges of leadership. Resilience is, like a sturdy ship, built to withstand the storms that come out of nowhere and get stronger on either side of this trouble. The leader's change acceptance, positive thinking, the creation of a support network, self-care, and learning from setbacks form a basis of his or her self-cultivation of resilience. In addition, such resilience enables leaders to challenge adversity with clarity, adaptability, and determination, meaning that any obstacle, no matter how tough, can be overcome.

Furthermore, resilience is not just a question of survival but a question of thriving amidst adversity. In such a way, leaders that are successful are able to lead their teams with respect to strength, solidarity, and optimism, providing a strong foundation for their teams to endure any trials that may come their way.

Perseverance, on the other hand, is the fuel that propels us forward towards our long-term goals. Leaders who set clear goals, stay committed, being flexible, staying positive, and seeking support are able to take advantage of the power of perseverance in transforming their dreams into realities.

In conclusion, effective leadership is by no means going to be enough just to reach the end but by taking this journey with resilience and perseverance in such a way as to translate some of the trip along the way as well. We need to cultivate these essential qualities and use them in our day-to-day lives as we embark on the leadership journey.

In other words, leadership is not just about having got there, but it's about the journey—the journey of growth, learning, and change. When equipped with resilience and perseverance, we can navigate the tumultuous seas of uncertainty with an iron fist of confidence and resolve, emerging triumphant on the other side stronger, wiser, and more resilient than ever before. So let us set sail on this voyage of leadership, guided by the guiding stars of resilience and perseverance, knowing that no matter what challenges lie ahead, we have the strength and the determination to overcome them.

End of Chapter 22

Chapter 23

Setting an Example Through Leadership Behavior

The importance of leadership behavior in the aspects of management cannot be understated; every action you take as a leader breeds in attitudes, behaviors, and performance. This chapter revolves around the big influence by leading by example, nurturing conducive behaviors, and role-modeling positive leadership features that drive success within an organization.

Leading by example is not just a recommendation; it's a basic rule to lead successfully. Your actions express loudly what is written in your words, influencing the conduct and morale of your team members. On the other hand, by exhibiting fair, respectful, and humble behavior, leaders establish standards of conduct that others imitate. We shall review how leaders can create a culture of trust, integrity, and accountability through consistent virtuous conduct.

Developing behaviors that engender loyalty is a strategic imperative for leaders who want to build cohesive and high-performing teams. Loyalty is earned through honesty, consistency, and supportiveness. We will delve into transparent communication, reliability, and empathy in fostering a feeling of belonging and commitment. We shall unravel practical strategies on how to cultivate loyalty and foster a culture of mutual respect and appreciation.

Emulating positive leadership traits is a transformative pursuit and can drive organizations towards greater success and resilience. Empathy, resilience, and optimism are just a few of the traits that greatly affect employee engagement, innovation, and organizational adaptability. We will shed light on the essence of these traits and their importance in advancing a culture of collaboration, adaptability, and continuous improvement. By embracing these traits, leaders are able to inspire confidence, motivation, and creativity among their teams, consequently leading to enhanced performance and sustained competitive advantage.

In short, this chapter can be defined as a guiding compass towards the uneven terrain of management for leaders. Whereas the understanding of the concept of leadership behavior and its implications towards organizational dynamics would help leaders in influencing their approach to management such that it fosters a culture of excellence, integrity, and innovation. Through introspection, learning, and deliberate practice, leaders are able to grow behaviors and traits that inspire loyalty, drive success, and inspire a long-lasting legacy of positive impact. Let's continue on this journey of unravelling the secrets to effective leadership behavior and how it may have profound implications for organizational success.

Leading by Example Through Fair, Respectful, and Humble Behavior

Leading by example: It involves showing others how to behave by what you do, through your actions. This is about doing it right and with fairness, respect, and humility in dealing with your team. Here's what each of these behaviors looks like in practice:

Fairness:

Fairness is the bedrock of effective leadership that ensures every team member gets treated equally, creating an environment where trust and equity are evident. This includes providing equal opportunities for growth and development, rewarding performance fairly based on merit, and resolving concerns or grievances with impartiality. Fairness also includes giving every team member equal opportunity to participate and share their ideas openly without discrimination. When leaders are fair in their actions and decisions, they create a culture that is inclusive and respectful of the contribution of each one of them.

Respect:

Respect is the bedrock of strong leadership, an appreciation for the individual's worth and contribution of each team member. The good leader shows respect by recognizing that each member is unique in terms of their skills, talents, and viewpoints. He creates an environment in which everyone has good value and heard what they have to say, creating a sense of camaraderie and a feeling of belonging. They actively listen to their team members' ideas and concerns, with a desire to really understand and solve those problems with empathy and care. This respect for diversity and stewardship of every person draws respect as a conclusion toward creating a culture of mutual respect and trust, a ground for one to succeed collaboratively.

Humility:

Humility is the hallmark of an effective leader who admits the fallibility of their plans, accepting mistakes as a learning opportunity. Leaders who embody humility, authenticity and vulnerability, and admit when they are wrong, creating an environment of openness and trust amongst their team members. By doing so, they set aside their ego for the collective success of the team and organization over personal pride. Humble leaders sought feedback and actively sought ways to improve themselves, realizing that continuous learning is critical for growth and innovation. Their humility drew loyalty and respect from team members and instilled a culture of accountability and collaboration.

When you lead with fairness, respect, and humility, a positive work environment is created where people feel valued and motivated. Trust and respect for your team increase, resulting in loyalty and productivity.

Developing Leadership Behavior That Fosters Loyalty

Loyalty is critical in forging a strong and cohesive team. As a leader, one can develop behaviors that build trust and inspire confidence. Here are some key behaviors that leaders should focus on:

Honesty:

Honesty forms the bedrock of trust within any team or organization, by engendering an environment that is transparent and has integrity. The honest leaders communicate openly and truthfully with their team members, sharing information without withholding or distorting facts. Being honest in addressing concerns and issues helps them build credibility and trust among team members. This straight, honest communication fosters a culture of accountability and mutual respect, within which team members can contribute their ideas and opinions while feeling valued and empowered to carry out work. Finally, honesty strengthens relationships and fosters a positive work environment conducive to success and growth.

Consistency:

A cornerstone of reliability and dependability in leadership is consistency in the actions and decisions made. This display by the leader creates a sense of stability and predictability amongst his team. By living up to certain principles and values, such consistency produces trust and confidence amongst team members, knowing that their leader is going to act consistently. Accountability, fairness, are also reinforced through consistency in standards and expectations. Consistency builds cohesion and unity within the team, thus enabling them to work together effectively in moving towards common goals with clarity and confidence.

Supportiveness:

Supportiveness is an important determinant of effective leadership; it brings about developing a sense of trust and loyalty within the team. Supportiveness by the leader shows the members that they are valuable and revered, and the working place becomes more positive and motivating. By providing support and encouragement, leaders provide power to their members to find their way in situations and achieve at a very high level of confidence. Being there in trying times helps to build resilience and strengthen the bond among team members. End of all, supportiveness is one of the key traits that enables leaders to inspire and motivate their team to achieve greatness.

Demonstration of these behaviors consistently will make the team earn your trust and loyalty. They will be willing to go that extra mile for you and the organization knowing that you have their best interests at heart.

Emulating Positive Leadership Traits for Organizational Success

These positive traits in a leadership profile are very necessary in influencing organizational success. You, as a leader, can mimic these traits to establish a positive and productive work environment. Here are some key traits to focus on:

Empathy:

Empathy can be the bedrock of strong leadership, since it allows leaders to connect with the people who are in their team at a deep and meaningful level. By understanding and feeling with their thoughts, feelings, and experiences, leaders may develop trust and rapport with their team members. Showing care and concern by compassionately supporting them is an empathetic move that shows leaders are committed to their team's welfare and would be willing to go to some extent to help when there is a need. To foster a good and supportive work environment, leaders actively listen to team members' problems and ensure listening to them and providing empathetic responses is done. Overall, empathy enables leaders to give a sense of belonging to their team and mutual respect, leading to increased morale and productivity.

Resilience:

Resilience is like a steadfast ship that soars through severe seas and weathered storms, evolving as a stronger vessel after every trial and tribulation. The resilience of the leader is key in overcoming challenges and setbacks for themselves and the team. Your fortitude inspires the team to persist in the face of such challenges. When strife arises, your ability to pivot through tough times and bounce back provides hope and a path to success for your team. Through resilience, you instill confidence and strength within the team members, pushing them to tackle the obstacles and grow stronger together.

Optimism:

Optimism is like a guiding light, lighting up the darkest path to offer inspiration and hope to those who follow. In the face of challenges, having a positive mindset as a leader helps one traverse them with ease. Optimism allows finding opportunities amidst problems and considerations to promote possibilities. Your optimism becomes infectious and spreads hope and confidence everywhere among the team. In spite of difficulties, your unswerving positivity serves as a beacon guiding your team to brighter horizons. Leading with optimism motivates your team to sustain themselves with renewed dedication and fortitude.

With emulation of these positive leadership traits, you are capable of creating a culture of success, where people will feel motivated and empowered to do their best work. Your positive attitude and behavior will motivate your team to reach new heights and achieve their goals.

Conclusion

In the realm of management, the significance of leadership behavior cannot be overstated. Every action a leader undertakes sends ripples throughout the organization, shaping attitudes, behaviors, and ultimately, performance. This chapter has delved into the pivotal role that leadership behavior plays in driving organizational success, focusing on three main aspects: setting examples, cultivating loyalty, and emulating positive leadership qualities.

Leading by example is not an option but rather a basic principle for having effective leadership. This is simply because, through fair, respectful, and humble behavior, leaders set the standards of conduct for others to emulate. Fairness provides equal opportunities and respect for all members of the team to build trust and inclusiveness. Respect goes a long way in acknowledging contributions that are unique to each team member, thus facilitating a culture that appreciates and belongs. Humility in authenticity and vulnerability encourages openness and cooperation. The three aspects, when put together, generate a well-safe working environment that flourishes trust and respect.

Loyalty is the most vital for developing behaviors that make teams work together towards success and high performance. Honesty, consistency, and support are some behaviors that help build trust and commitment within the team. When honesty is being upheld, being transparent and being accountable contribute to building trust, as consistency builds stability and predictability. Supportiveness manifests care and empowerment, thereby aiding in building stronger relationships and resilience. A leader's embodiment of such behaviors leaves a culture of trust and loyalty whereby team members are motivated to participate positively towards the team's growth.

However, at times, positive traits that embody positive traits are mandatory for an organization that seeks to have both success and resilience. Empathy, resilience, and optimism is what helps inspire and boost employees' resilience, creativity, and adaptability. Empathy fosters a relationship and understanding for teammates so that trust and rapport grow. Resilience stirs up encouragement and growth that can prepare any team to face difficulties with self-confidence. Optimism is able to raise the level of hope and possibility that could motivate creativity and ambition. When embracing these traits, the leaders' engagement in such environments increases confidence, motivation, and creativity that makes employees able in handling such environments better.

In conclusion, effective leadership behavior is the compass that guides organizations through the complexities of management. As long as a leader knows and understands the relevance of leading by example, building loyalty, and emulating positive traits, the culture is able to be crafted with greatness, honesty, and innovation. With reflexivity, learning, and ongoing practice, leaders would cultivate behaviors and traits that inspire loyalty, drive success, and leave a lasting legacy of positive impact. As we wind up this chapter, let us continue this journey of exploring the secrets to effective leadership behavior and its far-reaching implications on organizational success.

End of chapter 23

Chapter 24

Networking, Relationship Building, and Strategic Alliances

Foundational pillars to successful management comprise networking, relationship building, and strategic alliances. These components are critical in fostering organizational growth, enhancing innovation, and nurturing sustainability. In this chapter, therefore, we will understand the intricacies of these components and the significance of them towards driving organizational success.

While the relationship toward most of the stakeholders involved in the organization is the main pillar that strengthens effective management. These include employees, customers, suppliers, and investors—each with different roles they play in keeping the organization run smoothly. Building alliances with the stakeholders is essential to improve the management cycle. It focuses on developing close, constructive, and productive relations with every stakeholder. This chapter explores, among other things, strategies in building relationships, developing cooperation, and forming mutually beneficial relations.

On the other hand, strategic alliances serve as the tool for business growth and expansion. They enable businesses to achieve leverage with complementary strengths, establish new markets, and enhance their competitive advantage. We'll cover in detail how to form strategic alliances, from the use of partnerships that make more sense for businesses to negotiate terms and agreements.

Furthermore, one needs to be an expert in networking to become an effective leader. This is because networking avails one of valuable resources, insights, and opportunities. By building a strong professional network, a leader will expand his or her influence, keep up to date with the market trends, and facilitate cooperation across various domains. This chapter will uncover practical tips and techniques for honing networking skills and effectively channeling them towards leadership effectiveness.

In summary, this chapter is a guide to navigate a complex landscape that includes networking, relationship building, and strategic alliances to a successful management environment. Skillful leaders will, therefore, embed these pillars to propel their organizations towards greater growth and resilience in an ever-changing business world. So, join us as we explore the strategies and best practices that unravel effective management within today's dynamic business environment.

Building Relationships With Different Stakeholders

Getting along with different groups of people is important for the growth of any business. Stakeholders are people like workers, customers, suppliers, investors, the community, and the government. For good partnerships with all of these groups, follow these steps:

Employees:

Respecting and appreciating employees will go a long way in creating a positive work environment. When employees feel valued and heard, then they are more engaged and motivated to do their best work. Listening to their concerns will tell them that their well-being is under consideration. And providing growth and development opportunities help not only the employees themselves but also improve the organization overall. Acknowledging their contributions is a recognition of their efforts and the work they have done, helping build pride and loyalty among employees. End of all, being well with employees and boosting up their professional development directly leads to higher morale and productivity and helps create long-term loyalty.

Customers:

Understanding customers' needs and preferences is vital towards developing strong relationships. On the other hand, since listening is an effective approach in capturing their preferences and the challenges they face, you may mold your products or services according to their requirements efficiently. Excellent customer service, for example, remains being responsive, friendly, and helpful to guarantee a great experience every time a customer touches upon your services. Addressing issues or complaints promptly not only ensures customer satisfaction but also builds trust. As trust grows, customer loyalty increases, hence creating repeated business or positive word-of-mouth about the company, which is irreplaceable when it comes to picking up new customers and sustaining long-term success.

Suppliers:

Building open, honest communication with your suppliers is the key to the relationship. Holding regular contact and making sure that issues are discussed openly helps avoid misunderstandings. Negotiating fair terms and agreements ensures that the partnership works for both parties, values, and respects each other. Collaborating on ways to improve efficiency and quality can lead to innovative solutions and cost savings for both parties. Building strong partnerships with your suppliers ensures the overall performance and competitiveness of your organization, leading to a reliable supply chain.

Investors:

Keeping your investors well-informed about the performance, financial status, and future strategy of the company is an important part of creating trust and confidence in them. Regular reports and updates provided to them without fail show accountability and integrity, which are key factors in building a lasting relationship with your investors. The sincerity and honesty of communication help establish credibility and create a feeling of partnership between the company and its shareholders. Besides, sticking to your promises and meeting milestones, which you had offered earlier, would strengthen investors' faith in your organization and may entice them to invest more with you. Trust and confidence from such investment will surely see the long-term growth and success of your business.

Government Agencies:

Building a proper relationship with the government agency will be essential in managing regulatory requirements and foster a conducive business environment. This realization of adherence to laws, regulations, and the industry standard shows your sincerity towards compliance and ethical behavior. Engage with government agencies in an optimistic and constructive way, such as being involved in community activities and advocating for policies that resonate with the organization, thus helps in building relations and trust. This may mean that the interactions with regulatory agencies are smoother, processes are streamlined, and even open doors for opportunities such as grants or partnerships. In the end, this constructive relationship of the government agencies supports the entire community as well as your organization.

Community:

Engagement in the local community is not all about business; it's about corporate responsibility. Community events, local activities, and supporting charitable causes demonstrate your commitment to giving back and making a positive impact. By forming good relationships with community leaders, organizations, and residents, you create goodwill that helps to build up a strong reputation for your organization as a trusted member of the community. And these relationships also bring other benefits such as partnerships that are likely to give you more customers, more brand awareness, and more loyalty. It is every person who gets involved and invests that also raises the well-being of the society.

Creating Strategic Alliances for Business Growth

Strategic alliances involve partnerships between two or more companies that aim for shared objectives. They allow the participating companies to widen their market base, access new resources and capabilities, cut costs, and develop more competitiveness. Here are some ways to establish strategic alliances for growth in business:

Identify Potential Partners:

Identify potential partners through the identification of other organizations whose goals, values, and target market are coherent with your particular needs. Assess their reputations and the fact of that organization being well-skilled and being better placed in the available resources in relation to your own; this is for further engagement or dealing with one another. When partnering with organizations that have similar objectives and customer bases, it can benefit from each other's strengths and resources to realize common goals more effectively. A strategic approach for the purpose of partnering fosters collaboration, innovation, and enhances opportunity for success and growth.

Define Objectives and Expectations:

Defining objectives and expectations is clearly laying down of the goals, roles, responsibilities, and expectations of each partner in the strategic alliance. Clear metrics and milestones should be defined to measure progress and ensure that the partnership aligns with the overall strategic priorities of both organizations. It aims at facilitating transparency and avoidance of miscommunication and misunderstandings, which might cause friction and hinder the collaborative approach of mutual success. Clear objectives and expectations from the very beginning would allow partners to work in coordination, effective as ever, and go towards common goals in realizing mutually fruitful outcomes while at the same time ensuring the long-term sustainability of the alliance.

Negotiate Terms and Agreements:

Negotiations to be formed on terms and agreements involve entering into agreements that are favorable to all parties involved in the strategic alliance. This covers discussions on investments committed by the partner, revenue-sharing models, intellectual property rights, as well as exit strategies. Having had these issues discussed, potential risk can be minimized, and avenues for maximum profit can be determined. This way, during the course of the alliance, both partners' interests are protected and collaborated on—for the best working experience. Clear and neatly defined terms provide a basis for a good partnership that makes both parties feel confident for the objectives they are working towards, ensuring that their needs are clearly stated.

Implement and Monitor the Alliance:

The implementation and monitoring of the alliance imply making the agreed plan into effect, along with allocating appropriately needed resources for its implementation. Communication with the partner stakeholders is crucial in order to maintain all parties involved in achieving our desired outcomes. Monitoring performance metrics helps to track progress and identify any areas that may need further adjustments or improvement. By continuously monitoring the alliance's effectiveness, adjustments can be made to the strategy in order to optimize outcomes and align with the strategic objectives. This approach, proactive in nature, prevents losing momentum towards shared goals.

Networking Skills for Effective Leadership

Networking refers to developing and keeping relationships with such people who could be available to provide support, information, and opportunities that will promote both personal and professional growth. Effective networking skills are fundamental in leadership. Here are some tips for developing networking skills:

Be Genuine and Authentic:

Being true to self and the environment can involve displaying authenticity and sincerity. It means an interest in what other people are concerned with, using active listening for their perspective, and finding some common points to understand. Authenticity builds trust and credibility with other people, leading to stronger relationships and deeper connections. Sincere interactions form a sense of mutual respect and understanding, laying a basis for meaningful collaborations and partnerships. When a leader is authentic, he creates an environment where people feel valued and appreciated, leading to increased engagement and collaboration within the organization.

Be Proactive:

Proactive networking involves making a proactive effort towards expanding your professional networks and keeping up with existing ones. It entails attending networking events, joining relevant professional associations, and participating in online communities related to your field. Actively reaching out to potential contacts and keeping in touch with the ones you already have is a way of increasing visibility and collaboration opportunities, thus promoting progress in your career or business endeavors. It shows that you are enthusiastic and dedicated towards making connections that truly matter and might eventually result in very valuable partnerships, opportunities, and support.

Provide Value:

To provide value in networking involves helping, sharing relevant information, and connecting others with valuable resources or opportunities. Being generous with your time, expertise, and connections really helps you show that you're giving in to their success. By providing value, you strengthen your relationships within your network and build trust and reciprocity. When you consistently offer assistance and support without expecting an immediate return, you create a positive reputation and goodwill that can result in more collaboration, referrals, and mutual support in the long run.

Basically, it helps create a situation of reciprocity and generally enriches your network and makes for better professional relationships.

Follow Up:

After networking events or meetings, follow-ups are necessary for building and maintaining relationships. It shows that you value the connection and want to build upon it. Sending a follow-up email or message is personalized, thanking the person for their time and reiterating important things discussed at the time. The constant follow-up expresses the interest you have in the other individual and that you are interested in understanding their business better. It also keeps you at the top of their mind, which is why staying connected regularly, while sharing relevant updates or information, helps deepen the connection and form long-term professional relationships.

Be Patient and Persistent:

So essential in networking is patience and persistence because relationships do not develop overnight. It takes time and a great deal of consistent efforts. Patience will slow down the process to give such relationships the natural time for them to grow, without demanding immediate results or rapid growth. Persistence is about remaining committed to your networking goals and pushing through challenges, and that includes reaching out to new contacts as well as following up with connections that have developed. Patience and persistence pay off in growing your network, deepening relationships, and uncovering new opportunities for collaboration and growth.

Conclusion

It is in the fast-changing world of business, networking, relationship building, and strategic alliances that lay the pillars to success. In this chapter, it has been explained what significance these elements have played and brought insights into action, how to develop them effectively.

Networking is not about the accumulation of business cards or simply making nice chitchat but rather about establishing genuine contacts that open up opportunities for mutual benefit. Slow and persistent efforts will allow individuals to gradually develop their network and ensure lasting connections in anticipation of future collaborations and success.

Relationship building goes beyond mere transactions; it involves building a culture of trust, respect, and loyalty towards stakeholders like employees, customers, suppliers, investors, government agencies, or the community. The specific relationships need to be built only by having a proper form of structured communication, transparency, and empathy in the sense of leaders. Developing strong and everlasting relationships to fuel organizational success has been developed by leaders by emphasizing such elements.

Strategic alliances are indispensable tools for driving growth and fostering innovation in business. Two organizations having common goals and values partner together to leverage each other's strength and resources to the mutual benefit of achieving the objective. However, having well-defined objectives, creating fair terms, and setting reliable monitoring mechanisms to ensure the success of these alliances is very critical.

In summary, mastering the art of networking, relationship building, and strategic alliances is vital towards having a competitive edge in today's business landscape. This requires patience, persistence, and genuine connections that are meaningful. When one embraces these principles and takes on a strategic approach, then one can unlock new opportunities, foster innovations, and set a strong foundation for the long term in success. So, in the face of a tough business world, remember that success is a function of collaboration and interplay rather than single work.

End of Chapter 24

Chapter 25

Pushing Beyond Limits and Employee Dedication

In today's fast-paced and fiercely competitive business landscape, the demand for success is ever-present, leading organizations to seek not just skilled employees but also those who prove themselves time and time again with dogged determination to be at the forefront of all that business does. This chapter delves into basic elements when it comes to winning this war that must be waged through the provision of a workforce that leaves behind the concept of job descriptions and believes in itself that it is more than merely a job but something that involves living the challenge of an organization and contributing wholeheartedly towards its realization.

In the pursuit of sustained success, managers are more than mere overseers of day-to-day operations; rather, they become catalysts of motivation and ambition, urging their employees to reach milestones beyond their conventional boundaries. In this ever-changing competitive landscape, the drive towards success becomes highlighted more and more in the importance of employee dedication and commitment to organizational growth. Organizations recognize that true success does not stem from individual achievement alone; it lies within the collective effort of a motivated and empowered team with a common vision.

This chapter thus plays an imperative role in furnishing managers with a holistic understanding of strategies for nurturing a workforce whose intent is to outstand among themselves an unrelenting commitment to excellence. Through insights elucidated in this chapter, managers will appreciate insights on empowering their teams beyond their perceived limitations, embracing challenges as opportunities for development, and championing a culture of unyielding dedication and relentless pursuit of excellence.

Encouraging Employees to Go Above and Beyond Job Descriptions

Their job descriptions often define employees' functions, but for them to shine, they need support from their manager to get out of their comfort zones and take up new challenges. Managers can do this by encouraging employees to go beyond the routine that has been described in a job.

Setting a Clear Vision:

A clear vision has to be set up, so that every team member knows what she or he is supposed to do. The manager should state a credible vision that penetrates the psychological barriers of each team member to share a sense of purpose and direction in each individual. This way, the clearer the individuals' notion of the impact their contributions have on the general achievement, the more they will relate them to their individual responsibilities. A meaningful challenge for employees to engage themselves effectively is a larger perspective, encouraging the adoption of a mindset that can transcend the familiar boundaries of their given roles and thus see their work as cumulative towards the team's result. In simpler terms, the vision as the guiding light helps pave the way through the path ahead and helps direct the collective towards shared goals.

Recognizing and Rewarding Effort:

Effort-based rewards, to building a culture of excellence, is giving recognition and appreciation to effort in teams. Identification and appreciation for the contribution and hard work that employees bring forth enable them to feel their efforts are appreciated and validated, thus motivating them as they continue to make invaluable contributions. Whether through verbal, tangible, or personalized recognition, such gestures demonstrate that efforts are a valid basis for commendations. Critically, this recognition not only motivates the individuals being honored but also serves as a powerful example for others, inspiring them to emulate similar levels of commitment and excellence in their own endeavors.

Providing Opportunities for Growth:

It provides opportunities for growth to nurture a dynamic and skilled workforce. The managers need to avail various ways through which one can professionalize themselves in a wide range of topics, through training programs, workshops, and mentoring opportunities, in order to promote skill expansion and abilities development. These initiatives not only enhance the individual competence but also develop a culture of continuous learning and improvement in the organization. It is by doing so that the manager will enable his staff to be empowered in their respective workplaces while they continue to grow and develop together in a dynamic business environment. These are essentially not only investments that a manager makes in his/her workers but also strategic investments in both individual and organizational excellence.

Leading by Example:

Leading by example is a powerful way for managers to inspire their teams to push beyond limits. With the willingness to embrace challenges and strive for personal growth, managers set an inspiring precedent for their employees. Experiences of the manager, both of challenges and successes, give an insight into the relatable narrative of stepping out of one's comfort zone. Transparency and vulnerability by the managers help in creating an authentic and trust-based culture within the team that inspires people to emulate the proactive nature of self-improvement. The holistic lead eventually creates a shared ethos of resilience, ambition, and continuous growth that resonates with the team, pushing them toward collective success.

Motivating teams to contribute to organizational growth

For every team member to be involved in growing the business, it has to have the drive to succeed. Here is how managers can spur their teams to greatness.

Creating a Shared Vision:

The vision is another important aspect of building a team in a cohesive and motivated manner. By having each team member take part in the setting of goals and strategy development, the manager transfers power from his or her desk to the desks of the members, thus encouraging active involvement in shaping the direction of the organization. This cooperative approach generates the feeling that the employees have control over the vision and that they are indeed participating in its creation. When they identify that the goals and ideas they have as individuals relate to what is set as the organization's goals, people feel more motivated and committed to contribute their all and be on the same page. Finally, a shared vision creates unity in the team and alignment, which leads to collective success.

Providing Regular Feedback:

Feedback on an everyday basis will allow for creating a team culture focused on continuous improvement and progress. Regular feedback, in the form of positive accolades as well as constructive criticism, imparts certain insights to the employees regarding the influence of their contributions. Feedback on positive behavior builds up morale and inspires one to carry on working towards one's self-desired ambitions in line with the organization's vision. Constructive criticism, at the same time, offers a path to be more improved or productive in one's actions. This kind of balance in giving feedback provides a good environment for the employees, as it gives confidence that their work is valued, and it motivates them to perform even better, which in turn serves to encourage growth and success of the organization.

Encouraging Collaboration:

Collaborating is fundamental in accessing a team's full potential. The propensity for team members to collaborate, share ideas, and back one another up fosters a feeling of unity and camaraderie. Collaboration reduces silos and brings to the fore new ideas, hence innovation, good problem-solving skills, and applied teamwork. When an individual has a good feel about how much value they give to the team, they are more motivated to give their best, using their unique skills and wisdom for collective goals. The shared purpose propels the collective pursuit of success, ensuring members work cooperatively to meet objectives and nurture the spirit of excellence within the organization.

Celebrating Successes:

The celebration of successes helps to nurture an extremely positive, motivating work environment. By rewarding and celebrating milestones and achievements, managers propel a culture of value and recognition within their team. Even the smallest accomplishments should be recognized to maintain the overall progress and success of the organization. The celebration of successes definitely lifts the morale of the employees and fosters a sense of pride and accomplishment among them, which in turn motivates them to continue striving for excellence. This also leads to camaraderie and the sense of belonging among team members as they share in the joy of successes together. In conclusion, celebrating successes reinforces a culture of growth and the team's commitment to organizational success.

Cultivating a Culture of Dedication and Excellence Within a Team

Creating a culture of dedication and excellence starts with strong leadership. Managers can cultivate this culture by:

Setting High Standards:

By a culture of excellence within a team is challenging to create. It should be on how managers meet expectations and the standards of excellence clearly. Managers point their team towards success when they define these standards and the roadmap to it. High standards allow working team members to expand their horizons, innovate, and contribute constantly with different organizations. This commitment to excellence is a powerful move that contributes to enhancing not just the individual performance but also the success and repute of the organization.

Promoting Accountability:

Holding team members accountable for their behaviors and outcomes is imperative in proving an environment that promotes accountability and promotes excellence. Managers establish clear standards to ensure that tasks are undertaken with integrity and diligence. Encouraging employees to take ownership of their work creates a sense of ownership and pride, as they realize the role that their contribution will play to the team's success. When a team member takes accountability of their action, then there is an increased chance of showing initiative, adapting to challenges, and striving for continuous improvement. In the end, this creates a culture of high performance that flourishes with excellence.

Providing Support and Resources:

Empowering team members is a manager's imperative because it brings out their best. The manager must see to it that members have the tools, training, and information required to execute their roles effectively. A good manager invests time and energy by implementing training programs and workshops that imbue employees with necessary skills and knowledge. Besides, access to up-to-date information and technology can empower individuals to make valid decisions and implement tasks with efficiency. A well-supportive work environment that champions value and encouragement breeds creativity, teamwork, and job satisfaction. In the end, provision of suitable support and resources will boost employees' potential for realization and contribution to the organization.

Fostering Open Communication:

This is very important in strengthening the core values of the organization while creating a more collaborative and inclusive team environment. Creating an environment where team members openly share their views, experiences, and problems promotes openness within the team. Communication that's open allows team members to freely express opinions and ideas and provide constructive feedback. The diversity of ideas allows innovation, and problems are worked on. It also does enable the employees to address some of the rising issues quickly and promptly to avoid feeling overwhelmed and conflicted. In essence, fostering open communication gives a sense of belonging and unity, drawing the team towards shared goals and success.

Conclusion

In today's dynamic, competitive business environment, the need for organizations to push beyond limits and cultivate a culture of commitment and excellence within their teams has never been more important. As witnessed in this chapter, success demands more than skillful employees; it calls for dedicated, motivated, and driven individuals who go beyond their job description to contribute to the growth of the organization. Managers play a key role in nurturing such a workforce—not merely overseers of the day-to-day operations but catalysts for motivation and ambition. By developing visions, recognizing, and rewarding effort, giving opportunities for growth, and leading by example, managers motivate their teams to strive for excellence and push beyond imagined limits.

To foster a culture of commitment and excellence, encouraging collaboration, providing regular feedback, and celebrating successes is also essential. In collaboration, there is teamwork and innovation; feedback helps individuals understand the impact and areas that need improvement; and celebrating successes raises morale and reinforces the culture of achievement and recognition.

Setting high standards, promoting accountability, providing support and resources, and creating open communication are some of the practices that help cultivate a culture of commitment and excellence. High standards can cause expectations for performance to be exceeded, while accountability ensures that the tasks are done with integrity and diligence. Support and resources facilitate empowerment in roles, and open communication makes for a collaborative and inclusive team environment.

By implementing these strategies and practices, managers would create a work culture that motivates employees to perform and develop further, with dedicated commitment to organizational success and the realization of organizational goals. This culture of dedication and excellence not only supports individual employees but also drives organizational growth and success. Fostering such a culture will turn out to be vital in modern businesses while they face the problems that come with the terrain.

End of Chapter 25

Chapter 26

Continuous Improvement, Learning, and Resource Management

Welcome! In this chapter where we shall explore three critical aspects of being a great leader: always striving to better yourself, always keeping up with new trends, and smartly using what you have. We shall learn all of this from Ramayana, where Rama had to lead a great battle against a villain named Ravana. Rama made several smart decisions during the war that helped him during the war, and we can definitely learn something from how he handled things. So, why are we discussing this? Today, being a leader could be challenging: competition is fierce, markets are changing rapidly, and the unexpected always strikes us. However, we can learn a lot from how Rama handled tough situations and apply that to our own challenges.

Firstly, we will discuss about always striving for improvement. This means striving for continuous improvement by looking for better ways to work today compared to yesterday. It's about finding small ways to make ourselves, our teams, and our businesses stronger and more successful.

Next, we'll dive into learning. Learning is not something we do in just school; it is a practice that we ought to have every day of our life. It is about keeping curious, asking questions, and being open to new ideas. The more we learn, the more adequately we shall equip ourselves to face whatever comes our way.

Finally, we will talk about resource management. This is all about using what we have – money, time, and people – effectively. It's all about not wasting anything and making the most out of what you've got.

Our goal here isn't just to talk about these ideas; it's to give you some practical tips and strategies that you can actually use in your own work. We want to help you become a better leader, someone who can handle challenges, inspire others, and make your business or team a success. So, get ready to learn some valuable lessons from an old story that still has a lot to teach us about leadership in today's fast-paced world!

Lifelong Learning for Leaders

The Importance of Lifelong Learning

Lifelong learning forms the bedrock of effective leadership, offering the leaders tools for a dynamic business environment by equipping them with consistent learning. As leaders continue to seek knowledge and skills, they maintain adaptability in the face of dynamic conditions. Coming from more of a growth mindset, learning has become a top priority that encourages leaders to take up challenges as growth avenues instead of obstacles. That kind of mindset fosters a culture of curiosity, innovation, and constant improvement in organizations, where employees are encouraged to come up with fresh ideas and push the limits of what's possible. Learning continuously, leaders shall derive quality insights and experiences that shall form the basis of making sound judgments, increasing their strategic foresight capabilities. Consequently, the continuously curious leaders will find themselves at the forefront of staying ahead in regards to the curve of the future of their organizations by working with others and being ready for new changes.

Embracing a Growth Mindset

It is true that to lead companies successfully today and further in the future, leaders need to nurture a growth mindset. This mindset can be defined by an important belief that one can learn and grow through all the difficulties of life. By adopting a growth mindset, leaders, in turn, stimulate resilience not only for themselves but also in their teams. By allowing risk-taking, such leaders push people outside their boundaries to create an environment that employs innovation, providing both new ideas and approaches that could be judged as substandard. Besides, the leaders who embrace a growth mindset fostered a culture of continuous learning and development within their organizations. Investing in employee growth through providing an opportunity of skill development, these leaders encourage creativity and dedication to excellence among their teams. This commitment to growth and development not only brings forth such individuals but also takes care of the collective organism's success in the long run. Because it is the embracing of a growth mindset that unlocks the full potential of teams to lead innovation and success in the competitive business world today.

Learning from Experiences

In the development of leadership, experiences learned are very essential; these include both successes and failures as experiential lessons. There is always great relief in enjoying success, but at the same time, there are learnings that can be derived on how successful outcomes have been achieved and why. By analyzing the factors that helped bring about success, leaders may not only strengthen successful strategies but also boost replication of good behavior within their teams. Conversely, failures present an opportunity to learn from mistakes and missteps. If things don't go as planned, leaders must reflect and identify the root causes, not only to focus on achieving those objectives but also to know what went wrong. Embracing failure as a learning experience, not a setback, provides important learning experiences that help develop resilience in tough circumstances. Looking back at earlier experiences, help leaders refine their leadership style and adapt their strategies to meet future challenges. The continuous attitude of self-improvement through the experience of their leaders could provide them with the awareness needed to navigate challenges more effectively and provide organizational growth. Finally, by learning from successes and failures, a leader gains the ability to effectively use leadership skills, inspire his team, and bring out sustainable growth and success.

Creating a Culture of Continuous Improvement

Fostering a Culture of Innovation

Creating a culture of innovation is crucial for the organizations that seek to achieve the improvement and success over time. An environment, which is creative, provides an opportunity to try out any new ideas or approaches with no fear of failure. It is a pragmatic way of enabling the teams to innovate, by bringing out a new set of solutions, to take controlled risks so as to minimize the risk to the organization. Celebrating success and learning from failure are essential for crafting a culture of constant improvement. When success is celebrated and praised, it further raises the level of importance to innovate and provides space for more experimentation. Similarly, if failures are met with failure, the leader should bring out an open-door policy whereby the learnings that can be derived from such failures can be learnt in order to extract useful insights for improvement.

When an organization will fail to learn from failures and celebrate successes, such failures will only result in a long-term culture that never seeks to improve and to implement change. Such a culture breeds resilience, creativity, and adaptability that employees find themselves in, thus positioning the organization to thrive in today's fast-paced and competitive business landscape. In essence, fostering a culture of innovation will set the organization to tap into its full potential, which ensures that the teams are able to carry out meaningful change and progress.

Empowering Employees

Employee empowerment is a key issue with effectual leadership and organizational success. When employees have enough power to share their ideas, feedback, and are given the authority to do so, it would allow a more positive, creative, and collaborative work environment within an organization. Empowering leaders trust and involve their employees. Their confidence, when making decisions through delegation of the authority and responsibilities, creates greater ownership and accountability of their employees. When employees feel trusted and appreciated, it often makes them more challenging, problem-solving, and responsible for organizational success.

Furthermore, the development and growth opportunities should be available for inspiring employees to change, solve problems, and get involved in the organization. Such investment in their employees' development through training, development of skills, and career opportunities by the organization tells them that the organization cares about them and it wants them to develop the people and talent for the benefit of both the employee and the organization. This not only increases the satisfaction of the employees but also helps to create a learning and development culture that drives growth and innovation within organizations.

Regular Evaluation and Refinement

Consistent evaluation and refinement are a common foundation of ensuring ongoing improvements within an organization. It is meant to continuously review and improve procedures, systems, and strategies to be aligned with the organization's goals and objectives.

Leaders, therefore, who prioritize data-driven decision-making and performance metrics hold the key to making this possible. Through proper data analysis and a general view of performance indicators, leaders will be able to identify weak spots or underperforming areas where they can put in place elements needed to enhance performance. By using data analytics and performance metrics, leaders will have the ability to assess the efficiency of current processes and determine what should be done or redefined.

Furthermore, the process of evaluation and refinement should also entail soliciting feedback from employees, customers, and other stakeholders. Since those directly involved or impacted by organizational processes actively seek input on how things are being done. Feedback serves as an avenue for leaders to mine insights for improvement areas and possible concerns. Feedback from employees may detail areas of workflow inefficiencies or areas that may necessitate additional support or resources, while feedback from customers and stakeholders can offer insights into product or service quality, customer satisfaction, and market trends.

Through collaboration, which involves constant collaboration with feedbacks, organizations can make their decisions based on facts that can lead to success. With this process of continuous improvement, organizational processes can be reformed to keep pace with changing market dynamics, customer needs, and internal requirements that favor a culture of continuous improvement.

Rama's Resource Management Skills During the War With Ravana

Utilizing Available Resources Optimally

Utilizing resources strategically is a basic ingredient for leadership, especially when things get bad. Lord Rama's strategic resource utilization during the war with Ravana is an example of how effective leadership can navigate adversity with guile and effectiveness. First and foremost, leaders need to get a feel of the available resources at their disposal, be it human capital, financial resources, technology, and any other assets. With a clear sense of strengths and weaknesses relating to these resources, leaders can formulate proper strategies to effectively channel these resources towards organizational objectives.

Prioritizing key objectives is a prerequisite for resource optimization. Leaders should define their most critical priorities and channel the resources accordingly, in such a way that efforts are directed at activities that are aligned with the strategic objectives of the organization and bring forth the maximum impact. With proper focus on key initiatives, leaders may effectively maximize the efficiency of resource investment and ensure success for the organization.

Risk management is yet another important aspect that would lead to optimization in resource allocation. Leaders should anticipate the risk factors that may arise in the process and proactively do countermeasures so that any related impact would be lessened. Identifying and fixing such risks earlier may reduce interruptions and deploy the resources well in order to achieve the set objectives.

Another is maximizing strengths to achieve optimization in resource utilization. Knowing what strengths of the members of their team are, a leader needs to encourage them to use their skills and experience to enhance performance and innovation. Besides, leaders could take advantage of technological tools and other products for the purpose of enhancing productivity and streamlining processes.

Strategies for Effective Resource Allocation

This could mean adopting policies and practices that are geared towards resource optimization or making informed decisions on exactly how much to invest in a certain part of the organization or project. In doing this, it means finding a balance between short-term objectives and long-term strategic needs. To ensure the best possible chance of success, a leader must take time to correctly reflect on which investments are precisely aligned with organizational objectives, hence guide resource allocation decisions appropriately. Leaders should also keep a close eye on performance, ensuring that resources are being used effectively and the desired outcomes are being achieved. The use of clear performance metrics and regular progress reviews can keep leaders informed of results and enable necessary adjustments for the best use of resources.

Technology and data analytics also can be a helping hand in fine-tuning the allocation of resources. Organizations can optimize resource utilization and provide insights into areas of improvement through data analytics. The use of technology can also streamline processes, enhance efficiency, and enable organizations to remain agile in responding to changing market conditions.

The Importance of Succession Planning

Succession planning is the bedrock upon which organizations build their continuity and ensure that they are capable of moving forward with a sense of stability. This must mean to all, a crucial tool in the current changing environment in business. Succession planning is not just about replacing the departing leaders; it is about identifying and grooming the next line of leaders who will guide the organization. Leaders, therefore, must take proactive steps to map out high-potential talent within the organization and give them room to grow and learn. Such organizations should invest in talent development programs, mentorship programs, and training opportunities to cultivate talent ready to step into leadership positions as they open up.

Secondly, succession planning ensures a smooth transition in leadership once the key positions have been vacated. By having a well-fashioned succession plan, an organization avoids risks associated with leadership turnover and minimizes disruptions to its operations. This ensures that the organization not only maintains momentum but also continues its thrust towards the organizational objectives.

Furthermore, succession planning cultivates a culture of leadership development within the organization. By actively grooming future leaders and providing the required supports and resources to succeed, organizations can build a pipeline of talent that is capable of leadership in the years to come.

Conclusion

In summary, the journey that has been experienced through the interwoven principles of continuous improvement, learning, and resource management as embodied in the epic tale of Ramayana provides a series of useful observations for the effective application of strategies for leadership in the complex arena of today's business market. Understanding the importance of lifelong learning will enable us to realize that leaders who harbor a growth mindset and propagate a culture of curiosity and innovation in their organizations are more likely to stay competitive when change surfaces and achieve sustainable success.

In overcoming challenges and going for successes, we become a much wiser and experienced leader who can learn from the future experiences of successes and failures to make smart decisions, improve the leadership style, and be innovative enough to withstand adversity. The adopting of the growth mindset develops a culture of growth and development, hence empowering organizations to remain ahead and remain competitive in the markets.

Continuous improvement as part of continuous progress is a crucial step towards having organizations that may be said to be in a new beginning in terms of innovation, adaptability, and resilience. Through the sharing of ideas, trying new approaches, and having a culture where the leader could learn not only through success but also failure, organizations may bring positive change and development.

Efficient and effective leadership through successful resource management entails the judicious mobilization of available resources towards the realization of organizational objectives. Leaders that focus on key priorities, manage risk, and optimize resource availability will drive organizational success.

Succession planning is of key importance to organizational continuity, knowledge preservation, and the development of leadership progenitors. Identifying and nurturing high potential candidates, providing opportunities for learning and development, are some of the ways organizations can source successors capable of leading in the next several years.

If the leaders adopt these principles, then they will be in a position to mitigate challenges, create value, and foster a culture of innovation that will lead to sustainable organizational success. The Ramayana's timeless lessons are a reminder that effective leadership guides organizations toward growth, resilience, and prosperity.

End of Chapter 26

www.ingramcontent.com/pod-product-compliance
Lightning Source LLC
LaVergne TN
LVHW061608070526
838199LV00078B/7215